Wisdom's Daughter

Dear Rob,

It gives me great pleasure to introduce you to Julian!

Enjoy!

Joan Keith

WISDOM'S DAUGHTER

The Theology of Julian of Norwich

Joan M. Nuth

Crossroad · New York

1991

The Crossroad Publishing Company
370 Lexington Avenue, New York, NY 10017

Printed in the United States of America

Library of Congress Cataloging-in-Publication Data

Nuth, Joan M.
    Wisdom's daughter : the theology of Julian of Norwich / Joan M.
Nuth.
        p.   cm.
    Includes bibliographical references.
    ISBN 0-8245-1132-8
    1. Julian, of Norwich, d. 1343.   I. Title.
BV5095.J84N88   1991
230'.2'092—dc20   91-18907
                                                                          CIP

To my father Joseph who gave me my love for learning,

and to my mother Rita who taught me patience and perseverence,

this book is gratefully dedicated.

Contents

Acknowledgments

Many people have supported me during the writing of this work. First thanks go to my family for their unflagging encouragement. My teachers and mentors at both Weston School of Theology and Boston College deserve mention, especially Harvey Egan, Brian Daley, and Ellen Ross, who read the manuscript in its early stages, offering much helpful advice, and Leo O'Donovan, who was instrumental in bringing the book to press. My colleagues at John Carroll University have been understanding, good-humored companions throughout the completion of this project, and the administration provided much needed time in the form of course reductions and summer faculty fellowships. Justus George Lawler's prompt and expert editorial assistance has been invaluable. My friends in the People of the Promise, Cambridge, and the Community of St. Malachi, Cleveland, have cheered the progress of this work for years. Finally, I wish to acknowledge my deep gratitude to Brian McDermott, whose constant friendship, trust, loyalty, and respect have meant far more to me than words can express.

Note on Citations

My chief textual source has been the Middle English critical edition of Julian's *Showings* published by Colledge and Walsh for the Pontifical Institute of Mediaeval Studies in 1978. However, for easier readability, quotations from Julian's work are in Modern English. For the most part, I have used the translation by Colledge and Walsh published by Paulist Press in 1978. However, I have emended their translation in the following ways: I have changed the spelling of certain words from the British to the American form, and removed capitalization from certain words. This has been generally done, and I have not noted such emendations. I have also tried to use more inclusive language in a few places, and have occasionally retained the original word used by Julian rather than the Modern English word substituted by Colledge and Walsh. Such word changes are enclosed in square brackets within the citation. Any place where I may have altered slightly the meaning intended by the translators, I have noted such change in the footnotes.

Citations contain the reference information necessary for locating them in any edition of Julian's work. Chapters are indicated by lower case Roman numerals for the Short Text, Arabic numerals for the Long Text. The inclusion of these is intended to aid those using a text other than the Paulist Press translation. After the chapter numeral is listed the page number from the Paulist Press edition (e.g.: ii:127; 3:179).

Scriptural citations are from the Revised Standard Version unless otherwise noted.

Frequently Used Abbreviations

C&W   Edmund Colledge, O.S.A. and James Walsh, S.J., eds., *A Book of Showings to the Anchoress Julian of Norwich* (Toronto: Pontifical Institute of Mediaeval Studies, 1978).

EETS   Early English Text Society

EETS ES   Early English Text Society, Extra Series

EETS OS   Early English Text Society, Original Series

PG   J. P. Migne, *Patrologia Graeca*

PL   J. P. Migne, *Patrologia Latina*

SPCK   Society for the Promotion of Christian Knowledge

ST   Thomas Aquinas, *Summa Theologiae*

TI   Karl Rahner, *Theological Investigations*

Introduction

"All these infinitely obscure lives remain to be recorded, I said . . . feeling in imagination the pressure of dumbness, the accumulation of unrecorded life."[1] Such was Virginia Woolf's response to women's silence in history, and today's student of theology is struck by the same phenomenon. The articulation of Christian theology over the centuries has been the exclusive preserve of men.[2] Though the twentieth century Roman Catholic Church named two women, Catherine of Siena and Teresa of Avila, doctors of the church, one does not study their works in a typical course of doctoral studies in systematic theology. They are relegated to the discipline of "spirituality," which is usually considered a poor step-sister to the kind of doctrinal theology respected in the halls of academe. They are considered devotional writers, rather than theologians, and any doctrinal insights born of their experience of God are neither noticed nor studied as such, because one does not expect to find them.

But is it true that there have been no women contributors to doctrinal theology until now? Granted, until relatively recently, most women have lacked the equivalent of "five hundred pounds a year and a room of one's own,"[3] to say nothing of the educational opportunities necessary for scholarship. But there were some women in the past, particularly in women's religious communities, who were privileged with the privacy, independence and economic stability needed to render scholarship possible.[4] Are we really to believe that none of them put such resources to bear on theological reflection and the production of the fruits of such reflection? Feminist historiography has shown that women have been more than simply the victims of male oppression throughout history; they have also been active participants in shaping the cultural and social structures of their times, although usually unnoticed and unsung. The recovery of such facts has led to a new awareness of what events ought to be considered important and recorded in history, and even to the possibility of a new historical periodization more adequately inclusive of the experiences of women.[5] The awareness of women's reflection upon their experience of God and the examination of their records of such reflection should have a similar effect upon Christian theology. Present parameters for what designates legitimate theology need to be stretched to include the more experientially oriented mystical and devotional writings, many of which were produced by women. Careful investigation might reveal in such writings valuable doctrinal insights to add to our record of how the Christian faith has been experienced and understood in history, thereby enriching our own experience and understanding.[6]

This is especially important for feminist theology, which has begun to address questions previously unasked: What does theology look like when done by a woman? Is it substantially different from that done by a man? In what ways, and why? What effect does it have upon our understanding of theology as such? The past twenty years of attempting answers to such questions have yielded a considerable volume of respectable scholarship.[7] But what of the past? Is there any continuity between past and contemporary women theologians? Are there no paradigms in the whole history of theology from whom contemporary women theologians can draw inspiration?

This book is an attempt to provide such a paradigm. It presents the doctrinal insights of a woman theologian of the Middle Ages, Julian of Norwich, who, in May of 1373, received a vision of the crucified Jesus accompanied by certain revelations about the love of God for humanity. She recorded this experience and her initial reactions to it in what is now called the Short Text of her *Showings*. But for twenty years thereafter, Julian engaged in a continual process of prayer and study on the meaning of her experience. The result was the Long Text, which ought to be considered an example of theology as reflection upon the experience of faith, revealing how the contemplative experience of God can overflow into doctrinal teaching.[8]

Julian's doctrinal teaching is the subject of my enterprise. In the Long Text, Julian does more than merely describe her religious experience; she attempts to explain its doctrinal significance. In the process, she gives expression to all the main areas of Christian theology: incarnation and redemption, ecclesiology, the one and triune God, theological anthropology, creation and eschatology. Furthermore, the relationships of these doctrines to one another emerge creatively, giving an inner coherence to Julian's thought to form a comprehensive unity. Besides describing Julian's reflections on the various areas of Christian doctrine, I hope to analyze the pattern of her theology as a whole. What I am attempting, then, is the exposition of an original theological system, and in doing so, am reading Julian's *Showings* differently from most past readings.[9] Like Catherine and Teresa, Julian has been considered a devotional writer, not a doctrinal theologian, even though many have noted her doctrinal leanings.[10]

In selecting Julian as a paradigm for contemporary women theologians,

I do not mean to imply that she was a feminist. Such a designation would be anachronistic, indicating a consciousness and methodology that would have been totally foreign to Julian. She was a woman of her age, and her writing reflects the influence of the medieval theological mainstream, particularly of the Augustinian tradition. Therefore, while there are aspects of her theology that will be appealing to contemporary feminists, Julian also takes for granted and uses symbols and concepts that feminist theologians generally try to avoid. Nor am I suggesting, in drawing a parallel between Julian and today's women, that there is some eternal feminine experience that is essentially similar for all women, spanning different ages and cultures. Women's experience in every age reflects much more than their femininity; categories of economic status, social class, religious and cultural diversity create essential differences among women, even within a given period of history.

It is the category of gender that can provide a link between Julian and contemporary women. As distinct from the term "sex" which designates biological differences, the term "gender" indicates those differences between men and women created by social and cultural forces. Feminist studies have shown that gender must be taken into consideration in any investigation. There is no such thing as gender-neutral history, literature, or theology.[11] Consequently, feminist religious scholars have concluded that the Christian theological tradition has been produced from an overwhelmingly androcentric bias, and Christian women in every age have had to live with symbols created and perpetuated by men.[12]

Yet revisionist Christian feminists claim that Christianity's central symbols are multivalent, containing a "surplus of meaning" that transcends their seemingly androcentric and patriarchal bias.[13] Even gender-specific symbols for God and Jesus never signify merely maleness or femaleness; they have the capacity to affirm or reverse gender, question or support it, or they may have nothing to do with male and female roles, indicating values other than gender. Further, men and women react to the same symbols differently.[14] It can be instructive to see how a medieval woman such as Julian received and reflected upon the traditional symbols of Christianity. Did her appropriation of them yield elements that can be appreciated by today's feminists as supportive of women?

Even more basically, today's women theologians can learn something from the fact that Julian asserted herself as a theologian at a time when such a claim was considered inappropriate, indeed even dangerous, for women to make. Passing over from our day to hers and back again can help strengthen women's creative resolve to make their experiences count, their voices heard.[15] Julian's Long Text of *Showings* is a priceless gem of women's theological scholarship, and deserves to be recognized as such, helping to relieve the "pressure of dumbness" surrounding women's theology in history.

My aim is chiefly to expose, describe, and systematize the theology present in Julian's *Showings*. Some effort to situate her in her own milieu is an intrinsic part of that exposition, but I am not engaged in an historical work as such. Nor have I attempted to track down in any consistent, detailed way what Julian's sources may have been, beyond where they were obvious to me or where such research became necessary for my understanding of Julian herself. While I believe there is value in comparing Julian's reflections with those of the men of her time and with those of contemporary women theologians, I have done this sporadically at best. What I hope to have accomplished is a clear presentation of Julian's theology in order to restore to history one woman's theological reflection upon her experience of God.

Part One

Preliminaries

1

Historical Background

Julian's Life

Little is known about Julian's life,[1] not even her given name.[2] Knowledge about her comes from three sources: from her text itself, from mention of her in wills, and from *The Book of Margery Kempe*.

From Julian herself we learn the year of her birth and the circumstances surrounding the writing of her text. She was born at the end of 1342, since she received her revelations on May 13, 1373 when she was thirty and a half years old.[3] Seven days before the beginning of her revelations, Julian had fallen ill to the point of death and had received the last rites. Her revelations occurred during the day on May 13 and she received the last on the following night.[4] We do not know when she wrote the Short Text, but it is assumed that she did so shortly after the experience it describes.[5]

Julian does tell us something about the composition of the Long Text.[6] In the Short Text, she had hinted at her desire to write more about her revelations, since there were parts of them that she was unable to describe or comprehend immediately (xxiii:167). Afterwards, she constantly prayed to understand them more completely, a prayer that was not answered for fifteen years (86:342). Thus the composition of the Long Text probably did not begin until 1388. But it was not until "twenty years after the time of the revelation except for three months," in February 1393, that Julian understood the parable of the lord and the servant, which radically affected her perception of all the revelations (51:270, 276). This important part of Revelation 14 is not mentioned in the paragraph summarizing that revelation at the beginning of the Long Text (1:177). Therefore, we may conclude that there was a "first edition" of the Long Text, composed between the years 1388 and 1393, which then needed to be revised to include the insights gained from the parable of the lord and the servant. This "second edition" was not begun until 1393 and was completed sometime thereafter.[7]

This is all Julian tells us about the events of her life. There is no indication that she received any further mystical revelations. We learn one more fact from the scribe who provided a preface to the Short Text: that in 1413 Julian was still alive and was a recluse at Norwich (i:125).[8]

This last fact is corroborated by our second source, the evidence from wills found in the archives of the Norwich Consistory Court. In 1404, Thomas Emund, a chantry priest of Ayslesham in Norfolk, left one shilling to "Juliane anchorite apud St. Juliane in Norwice." This is the most definite of the witnesses. There are three others, wills dated 1393/4, 1415, and 1416, each of which leaves small amounts of money to a recluse named Julian in Norwich. We can safely assume that Julian lived until at least 1416.[9] There is no evidence that Julian was an anchoress until 1393, although it seems logical to assume that she was enclosed sometime before the writing of the Long Text to provide herself with the solitude conducive to such work.[10]

Our final witness is Margery Kempe, who consulted an anchoress in Norwich named "Dame Jelyan,"[11] probably in 1413,[12] which suggests that Julian must have acquired a reputation for spiritual guidance by then. The reliability of this witness is borne out by the remarkable likeness between some of the advice Margery reports and Julian's own ideas. Julian tells Margery to follow the urgings of her soul as long as they are "not against the worship of God and profit of her fellow Christians." For "the Holy Ghost moveth ne'er a thing against charity, for if He did, He would be contrary to His own self for He is all charity." She counsels against doubt: "He that is ever doubting is like the flood of the sea which is moved and born about with the wind," and recommends steadfast faith in the fact that the Holy Ghost dwells in the soul. She claims that God and the devil are "ever at odds" and reassures Margery that "the devil hath no power in a man's soul." Twice she mentions scripture: "Saint Paul saith that the Holy Ghost asketh for us with mourning and weeping unspeakable" (Rom 8:26) and "Holy Writ saith that the soul of a rightful man is the seat of God" (for which no matching text can be found).[13] As we shall see, these are some of Julian's favorite themes.

Julian's Literacy and Sources

Colledge and Walsh, the editors of the critical edition of *Showings*, have convincingly argued that Julian was a woman of substantial learning, far exceeding what could normally be expected of women in her day. They note a congruity of expression between Julian's book and such Middle

English works as the *Ancrene Riwle*, translations of the pseudo-Bonaventure's *Meditationes Vitae Christi*, Richard Rolle's *Meditations on the Passion*, and Walter Hilton's *Scale of Perfection*. Further, by the time she wrote the Long Text, Julian was familiar with Chaucer's translation of Boethius' *Consolation of Philosophy*, and the anonymous *Chastising of God's Children* (both of which were written around 1380), the writings of the author of *The Cloud of Unknowing*, and the English translation of Ruysbroek's *The Treatise of Perfection of the Sons of God*. This evidence shows that Julian kept abreast of contemporary spiritual literature. In addition, she exhibits a knowledge of patristic writers like Augustine and Gregory, and, most interestingly, of the works of William of St. Thierry, which in her day were known only in learned circles.[14]

In my own analysis of Julian's theological ideas, I have been impressed by her thorough grasp of Augustinian theology. Whether she read Augustine directly is impossible to determine, because all medieval theology was rooted in Augustine, and whole sections of his works were copied, usually without citation, into contemporary treatises.[15] In any case, whoever taught Julian her theology made sure she had a firm grounding in the so-called "Augustinian synthesis."[16] I also suspect that Julian was influenced not only by William of St. Thierry, but by the twelfth century Cistercians in general, and by the Victorines, all of whom were themselves thoroughly Augustinian.[17]

Beyond this, Colledge and Walsh also believe that Julian could read Latin and was well-versed in the rules of classical Latin rhetoric.[18] The first conclusion is based on the fact that many phrases in Julian's text seem to be direct translations from the Latin Vulgate.[19] It is conceivable that Julian had at her disposal an English translation of the Vulgate, but efforts to find a text matching her phrases have failed.[20] The conclusion that Julian knew Latin is further supported by the fact that she was a highly accomplished rhetorician. Throughout their edition of Julian's text, Colledge and Walsh indicate the presence of the figures of classical Latin rhetoric.[21] They also note that Julian grew in her mastery of rhetoric between the writing of the two texts; the Long Text exhibits a greater variety of figures and a stronger expertise in the use of them.[22] In many cases, the rhetorical figure is so intimately connected with the meaning of the theological idea being expressed, that to remove the figure would destroy the meaning altogether.[23] Julian was a pioneer here, in that she was transcribing into English linguistic rules and conventions that had been devised for the Latin language.[24]

The style of life Julian chose for herself, that of an anchoress, provided her with that independence, privacy, and leisure which made a life of learning possible for women.[25] It is also likely that she was a nun before her enclosure as an anchoress.[26] Both lifestyles suggest that Julian was from a wealthy family, since poor women were generally unable to become nuns, and anchoresses needed some source of financial support to attain ecclesial approval for enclosure.[27] If Julian were wealthy, it is not surprising that she was literate in English. The latter half of the fourteenth century saw a gradual growth in vernacular literacy among the laity of the upper and middle classes, some of which was accessible to women, although women's education generally lagged behind that available to men.[28]

Julian's having been a nun, however, does not explain the extent of her learning. While English nunneries of the early Middle Ages were renowned centers of learning, by the end of the fourteenth century their standard of education had greatly declined. The ability to read English was not always accompanied by writing skills. Most nuns could not understand Latin, and few could read or speak French, a fact that corresponded to the level of learning of most lay men and women of the time.[29] It is true that this should be understood in light of the gradual triumph of the English language over French and Latin in the age of Chaucer, rather than being interpreted merely as a lack of learning.[30] Julian's choice of writing in English was doubtless due to this influence, as well as to her desire to make her revelations known to the simple folk (9:191).[31] Yet Latin remained the language of the scholar in the church, and if Julian were able to read Latin, she was extraordinary in her age.

There is no way to discover how Julian acquired her learning. The best we can do is speculate that since the city of Norwich possessed one of the best libraries in the country, and all the chief religious orders of men had houses there, Julian could have had access to the resources necesary for scholarship.[32]

A frequent objection to Julian's literacy has been made because of the way Julian describes herself in *Showings*.[33] In the Short Text, she denies that she ought to be considered a teacher, for she is "a woman, ignorant, weak and frail" (vi:135), and in the Long Text, she introduces herself as "a simple, unlettered creature" (2:177). In both cases, Julian could simply have meant that, lacking a formal university education, she was not a scholar in the strict sense.[34] Besides, such a disclaimer of learning and scholarship was a convention for writers in the Middle Ages.[35] Put beside the textual evidence of learning and rhetorical expertise, these two remarks form comparatively inconsequential evidence for denying Julian's literacy. Thus Julian rightly deserves recognition as the first woman of letters in the English language.[36]

Julian's Mystical Experience

The first three chapters of the Short Text give us Julian's account of the context within which her showings occurred. In her youth she had prayed for three graces from God: to "have mind" of the passion of Christ, to be given a bodily sickness, and to be granted three wounds (i:125).

Julian had a deep desire to come closer to the passion of Christ. Even though she appreciated the efforts of the church to teach about Christ's sufferings, she desired something more: she would have liked to have been with Magdalen at the foot of the cross and to have seen physically the suffering of the Crucified, so that she could have suffered with him as did those who loved him. She desired what she calls a "bodily sight" of the crucifixion so that she could have a "truer mind of Christ's passion." Julian also prayed for a bodily sickness, a sickness unto death, wherein she would experience no earthly comfort, but all kinds of pain, both physical and spiritual, along with the torments and temptations of the devil. She hoped that all this suffering would more quickly unite her to God (i:125–26). We need not look far to discover Julian's motivation for desiring these two favors. Devotion to the passion of Christ was all-pervasive in the Western church by Julian's time, and both visions of the Crucified and debilitating illness were regarded as profitable ways of sharing in Christ's suffering.[37] One text in particular, which Julian almost certainly knew, encourages such desires very clearly. In the *Ancrene Riwle*, written for three young women aspiring to be anchoresses, the author holds up as extremely profitable both the cultivation of an awareness of Christ's physical sufferings and the healing effects of illness sent by God.[38] While the desire to share Christ's suffering was valued by both men and women, visions of the Crucified and illness were far more prominent in women's spirituality, and Julian's desire for these would have been regarded by many women as a conventional expression of piety.[39]

Julian prayed for these two gifts on condition that they be God's will (i:126); she asked for the third, however, without this proviso. She prayed to be given three "wounds": contrition, compassion, and longing with her whole will for God.[40] Julian regarded these as God's will for her, and indeed the proper attitude of the creature before God. By contrast, the first two desires seemed to be special favors, and thus she prayed for them on condition that they be God's will. Julian tells us she eventually forgot about the first two requests, but constantly prayed for the third (i:127). Julian therefore considered visions and special physical phenomena (such as the illness she desired) as secondary in importance to the love of God. While she prayed for them in the initial fervor of her youth, even then she realized that they were not as important as her third request for the three wounds, and as she gained maturity she forgot about them.[41]

Nevertheless, when Julian was thirty and a half years old, she fell ill to the point of death.[42] The curate in attendance at her bedside held a crucifix before her eyes and urged her to gaze upon it (ii:127–28). As Julian looked at the crucifix, it suddenly occurred to her that she should wish for the second wound: that God would fill her with compassion for the sufferings of Christ, compassion in its literal sense—suffering, "feeling with" Christ what he felt in his passion.[43] She tells us she did not desire at this point a bodily sight,[44] as she had in her youth, but merely longed to suffer with Christ. Nonetheless, much to Julian's amazement, she does receive a vision of the Crucified:

> Suddenly I saw the red blood trickling down from under the crown, all hot, flowing freely and copiously, a living stream, just as it seemed to me that it was at the time when the crown of thorns was thrust down upon his blessed head (iii:129).

The context and starting point for Julian's mystical experience, as it will be for her theology, is the vision of the passion of Christ. This is the only "bodily sight" she receives; though it changes many times, the sight of the crucified Jesus remains virtually constant throughout the course of the revelations.

At the same time that Julian views the bodily sight, she also receives what she calls a "spiritual sight of his homely love" in which she "sees" that "he is everything which is good and comforting for our help." This is followed by the imaginative sight of a small object the size of a hazel nut lying in the palm of her hand. In reply to her wonder about its meaning, Julian is "answered in her understanding" and she "sees" three things about its significance (iv:130–31). In all, Julian sees six things in her understanding accompanying the first bodily sight (v:132–33).

Julian's revelations came to her, then, in three modes: bodily sights, spiritual sights, and words or ideas formed in her understanding,[45] and Julian is precise about classifying each revelation accordingly.[46] Her experience is fundamentally visual, which lends a pictorial quality to her later theological reflections. But her visions were accompanied by an intellectual perception which contained the seeds of what would become her doctrinal teaching, developed in the Long Text.

The visionary character of her revelations places Julian in the tradition of continental women visionaries who flourished during the thirteenth and fourteenth centuries.[47] It is difficult to prove conclusively that direct knowledge of such a tradition inspired Julian either to pray as she did or to publish her own account of her showings. Whether or not the works of women visionaries were known in England during Julian's time is a point that scholarship has yet to settle.[48] However, it is logical to suppose that Julian knew of such women mystics by word of mouth, whether or not she read their works. Norwich, because of the wool trade, was in constant contact with the Low Countries and the Rhineland where many of the visionaries lived.[49]

While Julian shared some facets of the visionary experience with these women, she is in many ways different from them. For one thing, most continental visionaries received many revelations throughout their entire lives, while, as far as we know, Julian had only one such experience. Elizabeth Petroff has analyzed the content of the visions of medieval women mystics, grouping them into seven distinct types or stages.[50] A comparison of Julian's experience with this typology yields the following results.

The purgative stage of a visionary's life is a time of penance, typified by extreme self-loathing, particularly of the body, and a desire for humiliation, often accompanied by nightmarish attacks by demons and violent acts of self-torture.[51] With the exception of the nightmare about the devil at the end of her revelations (67:311–12, 69:315–16), we find nothing like this in Julian's text. Her attitude towards the body is sound, and she explicitly advises against rigid acts of asceticism and any form of self-degredation (76:329, 77:330–31).

In the psychic type of vision, the mystic receives premonitions about the spiritual state of others, particularly sinners, and ways in which she may help them, along with visions of purgatory or hell.[52] There was nothing of this sort in Julian's experience. At one point Julian does ask about the ultimate salvation of someone she loves, but she is told it is not for her to know (35:236). Nor is she given the vision of purgatory and hell she asked to receive (33:234). These two requests may indicate her awareness of what other visionaries experienced.

Doctrinal visions were given in answer to a particular theological dilemma, usually in highly symbolic or parabolic form, a category to which Julian's parable of the lord and the servant obviously belongs. Here Julian far exceeds the others, not only in the doctrinal content of her revelations themselves, but in the way she describes her efforts to understand their meaning.[53] This marks the most significant difference between Julian and the majority of women visionaries. While their writings may have doctrinal significance, few of the continental mystics seem to have engaged in the type of theological speculation that interested Julian.[54]

The devotional type of vision arose from meditations on the life of Christ, Mary, and the saints, and is the most common form of vision among the continental mystics.[55] We find this in Julian's meditative vision of Christ's dying and his eventually joyous countenance on the cross, and in her vision of Mary.[56] However, Julian does not stay with this type of experience for long; rather, she immediately moves on to consider its doctrinal significance. Indeed, compared to other visionaries, such devotional visions are sparse in Julian's text. Julian mentions that she "saw" no one in her revelations but Jesus and Mary (25:223), while most continental mystics had in addition elaborate experiences of a variety of saints.[57] The fact that Julian makes note of this may indicate her awareness of how her experience differed from that of others.

Participatory visions are experiences in which the mystic actually participates in the life of Christ or the saints, particularly in Christ's passion. Often such participation begins with the desire to share the grief of Christ's mother or Mary Magdalene at the foot of the cross. From here the mystic moves into the experience of suffering with the crucified Jesus.[58] Julian prayed for this in her youth (2:177–78), and does indeed share in Christ's pains, both bodily and spiritual. However, by the time she wrote the Long Text, her focus was not merely to describe this experience, but to use it as a springboard for her development of its doctrinal significance.

Many continental visionaries moved beyond participatory visions into a fuller development of them, the unitive type of vision. Here the "wound of love" is often described in highly erotic detail, aided by language from the *Song of Songs* and courtly love poetry.[59] Julian does pray for wounds, and in a few instances, calls Christ or the Spirit the spouse of the soul,[60] but she does not develop this theme. One is hard put to find a single erotic phrase in Julian's text, in marked contrast to the rapturous quality of other thirteenth and fourteenth century visionary writings.

The final type of vision described by Petroff is the vision of cosmic order, in which the whole of heaven and earth, hierarchically arranged, is viewed, often with the Virgin Mother of God, crowned in glory, reigning over all. Petroff suggests that what is operable here is an inchoate, symbolic awareness of the feminine as the ordering principle of the cosmos.[61] Julian does experience a vision of the glory of Mary in heaven (25:221–23), but her revelations which best exemplify this type are her trinitarian vision of the three heavens (22:216, 23:218), her vision of the exalted Christ (26:223–24), her last revelation of Christ reigning in glory in the soul (68:312–14), and her vision of Christ wearing all the saved as his crown at the end of the parable of the lord and the servant (51:277–

78). It is definitely Christ, not Mary, who reigns over the cosmos, and the feminine as principle of divine ordering is boldly developed in Julian's doctrine of the motherhood of Christ.

We may well wonder why there was such a preponderance of visionary experiences among women in the thirteenth and fourteenth centuries. Some of the difficulty we find today in appreciating such phenomena is mitigated by the realization that visions gave validity to women's religious autonomy and authority in a day when these were not respected.[62] To speak in the name of Christ, who revealed religious truths to them, earned for many women an esteem and even veneration that would have been withheld had they spoken on their own initiative. Petroff suggests that medieval holy women were caught in the paradox of needing to fulfill the stereotype of the "good woman," which demanded self-effacement and submissiveness, and at the same time to provide evidence of exceptionality, which demanded autonomy and the exercise of authority over others. Attributing their exceptionality to God's power was a way to resolve this conflict.[63]

For the women themselves, the visions encouraged growth in self-confidence and provided an acceptable vehicle for self-expression. Mystical experience, understood as being in continuity with the ordinary life of grace, is always mediated by the bodily and historical situation of the believer.[64] Therefore, however much a woman might attribute her insights to Christ, it is nonetheless her own experience and her own appropriation of that experience that is being expressed. In visionary experiences women's deep longings for authenticity encountered the divine, and found there the affirmation of such longings, allowing for a gradual growth in the self-assurance necessary for creative self-expression. Julian's experience seems to have had this effect upon her. While in the Short Text she denies that she ought to be considered a teacher, and points to Jesus as the true author of her text, she eliminates these passages from the Long Text. Instead Julian herself is very much present there, confidently recounting how she gradually came to a deeper understanding of her revelations, and allowing us to view a creative mind at work.[65]

However, Julian's main motivation for writing, as it was for many women visionaries, was the strong conviction that her revelations were meant not only for herself, but for all Christians:

Everything that I say about myself I mean to apply to all my fellow Christians, for I am taught that this is what our Lord intends in this spiritual revelation. And therefore I pray you all for God's sake, and I counsel you for your own profit, that . . . you contemplate God, who out of his courteous love and his endless goodness was willing to show this vision generally, to the comfort of us all. And you who hear and see this vision and this teaching, which is from Jesus Christ for the edification of your souls, it is God's will and my wish that you accept it with as much joy and delight as if Jesus had shown it to you as he did to me (vi:133–34; cf. xxii:164–65).[66]

Julian's revelations were not of the sort that embroiled her in the political controversies of church or state, as they were for Catherine of Siena and Joan of Arc. In fact, the absence of references in Julian's text to the disasters of late fourteenth century England and world is somewhat remarkable, since these included the three episodes and long-ranging effects of the Black Death, the Hundred Years War, the peasants' uprising of 1381, the Lollard controversy, the troubled reign of Richard II, the prosecution of heresy throughout Europe, and the Great Schism.[67] Julian alludes to such troubles only once (in the Long Text alone), and at that obliquely: "Holy Church will be shaken in sorrow and anguish and tribulation in this world as men shake a cloth in the wind" (28:226). Yet she is tremendously concerned about the effects of sin and suffering on human faith in God; this, if anything, can be said to be the central theme of her showings.

Julian's Concern for Orthodoxy

In reading *Showings*, one is struck by the number of times Julian insists upon her faithfulness to the rites, customs, and teachings of the church. The Short Text makes it clear that Julian drew strength from the sacramental life of the church. Believing herself to be at the point of death, she received the last rites, a curate attended her at her bedside, and she told "a religious person" about her mystical experience (ii:127–28, xxi:162). She teaches that the soul is united to God through contemplative prayer, but also through the good works recommended by the church (xix:159). She alludes to the eucharist (viii:137), and stresses in particular the importance of sacramental confession as part of the process of conversion and the life of perfection (xvii:155, xxiv:168). All these are retained in the Long Text with some additions.[68] Belief in the seven sacraments is mentioned as part of the content of Christian faith (57:292) and the Christ of her revelations is identified as "all the health and the life of the sacraments, . . . ordained in Holy Church" (60:298).

Furthermore, Julian makes an extended apology for her writing in the

Short Text, insisting that she is not trying to call attention to herself, "the wretched worm, the sinful creature" to whom the revelations were shown. The fact that she was a recipient of revelations does not mean she is holier than anyone else; in fact, Julian is sure that there are many who never had such an experience, but simply followed "the common teaching of Holy Church," who are far holier than she will ever be (vi: 133–34). Above all, she strongly denies that she is claiming to be a teacher: "But God forbid that you should say or assume that I am a teacher, for that is not and never was my intention, for I am a woman, ignorant, weak and frail" (vi: 135). Instead, her book is meant to point to Jesus who "is everyone's teacher," and Julian does not think the fact that she is a woman should prevent her from doing that.

In the Long Text, Julian retains the statements about her equality with other Christians (8, 9: 191) but she drops the apology for herself as a woman daring to publish her revelations, along with the concern that she not be considered a teacher. Instead, these are replaced by an emphatic assertion of her orthodoxy:

> But in everything I believe as Holy Church preaches and teaches. For the faith of Holy Church, which I had before I had understanding, and which, as I hope by the grace of God, I intend to preserve whole and to practice, was always in my sight, and I wished and intended never to accept anything which might be contrary to it. And to this end and with this intention I contemplated the revelation with all diligence, for throughout this blessed revelation I contemplated it as God intended (9: 192).

Throughout both texts Julian repeatedly insists that her revelations and her reflections upon them are completely consistent with the teachings of the church. In the Short Text, when she tells of her desire for a bodily sight of the crucifixion, Julian says that her wish for something more does not deny in any way the adequacy of what the church provides as instruction (i: 125). In fact, her desire for the "three wounds" was inspired by a story about St. Cecilia which she had heard told by a man "of Holy Church" (i: 127). Actually, belief and trust in church teaching were an integral part of the revelations themselves. When Jesus identifies himself for Julian, he says "I am the one whom Holy Church preaches and teaches to you" (xiii: 147), and when he shows Julian that Adam's sin was the greatest harm ever done he continues, "this is plainly known to all Holy Church upon earth" (xiv: 149). At one point, Julian learns of the great pleasure God takes in all those who follow the preaching and teaching of the church, for God *is* Holy Church, its ground, substance, teaching, teacher, end and means (xvi:152–53).

The assertion of the orthodoxy of her revelations is just as frequent in the Long Text; many of the points made in the Short Text are repeated verbatim or with only minor changes.[69] Julian adds the stamp of orthodoxy to a few more doctrinal points made in her revelations: to the fact that humankind is made in the image of the trinity (10:194), to the fact that the church recognizes sinners who have become saints (38:242–43), and to the purpose of the atonement (53:283).

Julian is particularly concerned to assert the orthodoxy of two points of doctrine in her revelations: their teachings about sin and salvation. In answer to her perplexity about sin, Julian tells us that Jesus informed her of all that was needful for her to know, but she quickly qualifies this statement:

> I do not say that I need no more instruction, for after he revealed this our Lord entrusted me to Holy Church, and I am hungry and thirsty and needy and sinful and frail, and willingly submit myself among all my fellow Christians to the teaching of Holy Church to the end of my life (xiii:148).

Julian obviously does not want us to think she is in a specially favored position with respect to other Christians, or that her revelations replace church teaching. In addition, this strong apology coming in the midst of the revelation about sin alerts us to the fact that what is to follow may perhaps be construed as contrary to church teaching.

The second doctrinal point about which Julian is concerned is the revelation that "all will be well." In light of the harm caused by sin, she does not understand how all can be well. Julian realizes that part of the answer is disclosed for all to see, and can be found in the teachings of the church. The other part of the answer is hidden in God's "secret counsels" and is not for humans to know (xiv:150). But this too, that we are not meant to know God's secret counsels, Julian insists is church teaching (xv:152). Again, this assertion alerts us to Julian's consciousness that this particular point of doctrine, as she states it, might be suspected of unorthodoxy.

In the Long Text, Julian records her struggle to reconcile the teaching of her revelations about sin and salvation with church teaching. Her revelations taught that God does not look upon sinners with wrath, and that, indeed, sin suffered becomes honor to the saved in heaven.[70] Related to this is the doctrine that "all will be well," which hints at universal salvation.[71] Julian was not merely concerned that others might construe these ideas as heresy; she herself had a problem with their orthodoxy. In contrast to considering sin as honor and to anything resembling universal salvation, Julian knew well that the church taught "many creatures will be damned, . . . eternally condemned to hell" (32:233). Nonetheless, Julian was directed by her revelations to "keep myself steadfastly in the faith, as I had understood before," that is, the faith of the church (32:233). There seemed to be a contradiction within her revelations themselves: on the one hand, God seemed almost to overlook sin as cause for damnation, turning it to honor, while uttering the somewhat ambiguous promise that "all will be well"; on the other hand, Julian is told repeatedly to stand by the teachings of the church which certainly appeared to be in opposition to the former. A desire was born in her to reconcile these two apparently contradictory teachings about salvation:

> that I might see in God in what way the judgment of Holy Church here on earth is true in his sight, and how it pertains to me to know it truly, whereby they might both [the revelations and church teaching] be reconciled as might be glory to God and the right way for me (45:257).

Julian tells us that she eventually found her answer to this dilemma in the "marvellous example" of the lord and the servant (45:257).[72]

What are we to make of Julian's concern about orthodoxy? Was she afraid of being accused of heresy? At first glance, the answer appears to be no, because, in stark contrast to the rest of Western Christendom, England was free of heresy until the Wycliffite controversy of the late fourteenth century.[73] It was only then that anything resembling the inquisition was exercised in England.[74] Julian was a contemporary of Wyclif, but she could not have been thinking of the full-fledged heresy that grew out of his writings when she composed the Short Text around 1373. Wyclif was not investigated for the first time until 1377, and not officially banned from Oxford until 1382.[75] Popular Lollardy, which grew out of Wyclif's moral and practical reform ideas, became a significant force only in the 1380s and was prosecuted with relative mildness until the fifteenth century.[76] Thus while Julian may have been aware of the investigation of Lollard heretics by the time she wrote the Long Text about 1393, this does not explain her insistence upon orthodoxy in the Short Text.

Could Julian have been aware of continental heresy and the church's prosecution of it that occurred throughout the fourteenth century? Specifically, considering Julian's position as a woman and a mystic, did she know about the church's inquisition into the so-called "Free Spirit" heresy, a heresy of which even the most orthodox mystics could be suspect? Contemporary scholarship has established the questionable nature of the heresy itself.[77] Unlike Catharism or Waldensianism, there was no sect or organized heretical group known as Free Spirits, and, while beguines and beghards were most often suspected of it, there is no evidence connecting them inevitably to it.[78] There seems to have been a great fear of antinomianism on the part of church officials in the later Middle Ages. The very existence of unregulated religious communities such as beguinages was enough to subject their adherents to abuse and persecution, without any real evidence of doctrinal error. Women who dared to teach publically or to publish written works on their own authority were particularly suspect, and if unrepentent of their so-called "errors," could be burned as heretics.[79]

Although Julian makes no overt reference to heresy, I think it highly likely that she knew about the prosecution of those suspected of the Free Spirit heresy, whether or not she knew precisely all of its supposed tenets, and this is partly why she was so concerned to insist upon her own orthodoxy.[80] Norwich was a city in direct contact, because of the wool trade, with the Low Countries and the Rhineland, places where inquisition into the Free Spirit heresy was constant and extensive.[81] Further, after a comparative lull, a new vigor was injected into inquisition into the heresy between 1353 and 1377, immediately before and during the time Julian would have composed the Short Text.[82]

A comparison of the points for which Julian shows concern with the supposed tenets of the Free Spirit heresy might yield some connection between the two. Julian professed her faithfulness to the sacraments, but this cannot by itself establish her knowledge of Free Spirit tendencies. While the denial of the necessity of the sacraments was associated with the Free Spirit heresy, it was also a chief reason for the prosecution of every other medieval heresy.

Julian also knew that she, as a woman, ought not advertise herself as a teacher. The idea that women ought not teach in the church is as old as Paul's first letter to the Corinthians (14:34),[83] and throughout the Middle Ages, concern about unauthorized preaching by lay people, especially women, motivated church authorities to investigate such preachers and teachers for heresy.[84] However, there is a special connection to the Free Spirit controversy of which Julian may have been aware: she may have known about the decree *Cum de quibusdam mulieribus* of the Council of Vienne, cited throughout the fourteenth century as the authoritative document legitimizing the investigation of women "commonly known as beguines" who dared to "discourse on the Trinity and the divine essence," and in doing so, spread opinions contrary to the faith, leading simple folk into error under their pretense of sanctity.[85] The fact that Julian was not a beguine[86] would not have exempted her from suspicion; women who were not beguines were prosecuted under *Cum de quibusdam mulieribus*.[87] While Julian is clear about not advancing herself as a teacher, she does gently but courageously challenge the attitude towards women implicit in the mentality fostered by *Cum de quibusdam mulieribus*: "But because I am a woman, ought I therefore to believe that I should not tell you of the goodness of God, when I saw at that same time that it is his will that it be known?" (vi:135).

It is interesting that Julian drops the apology for herself as a woman teacher in the Long Text at a time when heresy was actually being investigated on English soil, especially since women who dared to preach or teach were frequently suspected of Lollardy.[88] One explanation could be that there is no evidence of Lollardy in Norwich until about 1428.[89] There was also a relative lull in the inquisition into the Free Spirit heresy in the 1380s, although it was resumed with even greater force in the next decade.[90]

Most of all, Julian was concerned about the doctrinal orthodoxy of her revelations. The doctrines she particularly notes as being orthodox do not match exactly the supposed tenets of the Free Spirit heresy as outlined in *Ad nostrum*, the list of errors drawn up by the Council of Vienne which was used as a checklist in most heresy trials connected with the Free Spirit throughout the century.[91] However, there are two points of convergence between Julian's remarks and the Free Spirit controversy. They concern the doctrinal points about sin and salvation, the material in her showings that caused Julian the most anxiety.

One of the supposed teachings of the Free Spirit heresy was that once the soul had reached a certain stage of perfection, it was impossible to sin.[92] By contrast, Julian makes a point of saying she was told by God that she shall sin (37:241), and she is emphatic about the fact that she is an imperfect creature, despite her mystical experience (8, 9:191). However, sin does seem to lose some of its horror if God does not look upon the sinner with wrath (48:262, 49:263–64), and if sin can become cause for glory rather than damnation (38:242–43). Julian also advises that the sinner ought not dwell upon past sin, becoming filled with anxiety, but should give more attention to the love of God (79:334), a position that could easily be interpreted as a disregard for one's sinfulness.[93]

In addition, Julian's understanding of "all will be well" seemed to question the existence of hell and purgatory, although she protests vigorously that she does not doubt church teaching concerning them (33:234). Those suspected of the Free Spirit heresy were thought to deny the existence of hell and purgatory.[94] Julian's persistent struggle to reconcile these points of her revelations with orthodox teaching about them suggests that she may have known of cases where saying something similar was cause for suspicion.

It is possible that the suspicion of heresy actually attended the early history of Julian's text, for, by contrast to other Middle English spiritual writings, Julian's book had a limited circulation both during and after her lifetime.[95] As a text written in the vernacular by a woman it could have been suspected of heresy during the harsh prosecution of Lollardy after 1414.[96] This could have discouraged copies of it from being made or caused those extant to be destroyed.[97] An interesting apologetical postscript to the British Museum manuscript (Sloane) 2499 gives some credence to this theory. The scribe-editor has written:

> I pray almighty God that this book may not come except into the hands of those who wish to be his faithful lovers, and those who will submit themselves to the faith of Holy Church and obey the wholesome under-standing and teaching of men who are of virtuous life, settled age and profound learning; for this revelation is exalted divinity and wisdom, and therefore it cannot remain with him who is a slave to sin and to the devil. And beware that you do not accept one thing which is according to your pleasure and liking, and reject another, for that is the disposition of heretics. But accept it all together, and understand it truly; it all agrees with Holy Scripture, and is founded upon it, and Jesus, our true love and light and truth, will show this to all pure souls who meekly and per-severingly ask this wisdom from him (86:343).

The significance of Julian's struggle to reconcile the truth of her own experience with church teaching ought not to be lost on contemporary women. Feminist theology today is engaged in an attempt to counter hundreds of years of tradition which ignored or denigrated women's religious experience. Julian provides a courageous example of one who, based upon her own experience of God, dared to question church teaching, in a spirit of love and loyalty to the church, in a day when such question-ing was often construed as heresy punishable by death. In articulating her theology, she appropriates church tradition selectively, emphasizing those points of doctrine compatible with her own religious experience. Her courage to do this arose from the fact that she trusted absolutely in her revelations as indicative of God's will for herself and the whole church. She published her text as an effort to lead others, in a time preoccupied by the momentous questions of sin and salvation, to that same confidence in the great love of God which she had learned through her revelations, a love which promises, always and everywhere, "all will be well."

2

Julian's Theology

Having established that Julian deserves to be considered a theologian, it now remains to describe in what sense this is so. Hers is a theology which focused upon the chief doctrines of the Christian faith, and in a comprehensive way. Today the term "systematics" usually designates this type of theology, and indeed, it is from the perspective of contemporary systematics that I am examining and analyzing Julian's work. However, calling Julian's theology "systematic" without qualification can be misleading. It is not systematic at all, if "systematic" means a deliberate attempt to arrange the truths of faith into a comprehensive whole by planning in meticulous detail their place within an overarching design or conceptual framework.[1] Nonetheless, Julian's theology could be considered systematic if by "systematic" one means the emergence of a comprehensive system as the end result of a process of addressing particular questions of moment. Here a unified system gradually emerges by the recurrence of certain basic themes and ideas that become ever more closely interwoven in the discussion of particular theological issues.[2]

However, the term "systematics" as used today usually implies more than mere comprehensiveness. It indicates the deliberate use of some philosophical or scientific framework and a level of reflection several steps removed from the experience upon which it is based.[3] While Julian does considerably more than merely describe her experience, her reflections are not at the level of philosophical sophistication that is usually implied by the term "systematic theology." Nonetheless, I would argue that Julian does engage in some rigorous speculation, upon issues that puzzle her, in a way that resembles systematics properly so-called.[4]

A more useful way to situate Julian's theology is to employ Jean Leclercq's distinction between the scholastic and monastic theology of the Middle Ages.[5] Scholastic theology engaged the power of natural reason to construct coherent rational arguments for the truths of faith. Understanding, though set in the context of faith, was more nearly an end in itself. By contrast, monastic theology's main concern was nurturing the spiritual development of believers. It was based upon *lectio divina*, the meditative reading of scripture, out of which grew the insights gained through contemplation. While scholasticism eventually replaced monastic theology as a legitimate academic discipline, in Julian's day the two traditions continued to flourish side by side. Julian obviously belongs to the monastic tradition.

One of the hallmarks of monastic theology is that the inchoate, indescribable insights of contemplation come to expression not in clear, rational arguments, but in image-filled descriptions of God and the human before God. The emotional intensity of the original experience remains an intrinsic part of its rational articulation. But this certainly does not prevent monastic theology from arriving at original expressions of the doctrines of faith, nor does it inhibit the theological precision of the points being made. Indeed, it could be argued that such theology remains more precisely true to its object, the incomprehensible Mystery of God. It is also a theology compatible with the aim of contemporary feminism to be more holistic, integrating the affective with the rational, and remaining close to human experience. Grace Jantzen has described Julian's theology as a theology of integration. Although theologically sophisticated, Julian's reflections never lose touch with their source, her experience of God in the midst of suffering, and with their purpose, the pastoral comfort of her suffering contemporaries.

From Short Text to Long Text

The Short Text contains Julian's immediate reflections upon her mystical experience, the seeds from which her theology developed. At first glance it appears to be a collection of random ideas and comments, with no apparent order. However, the sequence of the revelations does reveal a pattern of sorts, helpful for understanding Julian's theological method.[6]

The pattern of Julian's theology is not a linear one. Rather, it is produced by a central image which holds together within it various doctrinal realizations. In the beginning that central image was the vision of the suffering Christ; thus the starting point of Julian's theology is christology, specifically Christ's passion. In chapters iv to vii the passion of Christ reveals all these things in a moment: the trinitarian nature of the God of love, the true meaning of creation and human nature, and the union of God and humanity that is salvation. Julian herself says of this showing:

> In this was contained and specified the blessed trinity, with the incarnation and the union between God and the human soul, with many fair revelations and teachings of endless wisdom and love, in which all the revelations which follow are founded and connected (1:175).

The doctrinal content of what Julian gradually unfolds piece by piece is contained all together in the sight she received at the beginning: the crucified Christ crowned with thorns.

In chapters vii and viii the passion of Christ also reveals sin and evil in contrast to the goodness of God and creation. In chapters ix to xiii the passion is explicitly linked to heaven and salvation; here a fuller examination of christology takes place with stress on the relation between the divine and human in Christ. Chapters xiii to xviii thoroughly examine the problem of sin in relation to the doctrine of salvation, and chapters xix to xxv offer some practical applications of this doctrinal content for Christian life and prayer. In addition to this basic pattern, two important themes are introduced in the first seven chapters: the theme of the trinitarian nature of God and the theme of the unity in Christ of all who will be saved. These two themes are thereafter related to every subsequent idea that is introduced. The result is a complicated synthesis in which each theological doctrine is always seen in its relationship to all the others, even when there is an attempt to isolate one or another of them for detailed discussion. Finally, Julian raises questions that bother her, and examines them from every angle. Three are treated in the Short Text: What is sin in relation to the goodness of God and creation? What is the relationship between suffering and salvation? How can all be well, given the great harm that sin causes us?

If by pattern one means a linear movement from one dogma to the next in an obviously organized progression, we will find nothing of the kind in Julian's theology. Yet there is an order and harmony in her reflections: they are held together organically in a central image; when one idea is developed in some detail, all else that has gone before is carefully related to it; and questioning of details occurs when something is not completely clarified. There is a good deal of repetition of themes, but in a progression towards an ever greater understanding of what was stated at the outset in the central image that contains all.

The Short and Long Texts Compared

The first noticeable difference between the Short and Long Texts is that

Julian has organized the latter into sixteen distinct showings, and she provides an outline and short description of each in Chapter 1 of the Long Text (1:175–77). The following summary of these revelations indicates the chapters in the Long Text (LT) which they comprise and the chapters in the Short Text (ST) to which they correspond.[7]

Revelation 1: The vision of the Crucified crowned with thorns, which reveals the mystery of the trinity, the incarnation, and the union between God and humanity (LT:4–9; ST:iii–vii).

Revelation 2: The discoloring of Christ's face in his passion (LT:10; ST:vii).

Revelation 3: God, almighty, all wisdom and all love, has made all that is and does everything that is done (LT:11; ST:viii).

Revelation 4: The scourging and shedding of Christ's blood (LT:12; ST:viii).

Revelation 5: The fiend is overcome by Christ's passion (LT:13; ST:viii).

Revelation 6: God rewards all the blessed in heaven with thanks (LT:14; ST:viii–ix).

Revelation 7: We are kept in love, in good times and bad, by the goodness of God (LT:15; ST:ix).

Revelation 8: The last pains and the dying agony of Christ (LT:16–20; ST:x–xi).

Revelation 9: The delight of the trinity in the redemption accomplished by Christ, a joy and delight that we share in now through grace, and will do so more fully in heaven (LT:21–23; ST:xii).

Revelation 10: The heart of Jesus cloven in two by love (LT:24; ST:xiii).

Revelation 11: Spiritual showing of Christ's mother (LT:25; ST:xiii).

Revelation 12: Our Lord God is all sovereign being (LT:26; ST: xiii).

Revelation 13: We ought to have great regard for God's deeds: both creation and redemption. By the same might, wisdom, and goodness that accomplished these, God will make all things well (LT:27–40; ST:xiii–xviii).

Revelation 14: Our Lord God is the ground of our beseeching. Our prayer delights God and out of goodness God will fulfill it (LT:41–63; ST:xix).

Revelation 15: We shall someday be taken from our pain and woe and be rewarded with Jesus, fulfilled with joy and bliss in heaven (LT:64–65; ST:xx–xxi).

Revelation 16: The Trinity, in Christ Jesus, dwells endlessly in our soul, and we shall not be overcome by our enemy (LT:66–86; ST:xxii–xxv).

Little of substance was dropped from the Short Text. Chapters i through vii of the Short Text remain virtually the same in the Long Text, with a few rearrangements and a rather substantial addition to the Short Text's chapter iv. Beginning with chapter viii, every few lines of the Short Text are embellished with substantial additions in the Long Text. By far the most important addition, comprising one-third of the Long Text, is the material added to Revelation 14, very little of which is in the Short Text. It was probably added during Julian's third and final editing of the text, because it is not described in the summary of Revelation 14 in chapter 1 of the Long Text. This material contains the parable of the lord and the servant and Julian's trinitarian theology, including the theme of the motherhood of God. After Revelation 14, the rest of the Short Text is repeated, with substantial embellishments and additions as before. The final chapters of the Long Text, chapters 75 through 86, contain new material.

The Parable of the Lord and the Servant

Most of what Julian has added in the Long Text falls into the category of additional reflections upon the material in the Short Text. But in a few cases, she records for the first time something that was part of the original revelation but which she suppressed in the Short Text. The most notable example of this is the parable of the lord and the servant.

Julian herself tells us that the parable was part of the original experience. In the midst of the fourteenth revelation about prayer, Julian returns to the perplexity she had felt about the content of the previous revelation: that the church teaches we are sinners and deserving of punishment, yet God looks upon us only with love. She is so perplexed by the seeming contradiction between these, that she pleads for help:

> I cried within me with all my might, beseeching God for help, in this fashion: Ah, Lord Jesus, king of bliss, how shall I be comforted, who will tell me and teach me what I need to know, if I cannot at this time see it in you? (50:266–67).

Then, Julian tells us, "our courteous Lord answered very mysteriously, by revealing a wonderful example of a lord who has a servant." Julian then recounts the parable as it came to her, stopping at a certain point to say: "at this point the example which had been shown vanished" (51:267). All that occurs after this in chapter 51 records Julian's later reflections upon and interpretations of the parable.

Why did Julian suppress the parable in the Short Text? She recognized that it was an answer to her prayer for clarification. Yet she could not understand it: "the complete understanding of that wonderful example was not at that time given to me." While it is true that all her revelations contained secrets not fully realized by her immediately, this one was particularly unclear: it was "mysterious," in which the "secrets" were "deeply hidden" (51:269). Julian was also confused about its orthodoxy. It was given as the reconcilation of the apparent conflict between church teaching and her revelations, but because she did not understand it clearly she could not explain that reconciliation. She understood the "beginning of the teaching": she saw the lord looking upon the servant only with love; she saw no cause for blame in the servant, even though he had fallen into a ditch and could not serve the lord (51:271). These symbols simply corroborated her understanding of how God looks upon sinners as given in her revelations. But she did not see how contemporary church teaching, especially about the damnation of sinners, could be reconciled to it. Finally, because it was so mysterious and ambiguous, there is a suggestion that at first Julian passed over it as unimportant. But later, for twenty years after the showing, she received "inward teaching" that she should pay attention to the parable, even though it seemed mysterious and "indifferent" to her (51:270).

When Julian finally understood its meaning, the parable assumed a central place in the revision of her text. It clarified many things that were unclear, and it enabled her to develop her theology of the trinity and of the motherhood of God, both of which immediately follow the parable in the Long Text. In fact, most of the Long Text was edited in light of it.[8]

In the parable, Julian sees a great lord sitting in state, and a servant standing before him, ready to do his will. The lord looks upon the servant lovingly, and sends him on a mission. The servant goes eagerly, but falls into a ditch and is so severely injured that he cannot help himself in any way. His greatest hurt is lack of consolation, because he can no longer turn his head to look upon his lord; thus he allows himself to be plagued by the distress of his situation. Julian is amazed that the servant could suffer all this so meekly. She looks carefully to see if she can detect any fault in him, but she cannot. In fact, the only cause of his falling was his good will. He is still as eager to do the lord's will as he had been when he was standing in the lord's presence, even though he has fallen and is unable to do so (51:267–68).[9]

Meanwhile, the lord continues to look on the servant most tenderly, "with a double aspect." Outwardly, the lord looks upon the servant with compassion and pity. Inwardly, Julian sees more deeply into the motivation for this: the joy the lord has in the nobility he intends for his servant.

Indeed, the goodness and honor of the lord demand that his servant be rewarded, above what he would have been if he had not fallen. All the suffering that resulted from his falling will be turned into everlasting honor (51:268–69).

At this point the vision vanished, and Julian remained in perplexity about its meaning. She thought that the servant symbolized Adam, but she saw many characteristics in him that did not fit with church teaching concerning Adam (51:269). For twenty years thereafter, Julian was instructed to pay attention to every detail revealed in the parable, including the attitudes of the characters and the type and color of the clothing they wore. It should be noted that Julian's experience of this revelation is essentially visual; the parable is a silent moving story. The cognitive and theological content she eventually derives from it are the result of her concentrated attention on its visual details. What follows here is the actual progress of her reflections upon the meaning of the parable over a twenty year period.

Julian understood that the lord signifies God and that the servant is Adam, representing all humanity. Because of his injuries, the servant cannot climb out of the ditch to complete the lord's will, and he cannot see how the lord looks upon him in order to regain the proper perspective on things; only his will is continually preserved in God's sight. God continues to look upon him with love because of this good will, but he himself is blinded and hindered from knowing it. Thus he sees clearly neither his lord, nor what he himself truly is in the sight of God. This is "the beginning of the teaching" which Julian understood at the time the showing was given, concentrating on how God looks upon sinners: always kindly disposed towards them and longing to bring them to bliss (51:270–71).

Next Julian recounts how she examined the various details of the parable for their allegorical significance. The lord sits alone in the wilderness. This symbolizes the fact that the human soul was made to be God's dwelling place, but when Adam fell, humanity was unable to perform that office. Rather than prepare an alternate place, God is content to sit on the ground and wait until a proper city is restored. The lord's clothing is azure blue, signifying God's steadfastness; it is wide and ample, signifying that God possesses endless joy and desires to restore this to the servant through grace. The lord's demeanor is merciful, revealing love and pity. The loving gaze which the lord keeps on the servant has a dual significance: part is compassion and pity, part joy and bliss. The compassion and pity are for Adam, but the joy and bliss are for the falling of God's Son, who is equal in every way to the Father (51:271–72).

Julian gradually comes to see a double significance in the servant as well. Outwardly he is dressed like a common laborer ready for work, clad in an old threadbare tunic, which Julian thinks unfitting for the servant of a great lord. But inwardly, she sees in him a ground of love, the love he has for the lord, which is the same as the love the lord has for him. The inward wisdom of the servant makes him see that there is one thing which will pay honor to the lord, and out of love, with no regard for himself, the servant rushes off to do the lord's will (51:272–73).

Then Julian begins to understand more about the servant's mission. There was a treasure hidden in the earth which the lord loved, a food pleasing to him. The servant is sent to do "the greatest labor," that is, to be a gardener, tilling the earth, making streams to run, and fruit to grow. He is never to come back until he has prepared the food in a way pleasing to the lord. In the meantime the lord sits in the wilderness and waits for the servant's return. Julian tells us that she did not understand all that this meant, and wondered where the servant came from (51:272–74).

Finally, Julian reaches a new level of understanding. She realizes that the servant represents both the second person of the trinity and Adam, who includes all humanity. When Adam fell, God's Son fell; Adam fell from life into death and then into hell, but God's Son fell with Adam in order to save Adam from hell. Since God's Son and Adam are joined by an eternal union, they can never be separated. Jesus Christ has taken upon himself all human blame, and thus God does not assign any more blame to sinners than to him. Even though he was equal to God in his divinity, he willingly took upon himself all human sinfulness, with no regard for himself or the pains he would suffer. Christ's humanity therefore includes all who will be saved by the incarnation and passion of Christ (51:274–76).

Julian then interprets all the details of the servant's stance and garb for their allegorical significance. The wisdom and love in the servant represent the divinity, the poor clothing he wears the humanity. His rushing away symbolizes the divinity in its eagerness to accept human nature; the hurt he experiences as a result of his fall represents human flesh, in which he undergoes mortal pains. The tunic is Christ's human flesh, its scantiness signifying that there was nothing to separate the divinity from the humanity. The torn tunic represents the tearing of Christ's flesh, which Julian had witnessed in her visions. The writhing and moaning of the servant in the ditch symbolizes the fact that Christ could not rise until he had died and given over his soul into God's keeping, with all humankind whom he had been sent to save. At the time of Christ's death, while his body lay in the grave, he showed his power, first by going down into hell to join the souls there together with himself in heaven. On Easter morning the suffering ended forever (51:275–77).

As a result, human flesh, Adam's tunic, is no longer old, scanty, threadbare, and short, but new, white, and forever clean, fairer even than the clothing of the lord. The lord no longer sits on the bare ground, but in a rich and noble seat; the Son no longer stands poorly clad as a servant, but sits at the lord's right hand, richly clothed, with a precious crown upon his head. All the saved form Christ's crown: the Father's joy, the Son's honor, the Holy Spirit's delight (51:278).

Once we know the outline of the parable, we can see its influence throughout the Long Text. There are four intimations of it, also missing from the Short Text. The first is found in the first revelation when God's courtesy and "homeliness" are revealed; to facilitate Julian's understanding, God shows her an "example" of a great lord who welcomes a poor servant into his presence with great familiarity and love (7:188). The second occurs in the sixth revelation after Julian hears God thanking her for her service; she sees, in her understanding, God as a lord in his own house, entertaining all his friends at a great feast (14:203). The third appears immediately after this, when Julian describes the second degree of heavenly bliss wherein the blessed will witness God's gratitude for each one's service; again, Julian gives the example of a king thanking his subjects, a thanks that becomes more honorable if it is proclaimed to all the realm (14:204). The fourth is found in the sixteenth revelation where Julian describes how one is led from the contemplation of a noble lord's realm to seek the high place where the lord actually dwells (68:313).

There is a significant recapitulation of the end of the parable in the sixteenth revelation, which was recorded in the Short Text (xxii:163–64). Julian sees her soul as a fine city from which Jesus, clad in glory, rules heaven and earth (68:312–13). The parallel to the end of the parable is obvious, where "the Son, true God and true man, sits in his city in rest and in peace" (51:278). Julian considers this last revelation the conclusion and confirmation of all the revelations (66:310). The fact that the lordship imagery plays such a large part in it attests to the centrality of the parable of the lord and the servant.

Julian views the parable as the showing which gave clarity to the points of doctrine she was confused about (45:257), and she refers back to certain aspects of it after she has recorded it (52:280–81). Besides these specific references, once one is familiar with the parable, one can see intimations of it everywhere, especially wherever Julian refers to God's courteous love.

Generically, the parable of the lord and the servant is a medieval preacher's *exemplum*, a fact of which Julian was aware, since she always refers to it as an "example."[10] The medieval *exemplum* was a short, illustrative story used by preachers to emphasize the point of a sermon.[11] It took several forms: anecdotes or legends about biblical and classical heroes or saints; allegorical figures based in scripture; or stories, fables, and figures drawn from people, animals, and objects in the everyday scene.[12] Many *exempla* were combinations of the latter two types, as is Julian's. While these took their initial inspiration from scripture, they developed on their own in accordance with facts drawn from ordinary experience.[13] The figure of the noble king or lord, based upon the feudal ideal and characterized by affability and generosity, was frequently employed.[14]

From about the middle of the thirteenth century, *exempla* began to be collected, often arranged in alphabetical order according to topic, in so-called "example books."[15] The *exempla* included in them were usually only the bare bones, mere outlines, of anecdotes or tales.[16] They were meant to be inserted into sermons in order to illustrate a point taken from scripture and, usually, to teach a moral. But the scriptural point to be illustrated and the moral to be drawn were left to the discretion and ingenuity of the preacher and were not included in the example book.[17] These books were extremely popular in Julian's day.[18]

Julian's *exemplum* is the simple story of a noble lord who had a loyal servant, whom he sent on a mission. Though the servant was eager to do the lord's will, he fell into a ravine and was powerless to do so. Nonetheless, the lord continued to look upon the servant with love, even though the servant did not realize this and suffered because of his failure. This is the way the story would have been outlined in the example book. The preacher would embroider it with pictorial details, each of which would then be explained for its allegorical significance. Julian regarded God as her teacher, and here God acts as the kind of preacher she would have been familiar with, using a simple tale to illustrate the main point of the teaching.[19] However, in this case, the way the story is told is through pictures rather than words. Julian is not listening to a sermon, but seeing the story's enactment in her imagination. The story is there before her, visually, and its allegorical interpretation is the product of her own reflection.

Julian's *exemplum* has scriptural ties. When we begin to examine this aspect of it, the apparent simplicity of the story acquires a surprising depth of meaning. The point of Julian's revelations centered around the message of consolation which the passion of Christ was meant to give. In spite of the hurt and suffering caused by sin, Christ's passion encourages the faithful not to fear; because of it, God gives the reassurance that all will be well. The parable goes immediately to the heart of this message and is meant to illustrate it clearly.

In its surface meaning, Julian initially sees the parable as representing Adam's fall as recounted in Genesis. The part she cannot reconcile with contemporary church teaching is the attitude of the lord, who represents God. She had been taught that God was justly angry with Adam who was deserving of punishment because of sin, but the parable shows nothing of this in God. Looking at the servant from God's point of view, she also sees no blame in the servant. In order to understand this, Julian must go far beyond the immediately obvious meaning of the story, a simple metaphor for the fall. Her reflection leads her deeper into its hidden meanings, and consequently into its further relationship to scripture. As a result, the simple *exemplum* becomes an exceedingly rich symbol with several layers of meaning, all full of scriptural allusions.

Medieval Exegesis

Medieval scriptural interpretation was dominated, in both scholarly circles and the popular imagination, by the allegorical method, summed up in the mnemonic device: *Littera gesta docet; quid credas, allegoria; Moralis, quid agas; quo tendas, anagogia.*[20] This method of exegesis understood the historical events portrayed in scripture as holding deeper symbolic meanings. Old Testament events allegorically prefigured Christ, church, and sacraments; both Old and New Testament events tropologically (morally or mystically) represented the spiritual relationship between God and the individual soul, and anagogically foreshadowed heaven and the last things. Though discredited in modern times, the allegorical method was actually capable of great depth of thought, reaching to the heart of the scriptural message in a way that mere literalism, or even anything resembling modern historical criticism, could never do.[21]

When Julian contemplated her parable over a twenty year period, she treated it as a visual representation of the scriptural story of salvation, understood in terms of the four senses of medieval exegesis. Literally, it was an imaginative tale, meant to illustrate a point of doctrine, which Julian recognized as a metaphor for Adam's fall and for how God looks upon sinners. We are already in the realm of allegory, but the allegory goes deeper. Julian's discussion of the double aspect under which she viewed the parable testifies that she was aware of this: the vision "was shown doubly with respect to the lord, and . . . doubly with respect to the servant." One part was "spiritual in bodily likeness," the other "more spiritual without bodily likeness." A deeper, more spiritual meaning accompanied the more immediately apparent, "literal" sense of the imaginative vision (51:267).

Allegorically, Adam was a figure of Christ, and Julian eventually recognizes that the servant is also the suffering Christ she has seen in her visions. Tropologically or mystically, the relationship between the lord and the servant represents the relationship between God and the human soul, clarifying for Julian why God looks upon sinners only with love, and enabling her to develop her understanding of the unity between Christ and humanity. Finally, this leads into the anagogical sense, which the end of the parable represents, and which is a central point in her revelations: the salvation of everyone "of good will" in Christ.

Lectio Divina

Julian's method of study was founded in *lectio divina*, the monastic tradition of sacred reading, which was practiced not to gain understanding for its own sake, but to attain an appreciation of God, its object.[22] *Lectio* and *meditatio* worked together hand in hand. *Lectio* meant "active" reading, demanding full participation of body as well as mind. The words were spoken aloud so that they were heard as well as seen, and felt by the moving of the lips. *Meditatio* meant "learning by heart," i.e., with the whole body, allowing the words that were seen, heard, and felt to become fastened in the memory and understood by the intellect, so that the will might desire to put into practice the message of the words. Thus *oratio*, the petition for God, and *contemplatio*, resting in the desire for God and the fruits of this desire, were the end and goal of the *lectio* and *meditatio*.[23]

In monastic meditation, the words of scripture were virtually "chewed over"; hence the word "rumination" came to be used for it, and the process was often described by the image of spiritual nutrition. As a result, the reader became deeply imbued with the words and themes of scripture, allowing for the phenomenon of reminiscence, in which a mere word or allusion could spontaneously elicit other passages from elsewhere in the bible. This had a great effect on literary composition. Certain words would set up a chain reaction of associations with other scriptural words or texts which had no actual connection to the topic being discussed. Thus, like the patristic authors, the medieval writer often strayed off the subject at hand, meandering freely about the topic, seeming to follow no plan other than the plan of association described above, although such seeming artlessness was often carefully contrived.[24] Another factor aiding rumination and reminiscence was the power of the medieval imagination to picture the colorful details of scenes suggested by a text. When this faculty was applied to scripture, the stories and events recorded there came vividly to life, thoroughly engaging the mind and emotions and leaving a strong impression on the memory. All of this had consequences for literary expression, causing writers to "express themselves spontaneously in a biblical vocabulary." Biblical reminiscences are often not quotations as such, but the words of the author who may not even be conscious of owing them to a source.[25] Thus a study of the influence of scripture on a given medieval work can never be restricted to the use of the bible as a source book for direct quotations.[26]

Julian lived in a world in which the language and content of scripture permeated every aspect of life and thought. The most ordinary animal, tree, or stone could call up some scriptural figure or event. Epic and chronicle were filled with biblical echoes. The bible was visually represented in the paintings and carvings on church walls and brought to life on the medieval stage through the mystery plays. Its realities were reenacted in the drama of the liturgy, the themes of which are reflected in medieval lyrics and poems. *Piers Plowman*, to name only one, is perhaps "the most profound example of a work written in imitation of the Bible."[27]

Julian's text is no exception; her literary expressions are "mosaics of Scripture borrowings," conflations of various biblical texts, many of which are carefully constructed for rhetorical effect.[28] The parable of the lord and the servant is an elaborate example of such a conflation of biblical texts, created by Julian's powers of reminiscence and pictorial imagination. While it is impossible here to cite all of its biblical allusions,[29] we can comment in broad strokes upon its most significant scriptural bases.

We have already seen that Julian first viewed the parable as an interpretation of the story of the fall in the third chapter of Genesis. The fact that Adam prefigured Christ led her to see the servant as the Crucified, recalling both the gospel accounts of the passion and the deutero-Isaian suffering servant, which in Julian's day was universally interpreted as a figure of Christ. Once the identification between the servant and Christ has been made, Julian reflects upon it with the help of the Johannine and Pauline writings. The love between lord and servant is described with allusions to the relationship between Christ and the Father in John's gospel. The willingness of the servant to leave self aside in order to do the will of the lord recalls the kenotic hymn of Philippians 2. The relationship between Christ and humanity, resulting from the identity of the servant as both Christ and Adam, is described in terms of the Adam/Christ typology

of Romans and the image of the body of Christ found in 1 Corinthians and
Ephesians. This identity also enables Julian to develop the notion of the
predestination of all the saved in Christ, with allusions to Ephesians and
Colossians. Finally, the eschatological finale of the parable echoes the
words and phrases used to describe the new Jerusalem of the Book of
Revelation. Thus the parable symbolizes the whole story of salvation told
in scripture, stretching from the beginning of humanity into the as yet
unfulfilled future.

While the practice of *lectio divina* enabled Julian to give the parable its
literary form and meaning, it also shaped the method she used to reflect
upon it.[30] In the midst of her exposition of the parable, Julian explains
three ways by which she understood it (and indeed all her revelations)
gradually over time: "The first is the beginning of the teaching which I
understood from it at the time" (51:269). This was her rudimentary
"reading" of the parable, the *lectio*.

"The second is the inward instruction which I have understood from it
since," which Julian describes in detail:

> For twenty years after the time of the revelation except for three months, I
> received an inward instruction, and it was this: You ought to take heed to
> all the attributes, divine and human, which were revealed in the example,
> though this may seem to you mysterious and ambiguous. I willingly agreed
> with a great desire, seeing inwardly with great care all the details and the
> characteristics which were at that time revealed, so far as my intelligence
> and understanding will serve, beginning with when I looked at the lord
> and the servant, at how the lord was sitting and the place where he sat, and
> the color of his clothing and how it was made, and his outward appearance
> and his inward nobility and goodness; and the demeanor of the servant as he
> stood, and the place where and how, and his fashion of clothing, the color
> and the shape, his outward behavior and his inward goodness and willing-
> ness (51:269–70).

This is a description of *meditatio*, the memorization of detail, which
enabled the parable, in a way similar to verses from the bible, to become
part of Julian. It illustrates the use of the pictorial imagination which was
part of that meditation and which enabled the medieval retelling and
reliving of scriptural stories with all the vividness of contemporary life.

Julian prayed to understand the meaning of the parable, thus *oratio*
accompanied her practice of *meditatio*: it was prayerful meditation. She
followed the instructions to meditate on the details of the parable "with
great desire" and the three ways of understanding together led her to the
prayer of faith and trust in God (51:269–70).

Finally, Julian's third way of understanding is "all the whole revelation from the beginning to the end, which our Lord God of his goodness freely and often brings before the eyes of my understanding" (51:269). This is very like the sudden insights of *contemplatio*, which are brief and fleeting and go beyond the ability of the mind to comprehend entirely or to express adequately in words.

Julian saw these three ways of understanding as part of one method: "And these three are so unified, as I understand it, that I cannot and may not separate them" (51:269), and this method bears a striking similarity to the monastic practice of *lectio divina*.

Julian's Theological Method

Paul Ricoeur's masterful *Symbolism of Evil* analyzes the process whereby "symbols give rise to thought." First, experience finds expression in a "primordial symbol," a symbol which is shared and reappropriated again and again sympathetically by the community of faith. Such a primordial symbol is spontaneously and immediately related to the experience which gave rise to it or to the reenactment of that experience by others. The second stage in the process is marked by the creation of myth, a more elaborate development of the primordial symbol in narrative form. This more elaborate symbol, which always contains within it the impulse and meaning of the primordial symbol, gives rise to the occasion for thought—more abstract, philosophical reflection on the meaning of reality as revealed by the symbol. This is not an "allegorizing interpretation that pretends to find a disguised philosophy under the imaginative garments of the myth," but rather "a philosophy that starts from the symbols and endeavors to promote the meaning, to form it, by creative interpretation."[31]

We can glimpse this process at work in Julian's creation of her theology, which has its starting point in her experience of God in the midst of suffering. The primordial symbol expressive of this experience is the suffering Christ, a symbol of the love of God meant to give comfort. This symbol dominates the Short Text, and it contains within itself implicitly a rich store of meaning which is not fully developed there. In the Short Text Julian remains close to the images and words of her revelations and does not travel far beyond them. The image that dominates the Long Text is no longer the Crucified, but the more elaborate parable of the lord and the servant, representative of the mythic phase of Ricoeur's process. This image places the symbol of the crucifixion within the larger context of the whole scriptural story of God's work of redemption. Both of these images, the crucified Christ and the parable of the mystery of salvation, are symbols from the heart of the Christian consciousness. Julian's experience is a "reenactment" of the communal Christian experience which gave preeminence to the image of the crucified Christ and the biblical story of redemption.

Finally, the "fanciful history" of the lord and the servant gives rise to the occasion for thought, providing answers to the perplexing difficulty of the inconsistency between Julian's experience and official church teaching. In her probing of this image over a period of twenty years, Julian touches upon essential theological questions: What is sin? Why didn't God prevent it? How can sin and suffering be reconciled to God's assurance that all will be well? Why does God look upon us only with love, when as sinners we deserve God's wrath? In her seeking the answers to such questions, we can glimpse, perhaps, a bit of the scholastic in Julian. They involve her in some speculation about the nature of God, humanity, sin and grace *as such*, not simply as they bear upon her contemplative life. They cause her eventually to form a theological synthesis, in which all the doctrines can be seen in relation to each other, which is one of the aims of systematic theology.

Yet, methodologically, Julian is no scholastic. She does not follow the strictly logical method of question, disputation, and conclusion practiced in the schools.[32] Nor is her aim simply knowledge as such, but the security of trust in God which enlivens faith. The method followed by Julian in her twenty years of reflection was the *lectio divina* of monastic theology. In the context of prayer, Julian returns over and over again to the images and words of her revelations allowing them to become part of her, through the memorization of detail that characterizes the *meditatio*, and through the relishing of the sudden insights given her in moments of contemplation. All of this was aided by study of traditional and contemporary theologians and spiritual writers, whose influence is evident in Julian's final synthesis.

Julian realized that the symbol of the lord and the servant, full of scriptural allusions, contained a "surplus of meaning" which no one interpretation could exhaust, for she returned to it again and again for newer and deeper insights into what had been revealed to her.[33] Thus, over a period of twenty years, the symbol yielded a richness of thought that rightly deserves the name of theology. Through this symbol, Julian is able to go beyond the rudimentary doctrinal explorations of the Short Text and develop them into a theology that is always carefully consistent with

Christian tradition and deeply reminiscent of scripture, but also highly original and creative, relevant to her historical milieu.

Julian would not have regarded herself as a creative theologian.[34] She wanted to publish the realizations she had learned from her revelations for the benefit of others. She believed she was transmitting God's special word to her, a word which captured in an essential way the true meaning of the gospel. In the process of transmitting this word, she found herself deeply involved in what we call theological reflection. The theological system which eventually emerged from this process of reflection is only implicit in her text. What I have attempted here is a more precise explication of that, allowing it to come to full view, so that we may better appreciate it for what it is, a disciplined reflection upon the experience of faith, truly deserving the name "theology."

Julian's whole work could be viewed as a commentary on the Johannine verse that God is love, and those who dwell in love, dwell in God and God in them (1 Jn 4:16). Part Two of this book examines Julian's theology of the love of God. It was first revealed as the love of Christ manifest in his suffering on our behalf; therefore Chapter 3 treats christology as the starting point of Julian's theology. The passion also revealed the depths of God's love, leading into a consideration of the other attributes of God, and especially God's trinitarian nature; Chapter 4 accordingly examines Julian's doctrine of God and of the trinity, which she describes as might, wisdom, and love. Finally, Part Three explores the effects of God's love upon human nature. Here Julian's reflections are founded on the notion that humanity is made in God's image, reflecting God's might, wisdom, and love. She emphasizes the relational aspect of the notion of image: being image of God means that humanity is held in relation to God through the operations *ad extra* of God's might, wisdom, and love. Consequently, Chapter 5 discusses the operation of God's might or the work of nature, Chapter 6 the operation of God's wisdom or the work of mercy, and Chapter 7 the operation of God's love or the work of grace.

Part Two

God Is Love

3

The Love of Jesus Christ

In the midst of her contemplation of the sufferings Jesus endured on the cross, Julian heard him say, "See how I love you" (24:221). These words sum up everything she saw, for every detail of the passion deepened her understanding of the intimacy, depth, and intensity of Christ's love for humanity. Julian's christology is mainly concerned with soteriology, with drawing out how Christ's act of redemptive love is beneficial for humanity.

By beginning with the passion and its soteriological implications, Julian shows great theological precision. In the Judeo-Christian tradition, it has always been the experience of salvation which reveals the meaning of God and creation: the Hebrew people recognized in the one who redeemed them from Egypt the God who had created the universe; experiencing the paschal mystery enabled the first Christians to articulate who Jesus was and who they were as his body, the church. Likewise, in the early centuries of Christianity, christological formulations were always soteriologically motivated. Gregory of Nazianzus summed up what was at stake in all the early doctrinal disputes about the person and natures of Christ: "what is not assumed is not healed, and what is united to God is saved."[1]

After Chalcedon, christology concentrated more and more upon the relationship between the divine and human natures of Jesus Christ. In the process, it became a technical and somewhat isolated discipline; its soteriological importance was at first taken for granted, therefore little emphasized, and then gradually ignored. The resurgence of interest in the humanity of Jesus, especially his passion, which dominated the theology of the tenth to twelfth centuries,[2] can be interpreted as an effort to reclaim the soteriological element so essential in the early christological debates.[3]

Preeminent in this development was Anselm of Canterbury, whose *Cur Deus Homo?* had incalculable influence, not only upon theology, but also upon the devotional life of succeeding centuries, in concert with the achievements of Bernard of Clairvaux and Francis of Assisi.[4] Julian inherited the legacy of these men. Like Francis she possessed a tender, passionate love for the crucified Jesus, which found expression in the longing to share his suffering. But she is even more like Anselm and Bernard in the fact that her meditation on the passion resulted not only in an increase of pious devotion, but also in a disciplined reflection upon its inner intelligibility. And like that found in the scriptures and patristic writings, Julian's soteriology is composed of a plethora of themes and images working together.[5]

The servant of the parable recalled to Julian's mind her visions of the suffering Jesus:

> By his tunic being ready to go to rags and to tear is understood the rods and the scourges, the thorns and the nails, the pulling and the dragging and the tearing of his tender flesh, *of which I had seen a part* (51:277; emphasis mine).

What had Julian seen? Her first vision was of the head of Christ, bleeding from the crown of thorns; the second revelation focused upon the discoloration of Christ's face during the passion; the fourth revelation depicted the scourging and the shedding of Christ's blood.[6] But mention of the torn and tattered tunic recalls most obviously the graphic description of the rending and drying of Christ's flesh as described in Revelation 8:

> The blessed body was left to dry for a long time, with the wrenching of the nails and the weight of the body; . . . through the great and cruel hardness of the nails the wounds grew wide, and the body sagged because of its weight, hanging there for a long time. . . . I saw that the sweet skin . . . was torn in pieces like a cloth, and sagged down, seeming as if it would soon have fallen because it was so heavy and so loose (17:207–8).

The image of Christ's flesh as cloth is also found in the parable:

> [The servant] was simply dressed like a laborer prepared [for travail] . . . ; his clothing was a white tunic, scanty, old and all worn, dyed with the sweat of his body, tight fitting and short, . . . looking threadbare as if it would soon be worn out, ready to go to rags and to tear (51:272–73).[7]

It represents not only the passion but the human nature of Jesus as such, for the servant says to the lord: "See, my dear Father, I stand before you in Adam's tunic" (51:275–76). The human nature of Jesus provides our entrance into Julian's soteriology. Two biblical themes dominate her discussion of it: the suffering servant and the new Adam.

Both of these themes are not without difficulty for contemporary feminist theology.[8] Certain interpretations of Jesus as the suffering servant who passively allowed himself to be sacrificed out of obedience to the Father have been used as justification for a servile attitude on the part of women towards men. While the figure of the suffering servant is essential to Julian's christology, she takes great care to emphasize that Christ was no unwilling, purely passive sacrificial victim to God's plan of salvation. Rather, Christ underwent his passion because of his own great desire for union in love with all human beings. Human service of others, flowing from the free choice of the will, can be viewed as an aspect of human growth in autonomy, not servility.[9] Christ's act of lowering himself to humanity's needs by assuming the human condition actually symbolizes, in Julian's theology, an opposition to any form of domination or subordination, rather than a justification for it.

Julian's use of the gospel tradition of Christ as the new Adam, the perfect image of God, could also be problematic for feminist theologians.[10] Historically, the humanity of Christ has been seen as the fullness of God's image, intimating that the nature of God is best understood as male. It should be remembered, of course, that this is a distortion of Christian doctrine, which has always taught that God's essence transcends all images and must therefore be considered as beyond sexuality and gender distinctions. Particularly troublesome is the Roman Catholic Church's present insistence on Christ's maleness as the essential element of his humanity to be represented by the celebrant of the eucharist. This is a novel idea when compared with the patristic arguments surrounding the Chalcedonian formula where Christ's sex was never the issue. In fact, the Church's early theologians were wary of allowing any of the particularities of Christ's historical existence or personality to be regarded as essential, a caution expressed in its notion of *anhypostasia*. It was important for them that everything human be seen as having been assumed by the Logos, so as to ensure the universality of the redemption proffered by Christ, and this, at least implicitly, includes sexual differences.[11]

Christ's human nature as the perfect image of God plays a central role in Julian's theology, but she never regards his maleness as particularly significant. In fact, unlike many women mystics who may have given her inspiration, Julian does not develop the bridegroom/bride analogy for the relationship between Christ and the soul, an analogy obviously dependent for its symbolism on Christ's maleness.[12] For her the servant of the parable signifies the human Jesus as taking upon himself all that Adam represents: the fullness of humanity which includes both men and women. This is never stated explicitly, for Julian simply assumes that she and all other women are included in the fullness of humanity who are one with Christ.

Further, when she searches for a symbol that best summarizes this redemptive act of Christ, she chooses to use the symbol of motherhood,
which she then develops in her doctrine of the trinity as revealing
something essential about the nature of God. While she sometimes uses
the traditional "Son," Julian never uses the masculine "Word" but always
the feminine "Wisdom" to designate the second person of the trinity. How
much of this was a conscious attempt on her part to present a picture of an
androgynous Christ is impossible to determine. But her theology certainly
provides a paradigm for the use of the biblical images of suffering servant
and new Adam in a way that is not detrimental to but inclusive of women.

The Suffering Servant: Salvation as Expiation

Julian's revelations helped her discover the connection between the
suffering of Christ and human suffering. When she first considered the
servant's fall and the pains he suffered as a result, Julian thought of the fall
of Adam and all resulting human affliction. Later, when she considered the
servant as Jesus, these same pains seemed to refer to his passion:

> The first was the severe bruising which he took in his fall, which gave him
> great pain. The second was the heaviness of his body. The third was the
> weakness which followed these two. The fourth was that he was blinded in
> his reason and perplexed in his mind, so much so that he had almost
> forgotten his own love. The fifth was that he could not rise. The sixth was
> the pain most astonishing to me, and that was that he lay alone. I looked all
> around and searched, and far and near, high and low, I saw no help for him.
> The seventh was that the place in which he lay was narrow and comfortless
> and distressful (51:267). [13]

Eventually, Julian saw an identity between Jesus and all humanity. Whenever she looked at the servant in "the poor laborer's clothing" she understood "Adam's humanity with all the harm and weakness which follow. For
in all this our good Lord showed his own Son and Adam as only one"
(51:273–75). This identity allows us to read all the passages about the
servant as referring to the earthly Jesus, and the focus is expanded from
Christ's death alone to the fact that he undertook "all the harm and
weakness" which are part of human experience because of the fall (51:277).
Julian's Jesus is the Jesus of Hebrews, able to sympathize with human
weaknesses, like us in all things but sin (Heb 4:15): "Jesus wished . . . to

make himself as much like us in this mortal life, in our foulness and our wretchedness, as one could be without guilt" (10:195).

Julian notes several times that the servant's greatest suffering was that he lost sight of the lord and the lord's love for him:

> This man was injured in his powers and made most feeble, and in his understanding he was amazed, because he was diverted from looking on his lord, but his will was preserved in God's sight. I saw the lord commend and approve him for his will, but he himself was blinded and hindered from knowing this will. And this is a great sorrow and a cruel suffering to him, for he neither sees clearly his loving lord, who is so meek and mild to him, nor does he truly see what he himself is in the sight of his loving lord (51:270–71).

This is why he suffers so much from the seven great pains. He experiences the lord as absent and himself as out of harmony with God. Applied to Jesus, this description recalls the Markan picture of the Crucified who cried out, "My God, my God, why have you forsaken me?" (Mk 15:34). Jesus suffered with all humanity even the experience of the seeming absence of God.

The stress Julian places on the details of Christ's human suffering gives color to the Pauline assertion that God "made him to be sin who knew no sin" (2 Cor 5:21). It is clear that the sufferings endured by Jesus were the result of sin, for the seven great pains are linked explicitly to Adam's fall. Jesus experienced everything human, including the effects of sin: "And so has our good Lord Jesus taken upon him all our blame" (51:275). The passion of Christ thus reveals the ugliness and horror of sin. In the second revelation Julian saw "frighteningly" the face of the Crucified bleeding, drying, and changing color throughout the course of his dying. She was given the insight that this horrible sight "symbolized and resembled our foul, black death, which our fair, bright, blessed Lord bore for our sins" (10:193–94).

The image of the suffering servant carries with it the idea of expiation: the innocent one suffers on behalf of the guilty by bearing all their blame. Like the deutero-Isaian suffering servant, as a result of sufferings patiently borne, he shall "make many to be accounted righteous" (Is 53:11). In Julian's words: "So was our Lord Jesus afflicted for us" (19:211); "he suffered for the sins of everyone who will be saved; and he saw and he sorrowed for everyone's sorrow, desolation and anguish" (20:213). To understand how such suffering can be "for us" we need to probe more deeply into the symbols of the passion.

Here Julian moves beyond the human Jesus in his earthly sufferings. The figure of the servant in the parable represents not only the humanity of Christ, but also his divinity (51:274). While her revelations began with the image of Christ's humanity, and while her reflections attempt to do justice to his human nature, Julian's christology could never be considered a "christology from below" in today's sense of the word. The Jesus Julian saw in his suffering humanity was never considered apart from his identity as the second person of the trinity.

The Details of Christ's Passion

Devotion to the passion of Christ in the latter Middle Ages was often expressed through an elaborate, sometimes gruesome, description of the details of Christ's passion, and the significance of each detail to the spiritual growth of the devotee.[14] While such devotion was common to both women and men, evidence suggests that it was more firmly at the center of women's piety. Devotion to the body, wounds, heart, and blood of Christ was also connected for many women to a deep devotion to the eucharist.[15]

It is obvious that Julian was influenced by this tradition, but her treatment of it is different from that of most visionaries. While she does describe some details of Christ's suffering, those which she had seen in her vision of the Crucified, she does so with quite a bit more restraint than is customary.[16] Although an affective element is certainly present in her descriptions, her main purpose is not so much to inspire devotion, as it is to investigate the doctrinal implications of Christ's sufferings. In trying to understand the expiatory nature of the atonement, she delves into the theological significance of two details of Christ's passion: his thirst and the shedding of his blood, both of which are connected to the broken heart of Christ.

The eighth revelation concentrated upon the drying of Christ's body, which called to Julian's mind his words on the cross: "I thirst" (Jn 19:28). Julian interprets this in a double light, both physical and spiritual. Christ's physical thirst represented not only the need for drink, but the fact "that the body was wholly dried up, for his blessed flesh and bones were left without blood or moisture" (17:207), recalling the gospel incident of the piercing of Christ's side and the pouring out of blood and water (Jn 19:34). Christ's spiritual thirst puts Julian in touch with his motivation for such suffering. He ardently longed to participate in human salvation and "voluntarily" went to his death (10:194).

In the parable the servant stands before the lord, desiring to do the lord's will, "all eager to hasten and run" (51:276). [17] There is not the slightest hint that Christ, out of obedience to God's will, allowed himself to be an unwilling or merely passive victim in God's plan of salvation. Rather, doing God's will meant also doing what Christ himself most deeply desired. In the tenth revelation, when he showed "his blessed heart split in two," Julian saw Christ's motivation for the passion:

> And for my greater understanding, these blessed words were said: See how I love you, as if he had said, behold and see that I loved you so much, before I died for you, that I wanted to die for you. And now I have died for you, and willingly suffered what I could. . . . For my delight is in your holiness and in your endless joy and bliss with me (24:221).

Christ's spiritual thirst is his "love longing" for us. The physical thirst of the earthly Jesus is over, but Christ's spiritual thirst is not yet at an end:

> [It] persists and always will until we see him on the day of judgment, for we who shall be saved and shall be Christ's joy and bliss are still here, and some are yet to come, and so will some be until that day. Therefore this is his thirst and his love longing for us, to gather us all here into him, to our endless joy (31:230). [18]

The work of salvation, won through Christ's sufferings and death, is not yet complete and thus Christ's spiritual thirst will not be satisfied until the end of time.

The other detail of Christ's passion which is given special treatment is the shedding of blood, the image with which Julian's revelations began. In the fourth revelation, Julian sees Christ at the time of the scourging, where "the hot blood ran out so plentifully that neither skin nor wounds could be seen, but everything seemed to be blood" (12:199). [19] Here Julian reflects upon the sacramental significance of the blood of Christ:

> God has created bountiful waters on the earth for our use and our bodily comfort, out of the tender love he has for us. But it is more pleasing to him that we accept for our total cure his blessed blood to wash us of our sins, for there is no drink that is made which it pleases him so well to give us (12:200).

The blood of Christ is powerful and plentiful enough to accomplish the whole work of salvation. At the time of Christ's death, "it descended into hell and broke its bonds, and delivered all who were there and who belong to the court of heaven." In the present, it continues Christ's redemptive work, flowing "over all the earth, and it is ready to wash from their sins all creatures . . . of good will." Like Christ's spiritual thirst, the pouring out of Christ's blood will not cease until the work of salvation is complete:

> The precious plenty of his precious blood ascended into heaven in the blessed body of our Lord Jesus Christ, and it is flowing there in him, praying to the Father for us, and this is and will be so long as we have need (12:200).

Julian linked the shedding of blood, along with the water from Christ's side, with the idea of his thirst for us. In the tenth revelation, this connection is made more forceful in her contemplation of the wounded side and broken heart of Christ:

> With a kindly countenance our good Lord looked into his side, . . . and there he revealed a fair and delectable place, large enough for all who will be saved and will rest in peace and in love. And with that he brought to mind the dear and precious blood and water which he suffered to be shed for love. And in this sweet sight he showed his blessed heart split in two. . . . And . . . said most joyfully: See how I love you, as if he had said, my darling, behold and see your Lord, your God, who is your Creator and your endless joy (24:220–21).[20]

Julian's reflections upon these two details of the passion, Christ's thirst and the shedding of his blood, add several things to the notion of expiation provided through her allusions to the suffering servant. They prohibit any interpretation of Christ's death as a passive expiatory sacrifice. They emphasize Christ's active role in the passion through his desire to fulfill the will of God, but more importantly they stress the fact that he suffered in order to fulfill his own desire. They reveal just what that desire of God's and of Christ's is: they reveal the depths and the nature of God's love for humankind. Finally, they suggest that the redemptive work undertaken by Christ is still continuing, especially through the sacramental mediation of the church, providing the way by which all the saved are included in the salvific act of Christ.

Philippians 2:5–11

The description of the servant in the parable is full of allusions to the hymn of Philippians 2:5–11. Julian's use of this text unites the notion of expiation in the suffering servant image with the idea of Christ's "love longing" in the images of his thirst and precious blood. The latter revealed a union of wills between God and the suffering Christ. If we return to the parable, we find that this union of wills is eternal:

> He was the servant before he came on earth, standing ready in purpose before the Father until the time when he would send him to do the glorious deed by which humankind was brought back to heaven. . . . with his prescient purpose that he would become man to save humankind in fulfillment of the will of his Father (51:275).

The servant is here identified as the Wisdom of God who eternally saw "that there was one thing to do which would pay honor to the lord," the act which would restore humankind to the lord (51:273):

> Even though he is God, equal with the Father as regards his divinity, . . . he stood before his Father as a servant, willingly taking upon him all our charge. And then he rushed off very readily at the Father's bidding, and soon he fell very low into the maiden's womb, having no regard for himself or for his cruel pains (51:275).

Note how exactly Julian's words in this passage reproduce the imagery and theme of the Philippians hymn:

> Though he was in the form of God, [he] did not count equality with God a thing to be grasped, but emptied himself, taking the form of a servant, being born in the likeness of men. And being found in human form he humbled himself and became obedient unto death, even death on a cross (Phil 2:5–8).

Julian makes other allusions to this hymn, both within the parable and throughout the Long Text: "The servant, for love, having no regard for himself or for anything which might happen to him, went off in great haste and ran when his lord sent him, to do the thing which was his will and to his honor" (51:273). This involved a "fall" which meant accepting all the sorrows and sufferings of humankind:

> The divinity rushed from the Father into the maiden's womb, falling to accept our nature, and in this falling he took great hurt. The hurt that he took was our flesh, in which at once he experienced mortal pains (51:277).[21]

This was a fall of the greatest extremes imaginable, "for he who is highest and most honorable was most foully brought low, most utterly despised"

(20:213), actually "becoming sin" for us. Above all, it reveals the strength of Christ's love for us:

> The love in him which he has for our souls was so strong that he willingly chose suffering with a great desire, and suffered it meekly with a great joy (20:214). . . . [and] he counts as nothing his [travail] and his [passion] and his cruel and shameful death (22:217).

Julian's prayer for a vision of the crucified Jesus had been motivated by her desire to have "the more true mind of Christ's passion" (2:178). This is an obvious allusion to Paul's introduction to the hymn, where he exhorts the Philippians to "have this mind among yourselves, which is yours in Christ Jesus" (2:5).[22] Julian understands Paul's intention in his use of the hymn when she views the attitude of Christ as the model for Christian conduct in this world. Not aspiring to the glory associated with divinity, but being content with human creaturehood and having compassion on human sinfulness become for Julian the proper attitudes of the human being before God. This is the attitude of Christ, the new Adam.[23]

The New Adam: Salvation as Recreation

So far we have described biblical themes which emphasize the suffering and brokenness of human nature, and the fact that Christ's passion reveals the horror of sin. But Jesus also reveals the true nature of humanity as intended by God. Julian uses the Pauline theme of the new Adam to emphasize this positive aspect of human nature.[24]

In the parable, the torn and ragged nature of the servant's tunic causes Julian to exclaim, "This is not fitting clothing for a servant so greatly loved to stand in before so honorable a lord" (51:273). This condition is certainly not what God intended for humanity:

> He [the lord] made the human soul to be his own city and his dwelling place, which is the most pleasing to him of all his works. And when we had fallen into sorrow and pain, we were not wholly proper to serve in that noble office (51:272).

The servant's task is to restore the city so that it will be a fitting habitation for the lord, a task described by allusions to Genesis. It is the same work once given to Adam: to till and keep the garden (Gen 2:15), by which Adam participated in God's creative activity. Because of sin, it will be done by "the sweat of his brow" (Gen 3:17–19):

He was to do the greatest labor and the hardest [travail] there is. He was to be a gardener, digging and ditching and sweating and turning the soil over and over, and to dig deep down, and to water the plants at the proper time (51:273).[25]

The servant's task is further described by the use of two more images operating together, buried treasure and food:

There was a treasure in the earth which the lord loved. I was astonished, and considered what it could be; and I was answered in my understanding: It is a food which is delicious and pleasing to the lord. For I saw the lord sitting like a man, and I saw neither food nor drink with which to serve him (51:273).

Thus the servant's task is:

to persevere in his [travail], and make sweet streams to run, and fine and plenteous fruit to grow, which he was to bring before the lord and serve him with to his liking. And he was never to come back again until he had made all this food ready as he knew was pleasing to the lord; and then he was to take this food and drink, and carry it most reverently before the lord (51:273–74).

This work of recreation is a doing over again, a reliving in the proper way of the original creation which was marred by sin, a bringing back to God of what had somehow strayed off course and become displeasing. Julian's reference to the "sweet streams" and "fine and plenteous fruit" are allusions to the recreation imagery of Isaiah, wherein "the desert shall rejoice and blossom" and "waters shall break forth in the wilderness" (Is. 35:1–2, 6–7). The image of the buried treasure brings to mind another scriptural passage: "The kingdom of heaven is like treasure hidden in a field" (Mt 13:44).[26] The treasure for which the lord longs in the parable is what he had once created to be his own kingdom, the lord's "own city and dwelling place." Working together, these images of water/fruit and kingdom/city recall one more scriptural image with its own allusions to Genesis:

Then he showed me the river of the water of life, bright as crystal, flowing from the throne of God and of the Lamb through the middle of the street of the city; also on either side of the river, the tree of life with its twelve kinds of fruit, yielding its fruit each month; and the leaves of the tree were for the healing of the nations. There shall no more be anything accursed, but the throne of God and of the Lamb shall be in it, and his servants shall worship him (Rev 22:1–3).

And God's kingdom or city, the food for which God longs, represents "all who will be saved," as Julian will make abundantly clear.

The one who is to bring about this restoration is Christ, whom Julian calls "the true Adam." Unlike the old Adam who is tired and worn out, "for it seemed by his outer garment as if he had been a constant laborer and a hard traveller for a long time," the true Adam is fresh to the task: "it seemed that he was newly appointed, that is to say just beginning to labor" (51:273–74). Julian focuses upon the will of the servant, the true Adam, to please the lord: "The servant stands before his lord, respectfully, ready to do his lord's will." And when the lord sends him on his mission, "not only does the servant go, but he dashes off and runs at great speed, loving to do his lord's will" (51:267). This union of wills between the lord and the servant is unchanging through the events of the earthly life and passion of Jesus. Even after the servant had fallen, "in spirit he was as prompt and as good as he was when he stood before his lord, ready to do his will" (51:268). The lord was thus able to "commend and approve" him for his constancy, and Julian can see no blame in him (51:270–71).[27]

This union of wills is described in terms of love: "inwardly, there was shown in [the servant] a foundation of love, the love which he had for the lord, which was equal to the love which the lord had for him," which love is the Spirit of God (51:273–74). The earthly Jesus, possessing the Spirit of God, always acted according to the Father's will, in spite of the weakness and temptations that are humanity's lot. In doing so, he recreated in himself what all humanity was called to be from the beginning: God's favorite "city and dwelling place," a comfortable home for God, wherein God and humanity are joined in love's unity. He is thus the true Adam through whose life the harm caused by the first Adam was healed and all humanity was recreated.

The work of salvation repairs and carries on the work of creation. There is a unity and continuity between them in Julian's thought which she describes throughout the Long Text, emphasizing, in the process, the great worth and value of human nature. God's creative activity continues to act in the work of restoration. This is precisely the message of the thirteenth revelation:

> Our Lord God wishes us to have great regard for all the deeds which he has performed in the most noble work of creating all things, and it treats of the excellence of human creation, which is superior to all God's works; and it is about the precious amends which he has made for human sin, turning all our blame into everlasting honor. Here he says: Behold and see, for by the same [might], wisdom and goodness that I have done all this, by the same

[might], wisdom and goodness I shall make all things well which are not well (1:176).

This unbroken connection between creation and redemption reflects the unchanging nature of God's love:

And he who created us for love, by the same love wanted to restore us to the same blessedness and to even more. And just as we were made like the trinity in our first making, our Creator wished us to be like Jesus Christ our savior in heaven forever, through the power of our making again (10:194).

Overcoming the powers of evil

Against such an eternally loving divine will the powers of sin and death ultimately have no sway. This is the content of Julian's fifth revelation: "the fiend is overcome by the precious passion of Christ" (1:175).

In Julian's day, the hour of death was viewed as a time when the Christian soul was particularly vulnerable to the temptations of evil spirits.[28] Believing herself to be on her deathbed, Julian says ". . . it seemed to me that I might well be tempted by devils . . . before I would die" (4:182).[29] Christ's passion becomes Julian's strength in the face of such temptations:

With this sight of his blessed passion, with the divinity which I saw in my understanding, I knew well that this was strength enough for me, yes, and for all living creatures who were to be saved, against all the devils of hell and against all their spiritual enemies (4:182).

Indeed, the suffering Christ is the only refuge from diabolical power: "apart from the cross there was no safety from the fear of devils" (19:211).

Julian connects the work of Christ's passion and death to the work of restoration by using the popular medieval tradition of Christ's descent into hell:

Adam fell from life to death, into the valley of this wretched world, and after that into hell. God's Son fell with Adam, into the valley of the womb of the maiden who was the fairest daughter of Adam, and that was to excuse Adam from blame in heaven and on earth; and powerfully he brought him out of hell (51:274–75).[30]

By this fall, the new Adam endured the old Adam's lot completely, allowing himself to come into contact even with the powers of hell.

Julian links the theme of the harrowing of hell with Christ's work of gardening. In hell the servant raises "the great root out of the deep depth," the great root of the treasure buried in the earth, the food that was pleasing to the lord (51:277).[31] His descent into hell rescues that root from all that prevented its growth, allowing it to flourish, despite the forces of evil that continue to work against it, though without effectiveness. The powers of evil have been overcome:

> God showed me that the fiend has now the same malice as he had before the Incarnation, and he works as hard, and he sees as constantly as he did before that all the souls who will be saved escape him to God's glory by the power of our Lord's precious passion. . . . [H]e can never do as much evil as he would wish, for his power is all locked in God's hands (13:201).

Therefore we are to "scorn [the devil's] malice and despise him as nothing," as God does, because "everything which God permits him to do turns to joy for us and to pain and shame for him" (13:201–2).[32]

O Happy Fault!

Because the work of Christ's passion and death has restored humankind from the debilitating fear of "endless torment in hell," we can look upon the passion with joy (23:220), recalling the notion of the "happy fault" celebrated in medieval song and liturgy.[33] Julian's ninth revelation shows "the delight which the blessed Trinity has in the cruel passion of Christ, once his sorrowful death was accomplished" (1:176), a delight we are meant to share: "it is God's will that we have true delight with him in our salvation" (23:218). In the parable the lord says:

> See my beloved servant, what harm and injuries he has had and accepted in my service for my love, yes, and for his good will. Is it not reasonable that I should reward him for his fright and his fear, his hurt and his injuries and all his woe? (51:268).

This passage means not only that Christ, the new Adam, is to be rewarded for his passion, but because the servant also represents all humanity, the sins we suffer from will be cause for our joy. Thus "the great goodness and . . . honor" of the lord require:

> that his beloved servant, whom he loved so much, should be highly and blessedly rewarded forever, *above what he would have been if he had not fallen,* yes, and so much that his falling and all the woe that he received from it

will be turned into high, surpassing honor and endless bliss (51:269; emphasis mine).

There is a clear allusion here to Romans where Paul points out the superiority of the work of redemption over the destruction wrought by sin:

> But the free gift is not like the trespass. For if many died through one man's trespass, *much more* have the grace of God and the free gift in the grace of that one man Jesus Christ abounded for many. And the free gift is not like the effect of that one man's sin. . . . If, because of one man's trespass, death reigned through that one man, *much more* will those who receive the abundance of grace and the free gift of righteousness reign in life through the one man Jesus Christ (Rom 5:15–17, emphasis mine).

Compare Julian's words:

> He taught that I should contemplate the glorious atonement, for this atoning is *more pleasing* to the blessed divinity and *more honorable* for human salvation, *without comparison*, than ever Adam's sin was harmful (29:228; emphasis mine).

The power of grace is infinitely greater than the power of sin, so powerful that it even uses the means of human destruction to effect an increase in human value beyond what would have been true if sin had never occurred. Sin is simply no match for the power of God's love:

> For wickedness has been suffered to rise in opposition to that goodness [which is in God]; and the goodness of mercy and grace opposed that wickedness, and turned everything to goodness and honor for all who will be saved (59:295).

Once again, Julian echoes Romans, where sin and grace are personified as two adversarial rulers, unequal in strength: "where sin increased, grace abounded all the more, so that, as sin reigned in death, grace also might reign through righteousness to eternal life through Jesus Christ" (Rom 5:20–21).

The crown of thorns which Christ wore at the beginning of Julian's revelations, representing the pain of human sin, is changed by the end of the parable into a crown of glory, representing all the saved in whom Christ eternally rejoices (51:278). In like manner, in the end, "sin will be no shame, but honor to us" (38:242). Just as the sufferings of Christ's passion, such as his thirst and the shedding of his blood, were the source of pain for him on earth and yet remain now in heaven as glorious reminders of his work of salvation, so it shall be with the sins humans suffer from:

> Our Lord Jesus takes them and sends them up to heaven, and then they are made more sweet and delectable than heart can think or tongue can tell. And when we come there, we shall find them ready, all turned into true beauty and endless honor (49:265).

Christians ought therefore to rejoice and take comfort in Christ's passion; because of it and in spite of the horror of sin, "all will be well" (27:225). And this famous phrase of Julian's may also owe its inspiration to Paul's letter to the Romans: "We know that in everything God works for good with those who love him, who are called according to his purpose" (Rom 8:28).

The Reason for the Incarnation

The last two themes, the overcoming of the fiend and the happy fault, indicate that the restorative effect of Christ's salvific work extends to the powers of evil. But is the overcoming of evil the only reason for Christ's incarnation and redemption? Julian does not explicitly treat the question whether God would have become human if there had been no sin.[34] But she intimates that the incarnation had a purpose other than repairing the damage caused by sin:

> Our reason is founded in God, who is nature's substance. From this substantial nature spring mercy and grace, and penetrate us, accomplishing everything for the fulfillment of our joy. These are our foundations, in which we have our being, our increase and our fulfillment. For in nature we have our life and our being, and in mercy and grace we have our increase and our fulfillment. . . . For we cannot profit by our reason alone, unless we have equally memory and love; nor can we be saved merely because we have in God our natural foundation, unless we have, coming from the same foundation, mercy and grace. For from these three operating all together we receive all our good, the first of which is the good of nature. For in our first making God gave us as much good and as great good as we could receive in our spirit alone; but his prescient purpose in his endless wisdom willed that we should be double (56:290).

Here the works of mercy and grace, which are brought into operation by the incarnation, were part of God's "prescient purpose" for humanity from the beginning.

Sin is a fact of human existence which cannot be denied and God actually uses it as one of the vehicles for human salvation, but it is not the cause of the outreach of God to humanity through the works of mercy and grace. Salvation involves more than the forgiveness of sins or the restoration of fallen human nature to its original state of justice. God willed that humankind be created in its "natural substance" and then be "increased" and "fulfilled" by being raised up into the very life of God. Viewing the incarnation as the fulfillment of God's plan for the increase of human nature places a very positive value upon human life in time.[35] God intended earthly life to be the means of human glory. This is salvation, something which Julian intimates would have occurred whether or not sin was a reality.

Cross and Resurrection

Julian has no detailed theology of the resurrection. Her brief treatment of it is related to the themes of recreation and the happy fault. She describes a change in appearance on the face of the Crucified in the ninth revelation. As she watches for the moment of Christ's death, "when by appearances it seemed . . . that life could last no longer . . . suddenly, . . . he changed to an appearance of joy" (21:214–15).

In the parable, once the servant has borne Adam's lot to the fullest extent by falling into hell, the moment of resurrection occurs. It marks the cessation of suffering and the full flowering of the work of recreation, the glorification of human nature:

> The body lay in the grave until Easter morning; and from that time it never lay again. For then the tossing about and writhing, the groaning and the moaning ended, rightly; and our foul mortal flesh, which God's Son took upon him, which was Adam's old tunic, tight-fitting, threadbare and short, was then made lovely by our savior, new, white and bright and forever clean, wide and ample . . . of a fair and seemly mixture, which is so marvellous that I cannot describe it, for it is all of true glory (51:277–78).[36]

When Julian saw Christ's visage change in the ninth revelation, she realized:

> In our Lord's intention we are now on his cross with him in our pains, and in our passion we are dying, and with his help and his grace we willingly endure on that same cross until the last moment of life. Suddenly he will change his appearance for us, and we shall be with him in heaven. . . . and then all will be brought into joy (21:215).[37]

This passage echoes Paul for whom Christians are "fellow heirs with Christ, provided we suffer with him in order that we may also be glorified with him" (Rom 8:17). Like Paul, the Christian should long to "know him and the power of his resurrection, and . . . share his sufferings, becoming like him in his death, that if possible I may attain the resurrection from the dead" (Phil 3:10–11).

For Julian, the glorious transformation that awaits the one who willingly suffers with Christ is the joyful other side of having "more true mind of Christ's passion." Cross and resurrection are inextricably united. Thus Julian could choose the suffering Christ for her heaven:

> So was I taught to choose Jesus for my heaven, whom I saw only in pain at that time. No other heaven was pleasing to me than Jesus, who will be my bliss when I am there. And this has always been a comfort to me, that I chose Jesus by his grace to be my heaven in all this time of [passion] and of sorrow (19:212).

In so doing Julian is once again in company with Paul who chose to glory only in the cross of Jesus Christ (Gal 6:14).[38]

Predestination in Christ: God's Eternal Salvific Will

As we have seen, the most perplexing question for Julian about her revelations was why God does not look upon humans wrathfully because of sin. She sensed that the answer involved a difference in perspective between God and human beings. Early in her revelations she had learned that everything which humans interpret by means of time sequence, cause and effect, or chance is not seen that way by God. In God all things are eternally present, therefore God sees sin and salvation from the perspective of eternal wisdom and love. What humans see in process is eternally accomplished from God's perspective (11:197–99). There sin is overcome; there humanity is God's own city and dwelling place, God's treasure and food, a source of delight and honor for God, eternally one with God.

Through the parable Julian learned that Christ is the key to this eternal union between humanity and God: "because of the true union which was made in heaven, God's Son could not be separated from Adam, for by Adam I understand all humankind" (51:274). Julian's reflection upon this truth is rooted in another theme developed from Pauline theology, the idea of the predestination in Christ of all who will be saved:

> For I saw that God never began to love [humankind]; for just as [human-kind] will be in endless bliss, fulfilling God's joy with regard to his works,

just so has that same [humankind] been known and loved in God's prescience from without beginning in his righteous intent. And . . . the
mediator wanted to be the foundation and the head of this fair nature, out
of whom we have all come, in whom we are all enclosed, into whom we
shall all go, finding in him our full heaven in everlasting joy by the
prescient purpose of all the blessed trinity from without beginning
(53:283).[39]

For Julian, Christ is the foundation and head of human nature, just as, for
the author of Colossians, he is "the image of the invisible God, the first-
born of all creation" (Col 1:15) for whom and in whom all things were
created. Furthermore, Julian's reference to the second person as Wisdom
recalls the female figure of the Book of Proverbs, actively present at the
creation of the universe, rejoicing and delighting in it (Prov. 8:22–31).
These two scriptural sources come together in her consideration of the
cosmic Christ, in whose image humanity is created and predestined to
eternal life with God.

Julian's view of human creation in and through Christ is succinctly
stated in the following passage:

God the blessed trinity, who is everlasting being, just as he is eternal from
without beginning, just so was it in his eternal purpose to create human
nature, which fair nature was first prepared for his own Son, the second
person; and when he wished, by full agreement of the whole trinity he
created us all at once. And in our creating he knit and united us to himself,
and through this union we are kept as pure and as noble as we were created
(58:293).

All humanity was created "at once" when God prepared a human nature
for the second person of the trinity. All human nature that was ever to be
in time (who would be counted among the saved) was united to God's
Wisdom in that instant, and this unity is never lost, even amidst the
vagaries and sinfulness of human life.

Julian sees the human soul as the fullness of human nature: "the noblest
thing which [God] ever made," and "the fullest substance and the highest
power is the blessed soul of Christ." Here Julian is indebted to the
Augustinian theme of the image of God, which will be discussed at length
in Chapter 5 below. In neoplatonic terms, the soul of Christ, itself created
in the image of the Logos, is the eternal form of the human soul, in which
all individual souls participate. The human soul of Christ "is preciously
knitted to him in its making, by a knot so subtle and so mighty that it is
united in God," thus it is "endlessly holy." But because all humanity was
created at once with the human soul of Christ, "all the souls which will be
saved in heaven without end" are also, in union with the soul of Christ,

"knit in this knot, and united in this union, and made holy in this holiness" (53:284). The cause of this union is the love of God:

> And for the great endless love that God has for all [humankind], God makes no distinction in love between the blessed soul of Christ and the least soul that will be saved. For it is very easy to believe and trust that the dwelling of the blessed soul of Christ is very high in the glorious divinity; and . . . where the blessed soul of Christ is, there is the substance of all the souls which will be saved by Christ (54:285).

God never looks upon humans with wrath, for God sees them only as eternally united to Christ.

In order to explain the changeable nature of the human being, Julian makes a distinction between the "substance" of the human soul, which is knit to God as described above, and "sensuality," the part of the soul closer to the body and affected by the vagaries of time and space.[40] But human sensuality is also meant to be God's dwelling place, and Christ plays a central role here. The triune God is able to enter into human sensuality, God's city, because Christ took that sensuality upon himself in the incarnation: "In the same time that God knit himself to our body in the maiden's womb, he took our sensuality, and in taking it, having enclosed us all in himself, he united it to our substance" (57:292). Humanity is thus doubly knit to Christ: in the creation of the soul's "substance" in his image, and in his taking upon himself human sensuality. In this "double knitting" God's work of creation and redemption are once again united. The following passage summarizes this, speaking of human substance and sensuality as higher and lower "natures":

> I saw that our nature is wholly in God, in which he makes diversities flowing out of him to perform his will, which nature preserves and mercy and grace restore and fulfill. And of these none will be destroyed, for our [higher nature] is joined to God in its creation, and God is joined to our [lower nature] in taking flesh. And so in Christ our two natures are united, for the trinity is comprehended in Christ, in whom our higher part is founded and rooted; and our lower part the second person has taken, which nature was first prepared for him (57:291).[41]

The union of Christ and all humanity is the new Adam, human nature increased beyond its original splendor by the fact of God's entering into human flesh. Human predestination in Christ is the secure guarantee of eternal bliss. Because God's loving will is effective to complete what God had planned from the beginning, one can trust that indeed "all will be well."

The Body of Christ: Salvation through the Church

For Julian the incarnation did not end with the resurrection and ascension of the historical Jesus; the Wisdom of God continues to live in human flesh through his body the church: "For all humankind which will be saved by the sweet incarnation and the passion of Christ, all is Christ's humanity, for he is the head, and we are his members" (51:276). Once again, Julian is indebted to Pauline theology, this time to the theme of the church as the body of Christ.[42] Julian's understanding of the church forms the foundation for everything she says about the Christian life of grace. God has done one act of salvation, through Christ, and insofar as an individual is part of that one act of salvation, by being united to Christ's body on earth, one is saved.[43] Julian thus speaks often of the "general" nature of salvation.

Christ is the perfect human, not only in the sense that the earthly Jesus qualitatively fulfilled the purpose for which humanity was created, but because in him we see humanity's quantitative fullness. Christ is the perfect human because he has "[knit] in himself everyone who will be saved" in his one body, the church (57:292). This is a different, fuller sense of "perfect human" than one finds in classical christology. It includes not only a full humanity for Christ as an individual, but all the saved as a race. While it would be anachronistic to apply the word "evolutionary" to Julian's thought, her notion of the quantitative perfect humanity of Christ is somewhat akin to the evolutionary christology of Teilhard de Chardin or Karl Rahner.[44] The human race reached its qualitative perfection in the human nature of Jesus, but all who will be saved must be "worked into him" (57:292), something that will not be finished until time's end. This is why Christ's thirst is not yet at an end, and why God must continually "draw us" to God's self.

The church is the body of that one human being, the servant of the parable who is both Christ and all who will be saved. It is thus both perfect and imperfect, reflecting both divine and human elements: "For insofar as Christ is our head, he is glorious and impassible; but with respect to his body, to which all his members are joined, he is not yet fully glorified or wholly impassible" (31:230).

The church is perfect because in Christ it already possesses all that is necessary for eschatological fulfillment: "All the gifts which God can give to the creature God has given to his Son Jesus for us, which gifts he, dwelling in us, has enclosed in him . . . until we have grown to full stature" (55:287).[45] The life of the church on earth, then, involves the gradual drawing of all its members into the life of Christ which it already possesses in fullness, insofar as he dwells therein as its head. This eschatological perfection of the church is never destroyed by sin; instead, it becomes the means by which sin can be overcome:

> For one single person may often be broken, as it seems to that person, but the entire body of Holy Church was never broken, nor ever will be without end. And therefore it is a certain thing, and good and gracious to will, meekly and fervently, to be fastened and united to our mother Holy Church, who is Christ Jesus. For the flood of mercy which is his dear blood and precious water is plentiful to make us fair and clean (61:301–2).

However, it is also true that the church on earth is imperfect: "We are not now so wholly in him as we then shall be" (31:230). Thus Christ continues to suffer on earth, in us and with us. Christ's thirst and love-longing for humanity are unsatisfied:

> For he still has that same thirst and longing which he had upon the cross, which desire, longing and thirst, as I see it, were in him from without beginning; and he will have this until the time that the last soul which will be saved has come up into his bliss (31:230–31).

Christ's work on earth, which the church continues for as long as time shall last, is therefore "to gather us all here into him, to our endless joy" (31:230).

This gathering into Christ is accomplished especially through the church's sacraments and preaching. As Jesus says to Julian: "I am he whom Holy Church preaches and teaches to you. That is to say: All the health and the life of the sacraments, all the power and the grace of my word" (60:298). Julian has no sacramental theology as such; she refers specifically only to the sacraments of penance and the eucharist. She stresses penance, in particular, as the means by which the wounds caused by sin are healed and turned into honor,[46] and her mention of the eucharist is linked to her discussion of Christ as mother (60:298).[47] Indeed the church itself is called "our beloved Mother in consolation and true understanding" because its actions are the continuation in time of Christ's office of motherhood toward humanity (61:301).

Through the preaching and teaching of the church, Christ continues his "pilgrimage" on earth, whereby "he is here with us, leading us, and will be until he has brought us all to his bliss in heaven" (81:337). If Christ is the foundation for the creation of human nature from the beginning, he is also the foundation for human life on earth through the mediation of the church. He is not only the suffering servant in union with whom humanity suffers from the consequences of sin, but also the new Adam in whom humanity lives as intended by God: "for Christ is mercifully working in us, and we are by grace according with him, through the gift and the power of the Holy Spirit" (54:286).

Julian expresses her faith in "everything . . . Holy Church preaches and teaches" (9:192) because God is the church's foundation, substance, teacher, end, and reward (34:235–36). She is therefore convinced that "everything which is profitable for us to understand and know our good Lord will most courteously show to us by all the preaching and teaching of Holy Church" (34:235).

The Motherhood of Christ: Summary Symbol of Soteriology

The theme of the motherhood of Christ was very common in the medieval devotional writings of both women and men.[48] Generally, the image expressed three aspects of the role of Christ in the work of salvation: the sufferings of the passion were compared to the pains of childbirth; the nourishment of the soul through the sacraments was compared to the nurturing function of motherhood; and Christ's love for the soul was compared to the tenderness and compassion of a mother toward her child.[49] All three of these analogies are present in Julian's own treatment of the motherhood of Christ, but she goes far beyond them in her use of the image.[50] Motherhood, for her, expresses the very essence, not merely certain incidental aspects, of Christ's activity towards humanity. It includes the whole economy of both incarnation and redemption, and is linked to her understanding of the second person of the trinity as God's Wisdom. Thus, Julian raises the image of Christ's motherhood to a new level of significance, allowing it to summarize her whole soteriology.[51]

Julian's understanding of the second person of the trinity as Wisdom could have its roots in the all-pervasive Augustinian trinitarian tradition, but she also could have drawn inspiration from scriptural sources. As deeply Pauline as we have found her to be, Julian surely would have noticed Paul's identification of Christ as God's wisdom in 1 Corinthians, an identification realized, paradoxically, through the cross:

> For Jews demand signs and Greeks seek wisdom, but we preach Christ crucified, a stumbling block to Jews and folly to Gentiles, but to those who are called, both Jews and Greeks, Christ the power of God and the wisdom of God (1 Cor 1:22–24).

Paul's wisdom christology is rooted in the wisdom tradition of the Hebrew scriptures. There Wisdom is a female figure who existed before the beginning of the world (Prov 8:22–31) and who is associated with the act of creation: "The Lord by wisdom founded the earth" (Prov 3:19). She is also responsible for the work of recreation: "while remaining in herself, she renews all things" (Wis 7:27), and the work of salvation: "the paths of those on earth were set right, and [they] were saved by wisdom" (Wis 9:18). She is involved in the work of sanctification: "in every generation she passes into holy souls and makes them friends of God and prophets" (Wis 7:27).[52]

It is not unlikely that Julian meditated upon the Wisdom figure of the Hebrew scriptures as a source for her theme of the motherhood of Christ.[53] For her, "the deep wisdom of the trinity is our mother, in whom we are enclosed" (54:285). The book of Wisdom calls Wisdom the "mother" of "all good things" (Wis 7:11–12), an idea made even more explicit by the voice of Wisdom herself in the Latin Vulgate's version of the book of Sirach: "I am mother of fair love, of fear and knowledge and holy hope. In me is all grace of the way and of the truth, in me all hope of life and virtue" (Ecclesiasticus 24:24–25).[54]

Julian's most thorough description of Christ as Mother, found in chapters 60 and 61 of the Long Text, is an elaboration of the analogy comparing God to an earthly mother found in Isaiah: "Can a woman forget her sucking child, that she should have no compassion on the son of her womb? Even these may forget, yet I will not forget you" (Is 49:15).[55] Compare Julian's extended analogy:

> We know that all our mothers bear us for pain and for death. . . . But our true Mother Jesus, he alone bears us for joy and for endless life (60:297–98). . . . The mother may sometimes suffer the child to fall and to be distressed in various ways, for its own benefit, but she can never suffer any kind of peril to come to her child, because of her love. And though our earthly mother may suffer her child to perish, our heavenly Mother Jesus may never suffer us who are his children to perish, for he is almighty, all wisdom and all love (61:300–1).

The theme of the motherhood of Christ was part of the material added after Julian understood the significance of the parable of the lord and the servant.[56] After recounting what the parable revealed about the love of God for humanity, it is as though Julian searched for an image to sum up her reflections on the salvific work of Christ, and the image of mother seemed to suit her purposes best. Since humans receive life doubly through Christ, through creation and salvation, the title of mother applies to Christ above all others: "this fair lovely word 'mother' is so sweet and so kind in itself that it cannot truly be said of anyone or to anyone except of him and to him who is the true Mother of life and of all things" (60:298–99). The symbol of Christ as mother, then, acts as a summary symbol for Julian's whole soteriology. As such, it is able to hold together all the themes and images described thus far.

In the symbol of Christ as mother the image of the suffering servant unites with that of the new Adam. In Genesis, the labor of Adam in tilling the soil by the sweat of his brow is paralleled by Eve's labor of bringing forth children in pain (Gen 3:16). Thus, "the greatest labor and the hardest travail," the work of gardening performed by the new Adam, is also language descriptive of childbearing. Julian takes advantage of the play on words associated with the word "labor" and with the general biblical tradition which correlated gardening images with sexuality and procreation. Similarly, she uses the play on words provided by "travail" and "travel" to equate Christ's whole journey through life with the process of giving birth.[57] Most unique to Julian's use of the motherhood theme is that it includes Christ's taking on himself our humanity, indicating a giving of himself in the incarnation to human flesh, comparable to a mother's giving of her bodily substance to the fetus within her womb.[58] Julian says of "our true Mother Jesus" that "in accepting our nature he quickened us to life, and in his blessed dying on the cross he bore us to endless life" (63:304). The pain and the shedding of blood endured by Christ in the passion finds a ready parallel in the pain of childbirth, thus incorporating the suffering servant image into the work of recreation. The "tossing about and writhing, the groaning and moaning" (51:277), words which Julian uses to describe the passion, can as easily describe a woman in labor. The work of recreation is basically a bringing to new birth, a work which requires labor and travail.

The details of the passion emphasized by Julian reappear in the motherhood image. Christ's thirst or love longing will not cease "until all his beloved children are born and brought to birth" (63:304). Therefore:

> He carries us within him in love and travail, until the full time when he wanted to suffer the sharpest thorns and cruel pains that ever were or will be, and at the last he died. And when he had finished, and had borne us so for bliss, still all this could not satisfy his wonderful love. And he revealed this in these great surpassing words of love: If I could suffer more, I would suffer more (60:298).

The blood of Christ with its sacramental significance appears again in the motherhood image, connected as it often is in medieval devotional works with the nourishing function of motherhood:[59]

> He could not die any more, but he did not want to cease working; therefore he must needs nourish us, for the precious love of motherhood has made him our debtor. The mother can give her child to suck of her milk, but our precious Mother Jesus can feed us with himself, and does, most courteously and most tenderly, with the blessed sacrament, which is the precious food of true life; and with all the sweet sacraments he sustains us most mercifully and graciously (60:298).

The open side of Christ reappears:

> The mother can lay her child tenderly to her breast, but our tender Mother Jesus can lead us easily into his blessed breast through his sweet open side, and show us there a part of the godhead and of the joys of heaven (60:298).

The motherhood image is used to make allusion to the Philippians hymn:

> Because he wanted altogether to become our Mother in all things, [Christ] made the foundation of his work most humbly and most mildly in the maiden's womb. . . . that is to say that our great God, the supreme wisdom of all things, arrayed and prepared himself in this humble place, all ready in our poor flesh, himself to do the service and the office of motherhood in everything (60:297).

Christ's motherhood also expresses well the idea that we are always held united to God, which is our natural place, through "a mother's love which never leaves us" (60:297). Because this is true we can regard our failings as happy faults:

> She [the mother] allows [her child] to be chastised to destroy its faults, so as to make the child receive virtues and grace. This work, with everything which is lovely and good, our Lord performs in those by whom it is done (60:299).[60]

Christ is identified with the church who exercises the nourishing and healing functions of motherhood:

> And therefore it is a certain thing . . . to be fastened and united to our mother Holy Church, who is Christ Jesus. For the flood of mercy which is his dear blood and precious water is plentiful to make us fair and clean. The blessed wounds of our savior are open and rejoice to heal us. The sweet

gracious hands of our Mother are ready and diligent about us; for he in all this work exercises the true office of a kind nurse, who has nothing else to do but attend to the safety of her child (61:301–2).

Since "the mother's service is nearest, readiest and surest," the image of motherhood can best express the closeness of the love that exists between Christ and us (60:297). We are always "enclosed in him" as in a womb: "our savior is our true Mother, in whom we are endlessly born and out of whom we shall never come" (57:292). The motherhood image is thus illustrative, in a rather different way, of the idea that Christians are of one body with Christ.

The work of Christ as mother goes beyond the work of mercy, for he shares in the operations attributed to the other persons of the trinity.[61] Julian uses the motherhood image to express the part played by Christ in creation as well as redemption: "the second person of the trinity is our Mother in nature in our substantial creation, in whom we are founded and rooted" (58:294). This recalls once again the figure of Wisdom present at creation and is linked to Julian's understanding of the predestination of all the saved in Christ.

Christ as mother also participates in the work of sanctification attributed to the Holy Spirit:

And in our spiritual bringing to birth he uses more tenderness, without any comparison, in protecting us. . . . [H]e kindles our understanding, he prepares our ways, he eases our conscience, he comforts our soul, he illumines our heart and gives us partial knowledge and love of his blessed divinity, with gracious memory of his sweet humanity and his blessed passion, with courteous wonder over his great surpassing goodness, and makes us to love everything which he loves for love of him, and to be well satisfied with him and with all his works (61:299–300).[62]

We owe our being to Christ our mother, as the foundation of our first creation. We owe our increase to her as well, in bearing us to new birth. And we will owe our final fulfillment to our mother Christ, who through the nurturing presence of her Spirit in the church, steadily leads us into the fullness of life of the trinity.

The Person and Natures of Christ

Julian reveals a precise knowledge of classical christology with respect to the person and natures of Christ. While she has no original development of it as such, she describes it concretely in a way which is pastorally pleasing. In the parable of the lord and the servant, the "two natures" of the servant are revealed in two distinct ways: by the lord's regard for him, and by the servant himself. In both cases, the "oneness of person" is preserved because there is only one servant.

The lord views his servant with a "double aspect," both "outward" and "inward" (51:268). Outwardly, the lord's "lovely regard" towards the servant was one of "compassion and pity"; inwardly it was one of "joy and bliss." In this double aspect we can see how God regarded the two natures of Christ. God's compassion and pity were for the sufferings of his human nature; God's joy and bliss were for the divine nature in its work of accomplishing human salvation. However, God's primary regard for the servant is one of joy, for "the joy and bliss surpass the compassion and pity, as far as heaven is above earth" (51:271). Thus Julian can say, as she often does, that the trinity rejoices in the passion of Christ.

In the servant also there is a "double significance, one outward, the other inward." Christ's human nature is seen outwardly in the "poor laborer's clothing"; his divine nature in his inner "wisdom and goodness," and especially in his love. Just as the joy of the lord's gaze is "higher" than his pity, so the inner goodness and love of the servant is stronger than his outer appearance would indicate (51:275).

In her description of the thirteenth revelation, Julian summarizes what she believed about the personal identity of Jesus Christ:

> Christ Jesus is both God and [human]; and in his divinity he is himself supreme bliss, and was from without beginning, and he will be without end, which true everlasting bliss cannot of its nature be increased or diminished. . . . And with respect to Christ's humanity, . . . with all the power of his divinity, for love, to bring us to his bliss, he suffered pains and passion and he died. And these are the deeds of Christ's humanity, in which he rejoices (31:230).

However, even in the midst of her meditations on the lowest depths of Christ's human sufferings, Julian never forgets his identity as the Son of God. In the twelfth revelation, she received a vision of Christ "more glorified" than she had seen him before, and he spoke to her repeatedly in words recalling the "I am" sayings of John's gospel:[63]

> I am he, I am he, I am he who is highest. I am he whom you love. I am he in whom you delight. I am he whom you serve. I am he for whom you long.

I am he whom you desire. I am he whom you intend. I am he who is all. I am he whom Holy Church preaches and teaches to you. I am he who showed myself before to you (26:223).

In this revelation, Julian was given to understand that in Christ is revealed the fullness of the Godhead.

Elsewhere, Julian comments further on the relationship between the divinity and the humanity in Christ:

He partly brought to my mind the exaltedness and nobility of the glorious divinity, and at the same time the preciousness and tenderness of his blessed body united with it, and also the reluctance that there is in human nature to suffer pain. For just as he was most tender and most pure, so he was most strong and powerful to suffer (20:213).

Because of "the union in him of the divinity," (i.e., the hypostatic union), the human Jesus had the strength to suffer "more pain than all who are to be saved" (20:213). As in classical christology, the divine personhood of Christ directs the human activity of the God-man, the human mind and will of Christ always acting in harmony with it because of the hypostatic union.

Julian exhibits a precise understanding of the communication of idioms of classical christology, as well as the circumincession of persons in the trinity. While "all the trinity worked in Christ's passion, administering abundant virtues and plentiful grace to us by him" (23:219), only "the second person, Christ Jesus" took our human nature (58:295). Though "only the virgin's son suffered" (23:219), a phrase emphasizing the human nature, Julian insists that "the most important point to apprehend in his passion is to meditate and come to see that he who suffered is God" (20:213).

Julian focuses upon the love of this divine personality: "the love in him which he has for our souls was so strong that he willingly chose suffering with a great desire" (20:214). In the Short Text, Julian had stated even more clearly that the love which motivated the earthly Jesus was divine and eternal:

But the love which made him suffer all this surpasses all his pains as far as heaven is above earth. For his pains were a deed, performed once through the motion of love; but his love was without beginning and is and ever will be without any end (xi:144).

The intensity of the love of Christ was first seen in the weakness and suffering of the human Jesus. But penetrating into the meaning of such a love led Julian to realize that love is the very nature of God. The passion of the earthly Jesus is the expression in time of the timeless love of God for humanity. Contemplating the love of Jesus therefore led Julian surely and steadily into the mysterious depths of the trinity.

4

From the Love of God to the Trinity

Julian was influenced and limited by the images and concepts of God prevalent in her day, but in spite of this, she advances some ideas about God that are surprisingly modern. One might expect that the lordship image for God in the parable of the lord and the servant, drawn from and elaborated according to the ideals of feudal society, would produce an understanding of God as patriarchal, hierarchical, and domineering. However, Julian's interpretation actually reverses the ordinary implications of that image to produce the picture of a God content to be on an equal footing with human beings. Although she seems to believe sincerely in the neoplatonic ideals of eternity and immutability, she nonetheless implies that the response of creatures has a real effect upon God. Over all, her picture of God is much more reminiscent of the God of the scriptures who is actively involved in relationship with human beings than it is of the more remote, immutable, transcendent God of classical Christian philosophy.

Julian creates her picture of God by focusing upon love as God's predominent attribute. All other attributes of God are seen in relation to God's love, elaborating and deepening her appreciation of it. And eventually, meditation on the meaning of God's love leads Julian into the mystery of the trinity, which she never considers apart from God's relation to humanity. Her doctrine of God is securely founded on the Johannine notion that God is love, and those who abide in love, abide in God and God in them (1 Jn 4:16).

God's Love

In the sixth revelation, Julian describes an imaginative vision which prefigures the parable of the lord and the servant:

> I saw our Lord God as a lord in his own house, who has called all his friends to a splendid feast. . . . I saw him reign in his house as a king and fill it all full of joy and mirth, gladdening and consoling his dear friends with

himself, very [homely] and courteously, with wonderful melody in endless
love in his own fair blissful countenance (14:203).[1]

The two words, "homely and courteously," with which Julian explains
how God entertains are the words she uses most often to describe the love
of God.

The Middle English word "cortaysye" is often thought to have had its
origins in the literary convention of courtly love, where it designates the
polite behavior appropriate to the deference due a high-born lady.[2] Actually, the word's origin may be more properly linked to the description of
Christian virtue.[3] The first recorded occurrence of the word is in the
Ancrene Riwle, where it signifies the desire to find pleasure in giving to
others.[4] In *Cursor Mundi* the word is used to indicate "the spirit of
kindness or consideration which will not deny another's request," a
meaning which remains central to the word throughout the fourteenth
century.[5] In addition, the word often denotes the avoidance of contention,
hospitality even to strangers, and strict adherence to the truth.

Courtesy, then, was primarily a virtue and, as such, mirrored God as
the source of all virtue. In medieval religious lyrics God is often described
as courteous, indicating God's desire to help and give pleasure to creatures. However, describing God as courteous does not mean God is simply
meek and mild towards humanity. It is a word able to describe charity and
kindness in such a way that justice is done to the responsibility incurred
by both parties to the love relationship; a courteous love is a love willing to
be generous and faithful, yet demanding a similar response.[6] The word
thus captures something of the relationship which ideally existed between
lord and vassal in feudal society, a relationship based upon personal love,
mutual respect, and fidelity to the obligations willingly assumed by both
parties.[7]

Julian's use of the word "courtesy" to describe God's love is consistent
with its root meaning as the gracious desire to find pleasure in giving to
others. This is evident in her description of God as a "cheerful giver":

> Always a cheerful giver pays only little attention to the thing which he is
> giving, but all his desire and all his intention is to please and comfort the
> one to whom he is giving it. And if the receiver accept the gift gladly and
> gratefully, then the courteous giver counts as nothing all his expense and
> his labor, because of the joy and the delight that he has because he has
> pleased and comforted the one whom he loves (23:219).

In God's courteous love human beings are welcomed into the pleasure of
God's company, invited into a relationship which provides comfort and
security against all affliction:

And this is a supreme friendship of our courteous Lord, . . . [who] shows himself to the soul, happily and with the gladdest countenance, welcoming it as a friend, as if it had been in pain and in prison, saying: My dear darling, I am glad that you have come to me in all your woe. I have always been with you, and now you see me loving, and we are made one in bliss (40:246).

The offer of friendship from such a God inspires devotion: "the more that the loving soul sees this courtesy of God, the gladder it is to serve him all its life" (14:204). Part of this service is the desire to fight against sin:

For the same true love which touches us all by its blessed strength, that same blessed love teaches us that we must hate sin only because of love. And I am sure by what I feel that the more that each loving soul sees this in the courteous love of our Lord God, the greater is his hatred of sinning and the more he is ashamed (40:247).

God's courteous love is a bulwark against sin, the common enemy of God and humanity; it indicates God's fidelity to the goodness of creation that cannot be undermined by the power of sin. Thus it is that "our courteous Lord comforts and succors, and always he is kindly disposed to the soul, loving and longing to bring us to his bliss" (51:271). This disposition is captured by the image of the lord in the parable, the blueness of the clothing signifying his steadfastness (51:272). Humanity's future with such a God is secure, "for our Lord God is so good, so gentle and so courteous that he can never assign final failure to those in whom he will always be blessed and praised" (53:282).

While God's own goodness "courteously" excuses sin, it is nevertheless important for sinners "meekly to accuse ourselves" (52:281). In order that they might do so, God's courtesy reveals their sinfulness in a compassionate and gentle way:

How courteously he protects us and makes us know that we are going astray . . . how steadfastly he waits for us, and does not change his demeanor, for he wants us to be converted and united to him in love, as he is to us . . . he in his courtesy measures the sight [of sin] for us (78:332).

God never leaves the soul alone in the contemplation of sin, but always reveals with it "a merciful compassion . . . and a courteous promise of a clean deliverance" (64:307).

Finally, God's courtesy rewards the human struggle against sin. In the parable, the lord's honor requires that the servant be rewarded for his suffering (51:269). Courtesy demands this; if the lord does not reward his vassal for his service he will seem "ungracious." Thus,

> as we are punished here with sorrow and penance, in contrary fashion we shall be rewarded in heaven by the courteous love of our almighty God, who does not wish anyone who comes there to lose his labors in any degree. For he regards sin as sorrow and pains for his lovers, to whom for love he assigns no blame (39:245).

God's courteous love is cheerful, kind, compassionate, friendly, generous, and faithful, but it also calls forth devotion on the part of God's creatures, a devotion that learns to hate sin and engage in the struggle against it, as an expression of trust and love.

While "courtesy" allows for friendliness and hospitality, it also evokes notions of majesty and nobility. God as courteous still maintains a certain distance from humanity, inspiring reverence, trust and gratitude, but this does not necessarily imply companionship. The other word Julian uses to describe God's love, "homely," puts us in touch with the amazing intimacy of God's love for humanity, a love, although noble, that does not despise lowliness. The Middle English word "homely," derived from "home," simply meant "feeling comfortable or at home with," and is best expressed by the modern English words "familiar" or "intimate."[8]

The revelation of God's "homeliness" was the part of her showings that most amazed Julian. When she records her first showing of the bleeding head, she tells us "I was greatly astonished by this wonder and marvel, that he who is so to be revered and feared would be so [homely] with a sinful creature" (4:181). Julian was first given the image of the lord in connection with this idea of homeliness:

> And so that I might understand this, God showed me this plain example. It is the greatest honor which a majestic king or a great lord can do for a poor servant, to be [homely] with him; and especially if he makes this known himself, privately and publicly, with great sincerity and happy mien, this poor creature will think: See, what greater honor and joy could this noble lord give me than to demonstrate to me, who am so little, this wonderful [homeliness]? Truly, this is a greater joy and delight to me than if he were to give me great gifts, and himself always to remain distant in his manner (7:188).

This simple example reveals that "he who is highest and mightiest, noblest and most honorable, is lowest and humblest, most [homely]" (7:188–89). This is true to such an extent that God does not "disdain to serve us in the simplest natural functions of our body" (6:186).[9]

God's homeliness means that God is our home, within whom we dwell. We have already encountered this idea in the image of Christ as mother in whom humanity is enclosed as in a womb, and in the related image of the open side of Christ. Julian also uses the analogy of clothing to express this idea:

> I saw that he is to us everything which is good and comforting for our help. He is our clothing, who wraps and enfolds us for love, embraces us and shelters us, surrounds us for his love, which is so tender that he may never desert us (5:183). . . . For as the body is clad in the cloth, and the flesh in the skin, and the bones in the flesh, and the heart in the trunk, so are we, soul and body, clad and enclosed in the goodness of God. Yes, and more closely, for all these vanish and waste away; the goodness of God is always complete, and closer to us, beyond any comparison (6:186).[10]

So close is God to humanity that "there may and will be nothing at all between God and the human soul" (53:284). In the parable, the lord's clothing points to the lord himself as "a secure place of refuge, long and broad, all full of endless heavenliness," calling up the image of a strong citadel (51:271).[11] The treasure in the earth has a secure foundation in the lord "in a marvellous depth of endless love" (51:274).

Julian interprets the homeliness of God's love quite literally. God's love is simply our home: "in this endless love we are led and protected by God, and we never shall be lost." We have been "treasured and hidden in God, known and loved from without beginning." Our soul has its foundation in God, "preciously knitted to [God] in its making" (53:284). This is "our natural place, in which we were created by the motherhood of love, a mother's love which never leaves us" (60:297).

On the other hand, we are God's home. The most obvious evidence for this is the fact of the incarnation, described in the last chapter. God made human reality the place where God chose to dwell. The idea of clothing plays a part here also, for Julian describes the incarnation as Christ's appearing in Adam's tunic. As a result of the passion and resurrection, all who are Christ's clothing are "made lovely by our savior, new, white and bright and forever clean" (51:278).

The restoration resulting from Christ's death and resurrection, however, is more frequently described using the image of God's city. Humanity was meant to be "God's city and dwelling place," and when sin made that city ignoble and unfit for God, the lord sat upon the bare ground until the servant had restored it (51:272). Once restored, it becomes God's favorite dwelling, God's "homeliest home" (68:313). Collectively, this city is Christ's church, "the fair maiden of endless joy," in whom Christ dwells as head (51:278). But it also represents the individual soul in which "the blessed trinity our creator dwells eternally" (1:177).

Julian's description of the mutual indwelling between God and humanity probably owes its inspiration to John's gospel. There, too, God is humanity's dwelling place. But human dwelling in God is possible only because the Word of God came to live in human flesh (Jn 1:11, 14). John's gospel is pervaded with phrases like "dwell in," "abide in," "be with," "stay with," emphasizing what Julian calls the homeliness of God's love.[12]

God's homely love is a love which simply wants to be with the beloved. It does not shrink from menial service or from a lowering of self in order to achieve the union of love. It is simple, domestic, humble, natural, comfortable, familiar and intimate. It reveals a God willing to be friend and companion to human beings, sharing their lot totally and equally.

The notions of courtesy and homeliness have been isolated in order to understand their contrast. But when Julian uses them together, as she frequently does,[13] a full picture of God's love emerges. God "is supreme [homeliness]," but God "is as courteous as he is [homely], for God is true courtesy" (77:331). God, who is at once high and noble, with all the connotations of majesty and glory associated with the word "courtesy," also does not disdain to become "homely" and intimate with human beings. While the parallel may not be exact, there is an intimation here of the picture of God that permeates the Judaeo-Christian tradition: God is both transcendent, far surpassing humanity in glory, and yet immanent in human history. God lowers self out of love, and in the process raises humanity to noble heights. The result is not that God becomes less, but that humanity becomes more.

The effect produced by the combination of the notions of courtesy and homeliness appears most clearly in the vision of Jesus as courteous lord ruling the universe from his homely dwelling, the human soul:

> And then our good Lord opened my spiritual eye, and showed me my soul in the midst of my heart. I saw the soul as wide as if it were an endless citadel, . . . a blessed kingdom, . . . a fine city. In the midst of that city sits our Lord Jesus, true God and true man, a handsome person and tall, highest bishop, most awesome king, most honorable lord. And I saw him splendidly clad in honors. He sits erect there in the soul, in peace and rest, and he rules and guards heaven and earth and everything that is. . . . And the soul is wholly occupied by the blessed divinity, sovereign [might], sovereign wisdom and sovereign goodness (68:312–13).

As a result of God's homely love, reaching down toward us and dwelling with us, we are lifted up into the everlasting glory of God. This is the "eternal life" of John's gospel which Christ's dwelling with us has made possible. Through him the Father is made known and present to us (Jn 14:8–9); through him the Counselor, the Spirit of truth, dwells with us (Jn 14:16–17).

The qualities of courtesy and homeliness, as descriptive of God's love, belong to the unity of God's essence. No one of the persons of the trinity can be said to be more or less courteous or homely than the others. Julian applies these qualities both to God as one and also, at various times, to each person of the trinity. Yet she also implies an appropriation of these qualities to the economic trinity. The word "courtesy" aptly describes the demeanor and actions of the lord of the parable, who represents the first person of the trinity. The servant is the second person who did not disdain to dwell in human flesh, thus the word "homely" expresses well God's outreach through the incarnation. But the one who makes this courtesy and homeliness immediately accessible is the Holy Spirit. The "wonderful courtesy and homeliness of our Father . . . in our Lord Jesus Christ" cannot be known by us, unless "by a great abundance of grace, given within by the Holy Spirit" (7:189).

The Holy Spirit, as the mutual love between Father and Son, and as the love with which Father and Son love us, brings God's courtesy and homeliness to us. While human existence is appropriated to the fatherhood of God, and recreation to God's motherhood, incorporation into the trinity, wherein humanity finds fulfillment, is attributable to what Julian calls God's lordship. And the notion of God's lordship, which is at once courteous and humble, most fittingly describes the action of the Holy Spirit.

Other Attributes of God

Justice and Mercy

Julian's discussion of God's justice and mercy is based upon the preeminence of God's love in her theology. God sees human beings only one way, through the eyes of love: "The . . . judgment which is from God's justice is from his own great endless love, and that is that fair, sweet judgment which was shown in all the fair revelation in which I saw him assign to us no kind of blame" (45:256). For Julian, as for Aquinas, God's justice is God's truth.[14] God always sees us as we truly are, "in our natural substance, which is always kept one in him, whole and safe, without end" (45:256). For God, humans are always the good and rightful recipients of

God Is Love

love. God's justice, then, is never wrathful toward humans, but is always turned lovingly toward them.

There is no conflict for Julian between God's justice and love. The notion of God's mercy, however, causes her some perplexity. Before her revelations she had understood mercy as the "remission of [God's] wrath after we have sinned" (47:260). But her revelations showed no wrath in God. Technically, since God always sees humans as good, without the blame caused by sin, God does not forgive (49:263). This is a unique and rather startling idea; to my knowledge, no one else in the Christian tradition says anything quite like this.

Julian found a solution to her perplexity about God's mercy in the difference between human and divine judgment. Unlike God's judgment which is based on our true "natural substance," human judgment is based upon "our changeable sensuality, which now seems one thing and now another." Human judgments are therefore "sometimes . . . good and lenient, . . . sometimes . . . hard and painful." To the extent that they are good and lenient, they match God's justice. But to the extent that they are hard and painful, they cause humans to experience something they describe as the wrath and forgiveness of God. As such, they need to be reformed by God's mercy and grace and brought into harmony with God's justice (45:256).

Like justice, God's mercy is founded in love. It is specifically "our preservation in love," against the forces of sin. It is "a sweet, gracious operation in love, mingled with plentiful pity." It works, "protecting us . . . [and] turning everything to good for us." It also "allows us to fail to a certain extent." Humans experience God's operation of mercy as a "protecting, enduring, vivifying and healing" activity. Through it they understand the tenderness and compassion of God's love, most adequately imaged by the symbol of mother (48:262). God's mercy will continue operating "so long as sin is permitted to harass righteous souls," that is, until all who will be saved are completely secure in the righteousness of God (35:237–38).[15]

In many treatments of the relationship between God's justice and mercy, God's justice explains why God punishes human sinfulness. In Julian's treatment, no such interpretation is possible. God's justice means simply that God loves humanity forever, since God always sees our essential lovableness. God's mercy maintains that essential lovableness against the powers of evil.

Being and Goodness

For Julian, "God the blessed trinity . . . is everlasting being" (58:293). God is "substantial uncreated nature" (53:284) or "nature's substance" (56:290); that is, "God is nature [or essence] in his being" (62:302). Like Aquinas, Julian equates God's existence with God's essence as the most basic description of God. [16]

Also like Aquinas and countless philosophers and theologians before him, Julian equates God's being, and indeed being itself, with goodness. [17] God is essential goodness: "that goodness which is natural is God"; this is what essential "being" or "substantial nature" is (62:302). The equation between being and goodness is very well expressed by Julian's use of the Middle English word "kynde," whose connotations and derivations include both the meanings "nature or essence" and "benevolence or kindness." [18] God's being is also love, rightfulness, truth, or justice, attributes which express various ways of looking at God's essential goodness.

All else that has being participates in God's being, thus God is the "true Father and the true Mother of natures" (62:302). Everything which participates in God's existence, then, is also essentially good. Julian enhances this thought by an allusion to the "I am who am" of Exodus 3:

> See, I am God. See, I am in all things. See, I do all things. See, I never remove my hands from my works, nor ever shall without end. See, I guide all things to the end that I ordain them for before time began, with the same [might] and wisdom and love with which I made them; how should anything be amiss? (11:199). [19]

Human existence depends upon its being held in this unchanging goodness of God. Thus there can be no wrath, the opposite of goodness, in God:

> If God could be angry for any time, we should neither have life nor place nor being; for as truly as we have our being from the endless [might] of God and from his endless wisdom and from his endless goodness, just as truly we have our preservation in the endless [might] of God and in his endless wisdom and in his endless goodness. For though we may feel in ourselves anger, contention and strife, still we are all mercifully enclosed in God's mildness and in his meekness, in his benignity and in his accessibility (49:264).

Rest and Peace

The fact that there can be no wrath in God puts us in touch with God's immutability, which Julian describes most often as rest and peace. In the parable, the lord "sits in state in rest and peace," the blueness of his clothing symbolizing his "steadfastness" or immutability (51:267, 272).[20] In fact, God *is* "true rest" (5:184). As such, God is the antithesis of wrath, for "wrath is nothing else but a perversity and an opposition to peace and to love," involving a lack of might, wisdom or goodness (48:262). Wrath implies change in God; peace and rest, on the other hand, indicate that "God's love does not change" (43:254).

Because God loves human beings eternally, they are included in the immutability of God. When sin tarnished human nobility, the lord of the parable continued to sit in exactly the same place until that nobility was restored. God's attitude towards humanity is unchanging:

> [God] never changed his purpose in any kind of thing, nor ever will eternally. For there was nothing unknown to him in his just ordinance before time began, and therefore all things were set in order, before anything was made, as it would endure eternally. And no kind of thing will fail in that respect, for he has made everything totally good (11:198–99).

The rest, peace, and immutability of God is what all human beings long for and move towards. Echoing Augustine, Julian says that we will never attain "perfect rest" until there is no created thing between God and us (5:183).[21] Our home is the rest and peace of God. God is "our steadfast foundation," where our substantial being is held in God's peace and rest unchangeably (49:265).

God's Joy

One of the unique aspects of Julian's theology is the extent to which she emphasizes God's joy.[22] The lord of the parable is a joyful lord, the joy of his countenance far surpassing the compassion and pity he shows the servant in his sufferings (51:271). At the end of the parable the servant too is "richly clothed in joyful amplitude, with a rich and precious crown upon his head," which crown, of course, is all the saved, "the Father's joy, the Son's honor, the Holy Spirit's delight" (51:278).

Joy is a component of God's courteous love. When Julian described the image of the lord reigning in his house, she saw him "fill it all full of joy and mirth . . . which . . . fills all heaven full of the joy and bliss of the divinity" (14:203). Joy is an essential attribute of God, yet eternally directed toward human beings:

> God rejoices that he is our Father, and God rejoices that he is our Mother, and God rejoices that he is our true spouse, and that our soul is his beloved wife. And Christ rejoices that he is our brother, and Jesus rejoices that he is our savior. These are five great joys . . . in which he wants us to rejoice (52:279).

The trinity "rejoices without end in the creation of the human soul, for it saw without beginning what would delight it without end." The human soul is "as beautiful, as good, as precious a creature as it could make," therefore the blessed trinity is "fully pleased" with it (68:313–14).

The trinity also rejoices in the passion of Christ. Through it God, the ever courteous "cheerful giver," finds joy and delight only in the fact that "he has pleased and comforted the one whom he loves" (23:218–20). Julian emphasizes to a great degree the joy of Christ, who "willingly chose suffering with a great desire, and suffered it meekly with a great joy" (20:214). In the ninth revelation, the suffering Jesus suddenly changes "to an appearance of joy" (21:215) in which he "counts as nothing his labor and his sufferings and his cruel and shameful death" (22:217).

Bringing all the saved into the joy of God is the special operation of the Holy Spirit. The "rest" we seek in God means entering into God, "acknowledging that he is full of joy, homely and courteous and blissful and true life" (26:223). Through the Spirit, God "loves us and delights in us, and so wishes us to love him and delight in him" (68:315). God's constant desire is "to bring us to the fullness of joy" (40:246); thus God takes "pleasure" and "delight" in our prayer (41:249) and in every good deed we do (43:253). Through these, "God rejoices in the creature and the creature in God, endlessly marvelling" (44:256). But God "will never have his full joy in us until we have our full joy in him" (72:320). God's work of salvation will not be complete until then. In the meantime, God joyfully anticipates the glorious fulfillment awaiting all who will be saved.

Julian's treatment of God's joy as an essential attribute of God effectively captures the God of Jesus as painted by the synoptic gospels. Julian's God reflects the joy of the shepherd upon finding the lost sheep, of the woman upon finding the lost coin, and of the father over the return of the lost son (Lk 15). The Jesus who feasted with sinners and outcasts, and who spoke of the kingdom in terms of a joyful celebratory banquet, revealed a compassionate and joyful God, who is adequately represented in Julian's theology.

The Incomprehensibility of God

Julian exhibits an exact understanding of symbol and theological analogy. The parable of the lord and the servant was "mysterious," with secrets "deeply hidden" in it; indeed every showing was "full of secrets" (51:269). Her showings were symbols revelatory of God given to her for her contemplation; they contained a "surplus of meaning" which was virtually inexhaustible, so that she needed to return to them again and again to understand them.[23] Yet, even though their meaning might be inexhaustible, Julian knew that these very rich symbols were mere analogies for the incomprehensible mystery of God.

Julian understood that "no one [can] see God and live afterwards . . . in this mortal life" (43:255). There are dimensions to God that are hidden, closed to human understanding, and the creature must always bow before the mystery of God. Julian returns to her feudal imagery to explain this: "It is fitting to God's royal dominion to keep his privy counsel in peace, and it is fitting to his servants out of obedience and respect not to wish to know his counsel" (30:228). When God gives a special revelation such as Julian's, it is carefully measured by God to contain what "is profitable for that time" (43:255). Humanity's place is to be "well satisfied both with what he conceals and what he reveals" (33:235).

In the thirteenth revelation, when Julian seeks to understand how all could be well in spite of sin, she acknowledges the limits of her understanding: "I saw hidden in God an exalted and wonderful mystery" (27:226). God tells her: "What is impossible to you is not impossible to me. I shall preserve my word in everything, and I shall make everything well" (32:233).[24] Through these words, Julian learns to rest content in God's promises without fully understanding how they can happen.

In spite of the love which causes God to enter into friendship and intimacy with human creatures, the majesty of God continues to inspire awe in human hearts:

> Out of wonder and marvelling, all creatures ought to have for God so much reverent fear, surpassing what has been seen and felt before, that the pillars of heaven will tremble and quake. But this kind of trembling and fear will have no kind of pain, but it is proper to God's honorable majesty so to be contemplated by his creatures. . . . And as good as God is, so great is he; and as much as it is proper to his divinity to be loved, so much is it proper to his great exaltedness to be feared (75:327).

No matter how "homely" God's love may be, the transcendence of God, intimated by the description of that same love as "courteous," causes God's creatures to bow low in wonder. No matter how extensive God's revelation of self may be, God always remains Incomprehensible Mystery.[25]

The Trinitarian God

In the first revelation, as described in the Long Text, the vision of the suffering Jesus immediately initiates Julian into the joy of the trinity:

Suddenly I saw the red blood running down from under the crown. . . . And in the same revelation, suddenly the trinity filled my heart full of the greatest joy, and I understood that it will be so in heaven without end to all who will come there. For the trinity is God, God is the trinity. The trinity is our maker, the trinity is our [keeper], and the trinity is our everlasting lover, the trinity is our endless joy and our bliss, by our Lord Jesus Christ and in our Lord Jesus Christ. And this was revealed in the first vision and in them all, for where Jesus appears the blessed trinity is understood (4:181).[26]

What enables Julian to make this paradoxical jump from the abject suffering of Jesus' humanity to trinitarian joy?[27] In her description of the same revelation in the Short Text, Julian reveals the missing link between Christ's passion and the trinity. It is the love of God:

Suddenly I saw the red blood trickling down from under the crown (iii:129). . . . And at the same time as I saw this [bodily] sight, our Lord showed me a spiritual sight of his [homely] love. I saw that he is to us everything which is good and comforting for our help (iv:130).

Then she sees the "little thing" as small as a hazel nut which represents all that is, owing its being and preservation to the love of God. God made it, keeps it, and loves it; God is creator, keeper, and lover (iv:130–31). Thus the passion of Christ, revealing as it does the love of God for humanity, puts Julian in touch with the threefold way God's love has affected creation.

This movement from God's love to the trinity is reminiscent of Augustine's "trinity of love" in the *De trinitate*.[28] For Augustine, the term "love" implies a threeness, including, besides itself, a loving subject and a loved object.[29] Contemplation of the love of God thus leads directly into the trinity. Because the Spirit is the bond or communion of Father and Son, "that mutual charity whereby the Father and the Son love one another," the term "love" can be especially appropriated to the Spirit, even though, as a term describing God's essence, it refers to the whole trinity.[30] This view of the trinity is apparent in Julian's parable. There, the lord is identified as the first person of the trinity and the servant as the second person.[31] The love between them is entirely mutual: "there was shown in [the servant] a foundation of love, the love which he had for the lord, which was equal to the love which the lord had for him," which love is the third person of the trinity, the Holy Spirit (51:273–74). This is the Augustinian understanding of the immanent trinity.

However, Julian does not describe this love of the inner life of the trinity apart from its inclusion of humanity. Throughout the parable the lord "sits in state, in rest and in peace," even though the external description of where he sits changes from that of wilderness to glorious city (51:267, 271, 278). Julian understood this constant sitting to represent the immutability of the divinity (51:276), yet it does not imply stasis because of the dynamic love with which the lord regards the servant. As we saw in the last chapter, the lord's regard had two aspects: the joy over the work accomplished by the servant surpasses the pity for the sufferings endured in the process. This joyful love for the servant motivates the lord to reward him with "the honorable rest and nobility" which he had chosen for him from before the beginning (51:271, 268). Furthermore, the lord's clothing, "billowing splendidly all about him" is described as being "wide and ample," signifying the fact that "he has enclosed within himself all heavens and all endless joy and bliss, . . . endless life and every kind of goodness," including the foundation of the treasure hidden in the earth (51:271–72).[32] But that treasure was "not wholly to his honor" until the servant had prepared it to his liking (51:274).

Here is the picture of a God who is immutable, a God of endless rest and peace, the antithesis of confusion or change. Nothing is lacking to this God; indeed all that exists has its foundation in God. Yet when we look at the relationship that exists between God and the servant, it is not described except in light of what the servant does, fulfilling the lord's will with respect to the treasure in the earth, something which involves a reaching out from within God's self to include humanity. Until the servant has accomplished this, there is wilderness around the lord and lack of food.

If we turn our attention to the servant, we find a similar phenomenon: the servant's relationship to the lord is also inclusive of humanity. In contrast to the sedentary lord, the servant is active. The quality of the servant's love for the lord causes him to disregard self and to endure suffering and hardship for love of the lord. But, as was amply shown in the last chapter, this love for the lord demanded a penetration into the lord's will to such an extent that the servant loved what the lord loved, the treasure in the earth that was destined to be their city and dwelling place.

The love that exists between lord and servant, a love identified as the Holy Spirit, is inclusive of humanity and is rarely described apart from it. The Holy Spirit is, therefore, not only the mutual love with which Father and Son love each other, but also the love with which they love human beings and the means by which all who will be saved are included in the love and life of the trinity.[33] The Father loves us by loving the Son through the Spirit; the Son loves us by loving the Father through the Spirit. And that mutual love in the trinitarian Godhead is what effects human creation, increase, and fulfillment.

Human beings appear as something radically important to God. Julian nowhere says explicitly that God needs humanity, or that human beings add anything essential to God. But the lord's dwelling place is certainly richer after the recreation of human nature wrought by the servant, and the servant is rewarded "above what he would have been if he had not fallen" (51:269) with "a rich and precious crown," which crown is all who will be saved (51:278). Furthermore, the glorified Son's clothing, which represents restored human nature, is "fairer and richer than the [Father's] clothing" (51:278). Human beings are seen to give something to God, if not to God's essence, certainly to God's rejoicing in the divine works accomplished in time.

Julian preserves God's immutability by stating that human creation, increase, and fulfillment were God's plan from before beginning, and that the final fulfillment of humanity is always held secure in God's intention. From God's standpoint, all the saved are eternally increased and fulfilled, and God eternally rejoices in this. But this means that part of the nature of God's love is its eternal extension outside of God towards the other-than-God. Since God always loved humanity from before beginning, when humans are finally united to God (from the human perspective), this is not an addition to God, but the increase and fulfillment of what exists outside of God which God always intended by the gratuitous nature of God's love. Because of the emphasis Julian places upon God's turning toward us, humanity never appears in her theology as the unnecessary afterthought of an utterly self-sufficient God, but as something precious to God in which God eternally rejoices.

The Unity of the Godhead

Julian accepted the classical doctrine of the immanent trinity, that God is one in essence and operation, and that the only distinction among the persons of the trinity is in their relations to each other.[34] For example, she clearly says that "the trinity [not the Father alone] is our maker, the trinity [not the Son alone] is our [keeper], the trinity [not the Spirit alone] is our everlasting lover" (4:181). God was one in the work of creation: "As well as the Father could create a creature and as well as the Son could create a creature, so well did the Holy Spirit want the human spirit to be created, and so it was done" (68:313). God was also one in the work of salvation: "All the trinity worked in Christ's passion . . . but only the virgin's Son suffered, in which all the blessed trinity rejoice" (23:219). Finally, God the trinity is one in the work of sanctification whereby humanity is united to God by love:

> And by the endless intent and assent and the full accord of all the trinity . . . before he made us he loved us, and when we were made we loved him; and this is made only of the natural substantial goodness of the Holy Spirit, mighty by reason of the might of the Father, wise in mind of the wisdom of the Son. And so is the human soul made by God, and in the same moment joined to God (53:283–84).

Julian also exhibits an understanding of the notion of *perichoresis* or *circumincessio* in the trinity, the idea that, because of their unity of essence, the three persons of the trinity interpenetrate or dwell within each other. "Where Jesus appears the blessed trinity is understood" (4:181), she says at the beginning of her revelations. Thus "the blessed trinity our creator dwells eternally in our soul in Christ Jesus our savior" (1:177). There the Son "sits in his city in rest and in peace, which his Father has prepared for him by his endless purpose, and the Father in the Son, and the Holy Spirit in the Father and in the Son" (51:278). Through sanctification, human beings participate in the perichoresis of the inner life of the trinity:

> We are enclosed in the Father, and we are enclosed in the Son, and we are enclosed in the Holy Spirit. And the Father is enclosed in us, the Son is enclosed in us, and the Holy Spirit is enclosed in us, almighty, all wisdom and all goodness, one God, one Lord (54:285).

Julian understood that the attributes used to describe God apply to God's unity. Consistent with classical thought, she knew that terms like "might, wisdom, and love" describe God's essence, and do not belong to one person of the trinity to the exclusion of the others.[35] Yet, in order to facilitate human understanding of the trinity in relation to humanity, it is appropriate, for example, to allow "might" to designate the Father, "wisdom" the Son, and "love" the Holy Spirit. It is within this latter framework that most of Julian's reflections on the trinity take place. Since her revelations emphasized the relationship of the trinity to humanity, Julian's trinitarian doctrine focuses almost entirely on the economic trinity.

The Economic Trinity

In the Short Text there are three triads which Julian uses to describe the trinity: might, wisdom, love; joy, bliss, delight; and maker, keeper, lover. These are developed further in the Long Text, where Julian added more descriptive triads as she grew in understanding of the trinity. We will discuss those found in the Short Text first, then move on to the others.[36]

Might, Wisdom, Love

The most frequent triad by which Julian refers to the trinity is not the traditional Father, Son, and Spirit, but might, wisdom, and love (or goodness).[37] In the third revelation she realized that "our Lord God almighty, all wisdom and all love" has made everything that is and does everything that is done. Further, by the same might, wisdom, and goodness that God has done all this, God will make well all that is not well (1:175–76). We can rest secure that even now, in Jesus Christ, the trinity dwells in our soul, "honorably ruling and commanding all things, [mightily] and wisely saving and preserving us out of love" (1:177).[38]

The might, wisdom, and love of God are sometimes designated by the verbs "may," "can," and "will." In the thirteenth revelation Julian records the comforting words of Jesus to her: "I may make all things well, and I can make all things well, and I shall make all things well, and I will make all things well; and you will see yourself that every kind of thing will be well" (31:229).[39] In reflecting upon these words, Julian finds a full-fledged trinitarian doctrine. "May" indicates the ability to accomplish a deed, representing the Father's might; "can" indicates the wisdom or knowledge necessary for the task, representing the Son as wisdom; "will" indicates the desire or motivation behind the action, the Holy Spirit as love. All three acting together are appropriately represented by "shall," expressing the idea that since God is mighty and wise to accomplish what God wills, the fulfillment of God's will is inevitable. Human inclusion in the realization of this will of God is indicated by "you will see yourself" (31:229).

Joy, Bliss, Delight

For Julian, God is joy, bliss, and delight. At the end of the parable the Son sits at the right hand of the Father, which means that he shares "in the highest nobility of the Father's joy" (51:278). The Son "is himself supreme bliss, and was from without beginning, and he will be without end, which true everlasting bliss cannot of its nature be increased or diminished" (31:230). And the Holy Spirit, as the love between them, is their mutual "delight."

However, as with the love of God, Julian rarely mentions God's joy, bliss, and delight without reference to humanity. "Heaven" refers to the mutual rejoicing that takes place between God and human beings. When Jesus said to her in the ninth revelation, "It is a joy, a bliss, an endless delight to me that ever I suffered my passion for you" (22:216), Julian was led to contemplate the way the trinity rejoices in the incarnation and recreation accomplished by Jesus Christ. She tells us that in these words she understood "three heavens":

> And all are of the blessed humanity of Christ. And none is greater, none is less, none is higher, none is lower, but all are equal in their joy (22:216). . . . By "joy" I understood that the Father was pleased, and by "bliss" that the Son was honored, and by "endless delight" the Holy Spirit. The Father is pleased, the Son is honored, the Holy Spirit takes delight (23:218).

The triad, "joy, bliss, and delight" describes the attitude of God towards those who are saved. They are "God's crown": "the Father's joy, the Son's honor, the Holy Spirit's delight" (51:278). To my knowledge, no one else has ever described heaven in quite this way. Traditionally, heaven indicates the state of joy experienced by the blessed in the beatific vision, that is, humanity's enjoyment of God. Julian uniquely extends the meaning of heaven to include the joy which the saved bring to God. Indeed, all the saved are the mutual gift exchanged between Father and Son in heaven:

> I saw that Christ, having us all in him who shall be saved by him, honorably presents his Father in heaven with us, which present his Father most thankfully receives, and courteously gives to his Son Jesus Christ. This gift and operation is joy to the Father and bliss to the Son and delight to the Holy Spirit (55:286).

But the Holy Spirit is also the mutual gift of love between Father and Son. Once again, we see that all who will be saved are included in the gift of the Spirit that Father and Son offer to each other, an interesting added dimension to the Augustinian treatment of the Holy Spirit.

Maker, Keeper, Lover

The triad "maker, keeper and lover" emphasizes the way God's might, wisdom, and love affect creation. In the "little thing" the size of a hazelnut which represents all creation Julian sees three properties: God made it, preserves it, and loves it. God is therefore our maker, keeper, and lover (5:183).[40]

Being, Increase, Fulfillment; Nature, Mercy, Grace

In the Long Text, Julian greatly expands upon the triad "maker, keeper, lover." Humanity receives *being* from the operation of God as *maker*, the result of the fact that God is *substantial nature* or being itself; humanity receives *increase* or *making again* [recreation] from the operation of God as *keeper*, which can also be called the operation of *mercy*; and humanity gains final *fulfillment* from the operation of God as *lover*, also known as the operation of *grace*.

Julian's inspiration for this way of describing the human being in relation to God lies in the notion, developed creatively by Augustine, that the human soul is made in the image of the trinity (10:194). In the might (or truth), wisdom, and love of the soul, humans image God's might (or truth), wisdom, and love. For example, Julian paraphrases Augustine's thought in the following passage:

> Truth sees God, and wisdom contemplates God, and of these two comes the third, and that is a marvellous delight in God, which is love. Where truth and wisdom are, truly there is love, truly coming from them both, and all are of God's making. For God is endless supreme truth, endless supreme wisdom, endless supreme love uncreated; and a human soul is a creature in God which has the same properties created (44:256).

However, instead of stressing the natural faculties of the soul as imaging God's trinitarian essence, Julian describes human likeness to the triune God in terms of God's actions toward humans in history. Human nature is like God as substantial being in its creation. But it is meant to become more like God in its recreation through God's wisdom or mercy, a work which reaches its fulfillment through God's love or grace. The progress of human life in time, both collectively and individually, mirrors the intention God had for humanity from before beginning, which has been acted out over the course of human history through the incarnation and sending of the Spirit. In such a view, God is seen to be dynamically active in human history, and the doctrines of recreation and sanctification are in continuity with the doctrine of creation.

Julian may be indebted here to Paul, whose message is strikingly similar: "those whom he predestined he also called [the work of nature]; and those whom he called he also justified [the work of mercy]; and those whom he justified he also glorified [the work of grace]" (Rom 8:30). There are also some similarities here to Augustine's "trinity of faith" in Book 14 of the *De trinitate*. There the essential *nature* of human beings is an ineradicable imaging of God; *grace* is the progressive recovery of the likeness which has been lost by sin; the goal and perfection of this likeness is the state of *glory*, which occurs only in the vision of God. But Julian emphasizes more than Augustine does the fact that the image of God in the human soul is something that grows gradually, reflecting the works of the economic trinity in time.

The following passage illustrates how Julian sees God's economy towards humanity in time as reflective of the trinitarian God:

> Our reason is founded in God, who is nature's substance. From this substantial nature spring mercy and grace, and penetrate us, accomplishing everything for the fulfillment of our joy. These are our foundations, in which we have our being, our increase and our fulfillment. For in nature we have our life and our being, and in mercy and grace we have our increase and our fulfillment. This is three properties in one goodness, and where one operates all operate in the things which now pertain to us. . . . For we cannot profit by our reason alone, unless we have equally mind and love; nor can we be saved merely because we have in God our natural foundation, unless we have, coming from the same foundation, mercy and grace. For from these three operating all together we receive all our good (56:290).[41]

The human being is made in the image of the trinity, then, but in the image of the economic trinity. The progress of Christian life is meant to include recreation and fulfillment as well as creation. Throughout the course of their individual lives, humans reproduce the pattern of how God has reached out to humanity in its communal history through the events of the incarnation and sending of the Spirit. This is a dynamic way of understanding human nature as the image of the trinity, emphasizing the importance of human life in time.

Fatherhood, Motherhood, Lordship

Julian provides titles to describe God's relationship to humanity through the operations of nature, mercy and grace. In contemplating the work of the trinity, Julian understood "three properties: the property of the fatherhood, and the property of the motherhood, and the property of the lordship in one God" (58:293).

In the fatherhood of God, we have "our protection and our bliss, as regards our natural substance, which is ours by our creation from without beginning." God as Father is "the high might of the trinity" in whom "we have our being" (58:293–94). In fact, Julian sometimes identifies God the Father as "being" itself: "our great Father, almighty God, who is being, knows us and loved us before time began" (59:296).

In the motherhood of God, "in knowledge and wisdom we have our perfection, as regards our sensuality, our restoration and our salvation." God as Mother is "the deep wisdom of the trinity," and is Mother in a twofold sense: "our Mother in nature in our substantial creation, in whom we are founded and rooted, and . . . our Mother of mercy in taking our sensuality." In God as Mother "we profit and increase, . . . [and] we have our reforming and our restoring, . . . in whom our parts are united and all made perfect" (58:293–95).

In the lordship of God, "the great love of the trinity, . . . we have our reward and our gift for our living and our labor, endlessly surpassing all that we desire . . . out of his great plentiful grace." God works, "rewarding and giving. . . . freely, by grace, fulfilling and surpassing all that creatures deserve." Thus, "through the rewards and the gifts of grace of the Holy Spirit we are fulfilled" (58:294–95).[42]

All human life images these three properties of the trinity—fatherhood, motherhood, lordship: "in the first we have our being, and in the second we have our increasing, and in the third we have our fulfillment. The first is nature, the second is mercy, the third is grace" (58:294). And again, "Our Father wills, our Mother works, our good Lord the Holy Spirit confirms. . . . For in these three is all our life: nature, mercy and grace" (59:296).

These terms do not define God with respect to the relations of persons within the Godhead; they refer to God's relations to humans. As such, they refer to God's unity of essence and not to the distinction of persons within God. It can therefore be inferred that the one and triune God, not only the first person, relates to us as Father in the creation of our being or nature; the one and triune God, not only the second person, relates to us as Mother in our recreation through the work of mercy; the one and triune God, not only the Holy Spirit, relates to us as Lord in our fulfillment through the work of grace.

Julian's awareness of this is apparent in the fact that she calls fatherhood, motherhood, and lordship "properties" and not "persons" in one God. Further, in an elaboration on the "I am" sayings, the glorified Christ speaks for the unity of the Godhead:

I am he, the might and goodness of fatherhood; I am he, the wisdom and the lovingness of motherhood; I am he, the light and the grace which is all

blessed love; I am he, the trinity; I am he, the unity; I am he, the great
supreme goodness of every kind of thing; I am he who makes you to love; I
am he who makes you to long; I am he, the endless fulfilling of all true
desires (59:295–96).

To the extent that the property of motherhood expresses particularly
well the labor Christ underwent in assuming and perfecting our nature, it
is appropriate to apply it to the second person, just as it is appropriate to
apply the property of fatherhood to the first person and the property of
lordship to the Holy Spirit, even though, in all cases, the properties
actually refer to the essence of the one God and not to the distinction of
persons.

What is unique here is Julian's understanding of the property of
motherhood as an essential attribute of the Godhead: "To the property of
motherhood belong nature, love, wisdom and knowledge, and this is
God" (60:299). Not only does she call Jesus our mother, but she has a
doctrine of the motherhood of *God*. The one and triune God can be said to
be our mother in her threefold function of motherhood toward us:

> I understand three ways of contemplating motherhood in God. The first is
> the foundation of our nature's creation; the second is his taking of our
> nature, where the motherhood of grace begins; the third is the motherhood
> at work. And in that, by the same grace, everything is penetrated, in
> length and in breadth, in height and in depth without end; and it is all one
> love (59:297).[43]

Many medieval devotional works employed the image of mother as an
incidental metaphor for Christ's actions toward us, but Julian is unique in
considering motherhood an essential attribute of God.[44]

Reprise: The Love of God

Julian's description of the one and triune God exhibits the influence of
traditional theology. She would not deny that God is the utterly transcendent, omnipotent, omniscient totally Other One, set over against all that
is by an impassible chasm of difference. But her deep reflection upon the
love of God alters this traditional picture of God to a considerable degree.
We can see this happening in the feudal imagery she uses. The lord is
above the servant, courteously bending down in kindness and generosity
from a superior height, worthy of reverence and respect. But any suggestion of domination and subservience in this image is removed by the

homeliness of the lord's love, a love which rejects the privileges of domination in order to be with the beloved, in order to function simply as friend and companion, rather than sovereign. God's love has an effect upon the other attributes of God. As Julian says herself, God's love "makes [might] and wisdom very humble to us" (73:323).

In Julian's theology, God as the omnipotent source of all that is, to whom everything owes its existence, becomes the creative and preserving love that constantly surrounds creation. Humanity is enclosed in God's womb of love, protected by God's clothing of love, always safe from harm. God's relationship to humanity is not vertical but circular, surrounding us, holding us in love's embrace. Humans never stand outside of where God is, needing to knock to gain entrance to God's presence. God is never distant, but the very matrix which sustains us, ever present to human needs. Julian's naming God "Mother" and her extensive use of that title reinforce this picture of God. The fact that she includes in God's mothering activity both the foundation of human existence and the renewal of human spiritual potential makes Julian's picture of God as mother very close to Rosemary Radford Ruether's revival of God as the Primal Matrix of all life, sustaining both matter and spirit, nature and history.[45] Julian's God also bears striking resemblance to Sallie McFague's suggested models for God as mother, lover, and friend.[46]

While Julian certainly affirms that God is the only necessary being, absolutely independent of everything else, God's love includes in its essence a reaching out beyond God's self towards the other than God. Within God is an essential "giveableness," a desire and capacity to give of self, present from eternity and finding expression in time in the works of creation, incarnation and sanctification. This idea was not absent in the tradition handed down to Julian; Augustine's description of the Holy Spirit as Gift expresses it well.[47] But Julian radically underlines its implications for how valuable human beings are to God. Humans are enclosed in God in another sense, as being crucial to God's happiness. Is God increased in any way by the addition of God's loved ones into eternal union with God? Julian's traditionalism prevents her from saying this outright, but perhaps we can find a hint here of the instinct present in contemporary process theology.

The point Julian wanted to stress is what is so frequently ignored in the consideration of the nature of God. As she puts it, we usually have no trouble believing that "God is almighty and may do everything, and . . . all wisdom and can do everything," but we hesitate to trust that God "is all love and wishes to do everything" (73:323). While I may readily acknowledge that God "is almighty, and may punish me greatly, and . . .

all wisdom, and can punish me wisely," it is difficult to believe that God "is all goodness and loves me tenderly" (77:330). Julian shrewdly penetrates into that basic human inability to accept the self as lovable; because of it, humans paradoxically seem to feel more comfortable with a God who keeps an account of all their failures and is waiting to punish them, than with a God willing to accept them as they are. Julian's revelations counteract this misconception of God, proclaiming that "God is as willing as he is [mighty] and wise to save humanity" (40:247).

Stress upon God's love also alters Julian's understanding of traditional trinitarian theology. Her concentration upon the economic trinity, the threefold way God is related to us, makes that core doctrine of Christianity meaningful to Christian life. Her revelations refer her back to the source of the trinitarian doctrine, to the experience of the early church, wherein through Christ, Christians knew God not only as the source and goal of all that is, but also as the one who saved them by being one of them, and as the Spirit present in their hearts. The proper articulation of this threefold experience absorbed the attention of the first five centuries of Christianity, during which time theologians gradually defined what it revealed about God. But after Augustine, the doctrine of the trinity became more like an exercise in theological geometry, intent on describing the life within God's self with little reference to humans.[48] Julian's strong emphasis upon the importance of the economic trinity anticipates the work of Karl Rahner in our own century.[49]

With such stress upon God's love, pneumatology receives an important place in Julian's theology, even though the Holy Spirit is mentioned explicitly only occasionally. In her meditations on the meaning of Christ's incarnation and especially his suffering and death, she is most concerned with the way by which humanity is incorporated into those mysteries. Thus she recognizes the proximity of the Holy Spirit to us. The title "lordship" as applied to the Spirit suggests a dynamic, active influence in the building up of the kingdom, through each individual soul's coming into union with God.[50]

In sum, Julian's God is a God always active in the world of time, which that God creates and loves eternally. God's whole being and activity are involved in the work of human salvation; to be this generous and outward-turning is part of the essence of God. Thus Julian's picture of God underlines the truth of the promise of her revelations: "All will be well." Julian's pastoral motivation is completely evident here: to correct the misconception of her age's stress upon a God who was demanding and vengeful, and instead to encourage trust in a God whose essence is love.

Part Three

The Effects of God's Love

Julian's vision of the Crucified revealed the love of God as the ultimate reality against which everything else must be focused in order to be understood properly. With respect to the human being, this love of God has three effects, corresponding to the persons of the trinity. The love of God performs the work of nature by creating humanity in God's image and all the world for humanity, and by sustaining in existence everything that is, holding the soul in an eternal union with God. The love of God performs the work of mercy by healing the damage caused by sin and by increasing God's image in human nature. The love of God performs the work of grace, fulfilling humanity by bringing it into union with the life of the Godhead, partially in this life, fully in the next.

While Julian uses the term "grace" to distinguish the work of the Spirit from that of the other persons of the trinity, all the activity of God in relation to creatures is "grace" in the broader sense of the word. It is impossible to talk about Julian's understanding of human nature apart from grace, and the work of mercy is also what we commonly understand by "grace." Therefore, rather than describing nature, sin, and grace as such, in isolation from one another, the following chapters describe the effects of God's love (i.e., grace) upon nature, sin, and the spiritual growth of Christians. Even these distinctions are fluid, since in Julian's thought God's works of nature, mercy, and grace are in continuity with one another.

It is also important to note that what follows in these chapters pertains only to "those who will be saved" (9:192). Julian repeats this qualification constantly in the development of her anthropology, for she claims that this is all that was shown to her. We will consider her treatment of the possibility of eternal damnation at the end of Chapter 7.

5

The Work of Nature

The Goodness and Order of Creation

Behind the notion of God as Love stands the idea of God as Being, the most basic description of God in all Christian philosophy. God alone is; all else is and continues to be held in existence because of God. As a result there is a radical contingency to everything other than God.[1] In relation to God as Being, all creation appears "little" to Julian, tending towards the nothingness out of which it was created:

> [God] showed me something small, no bigger than a hazelnut, lying in the palm of my hand, as it seemed to me, and it was as round as a ball. I looked at it with the eye of my understanding and thought: What can this be? And it was answered generally thus: It is everything that is made. I was amazed that it could last, for I thought that because of its littleness it would suddenly have fallen into nothing. And I was answered in my understanding: It lasts and always will, because God loves it; and thus everything has being through the love of God (5:183).[2]

Julian emphasizes Love, not Being, as the most precise description of God. For her Love expresses best the nature of the relationship that exists between God as Being and all else as beings in God. She prefers to say, then, that God's love is the cause of the existence and the continuation in being of all that is other than God.[3] The effect of this emphasis is to place the radical contingency of created reality upon a sure relational foundation. Creation's continued existence is assured because of the eternal trustworthiness of God's providential love. Created reality is radically contingent, always teetering on the brink of nothingness, but it rests in the security of being held in the love of God, who is the one sure reality, Being itself.

It is only because of their radical dependence upon God that Julian considers created things as "nothing." We need to "despise as nothing everything created," but only so that we may "love and have uncreated God" (5:183).[4] Otherwise, creation is always depicted as essentially good:

> I know well that heaven and earth and all creation are great, generous and beautiful and good. But the reason why it seemed to my eyes so little was because I saw it in the presence of [the one] who is the creator. To any soul who sees the creator of all things, all that is created seems very little (8:190).[5]

The goodness of creation is dependent upon God understood as essential Goodness. Just as God alone can be said simply to be, so God alone is good; all else is good by participating in God's goodness. Thus Julian can say, "God is everything which is good . . . and the goodness which everything has is God" (8:190). But Julian is concerned less with the ontological goodness of creation than with its dynamism: the goodness of God is everywhere active in creation.[6] In fact, as primary cause, God can be said to do everything which is done through secondary causes. Julian understands the distinction between primary and secondary causality, for she says, "God in his goodness . . . makes the planets and the elements to function according to their natures" (18:211). However, her revelations emphasized primary causality: "For at this time the work of creatures was not revealed, but the work of our Lord God in creatures; for he is at the center of everything, and he does everything" (11:197).[7]

Because God is essential goodness and can do no evil, Julian concludes that "everything which is done is well done." She knows that human beings do not always see things this way. Sometimes we think things happen by chance, with no apparent purpose; sometimes we regard things as evil (11:197–98).[8] In both cases, God's perspective and ours are not the same. When Julian "saw God in a point" in the third revelation, she received a fleeting glimpse of God's point of view. The basic difference between God's perspective and ours lies in the fact that God is eternal Being and we are temporal beings. For God everything is always ordered to a purpose which never changes:

> I saw most truly that [God] never changed his purpose in any kind of thing, nor ever will eternally. For there was nothing unknown to him in his just ordinance before time began, and therefore all things were set in order, before anything was made, as it would endure eternally. And no kind of thing will fail in that respect, for he has made everything totally good (11:198–99).[9]

Julian's revelations allowed her to penetrate momentarily into this order and purpose of God, where she saw that everything is done "by God's prescient wisdom" (11:197).[10]

Julian shared the hierarchical understanding of creation that was an essential part of the medieval world view.[11] She does not treat the lower levels of creation in detail, although she does reveal a sense of the order which exists among non-rational creatures:

> For it is easy to understand that the best of deeds is well done; and the smallest of deeds which is done is as well done as the best and the greatest, and they all have the property and the order ordained for them as our Lord had ordained, without beginning (11:198).

Julian does consider the place of human nature in relation to what is above and below it. Everything inferior to human nature was made "to serve us" and God protects it "for love of us" (42:252). But human creation "is superior to all God's works" (1:176), "the noblest thing which [God] ever made" (53:284). More precisely, the human *soul* is God's noblest work:

> If the blessed trinity could have created the human soul any better, any fairer, any nobler than it was created, the trinity would not have been fully pleased with the creation of [the human] soul. But because it made [the human] soul as beautiful, as good, as precious a creature as it could make, therefore the blessed trinity is fully pleased without end in the creation of [the human] soul (68:314).[12]

It should be noted that Julian does not express any dichotomy between male and female in the chain of being, evident in one strand of the Christian tradition.[13] She simply assumes that men and women are equal in their humanity.

The reason for the creaturely perfection of the soul is simply that this "fair nature was first prepared for [God's] own Son, the second person" (58:293). Indeed, "the fullest substance and the highest power" of human nature "is the blessed soul of Christ" (53:284). But since, in the creation of the humanity of Christ, God "created us all at once," all humanity is eternally one with the human nature of Christ, and, through him, eternally united to God (58:293).

Christ, the Wisdom of God, appears as the purpose and end of human creation. But because all non-rational creation was made to serve the human, Christ is also the ordering principle towards which the whole of creation tends. This is depicted in the parable of the lord and the servant where Christ does the work of a gardener, ordering and preparing the treasure hidden in the earth and bringing it before the lord. What was described above in Chapter 3 with respect to recreation can also be interpreted as divine Wisdom's work of ordering the original creation. Julian also considers the relationship between Christ and the created world when she mentions the effects of Christ's death upon the universe:

> All creatures which God has created for our service, the firmament and the earth, failed in their natural functions because of sorrow at the time of Christ's death, for it is their natural characteristic to recognize him as their Lord, in whom all their powers exist. And when he failed, their nature constrained them to fail with him, insofar as they could, because of the sorrow of his sufferings (18:210). [14]

In the hierarchy of creation, the human being, of whom Christ is the exemplar, is seen as a bridge between the material and spiritual orders of being. The body was created from the slime of the earth, while the soul was made from nothing material. Furthermore, the soul itself is bipartite, having "sensuality" and "substance," the former related to the physical body, the latter immediately to God. The human being is therefore a microcosm of the material and spiritual universe, [15] and it is through the human as such that non-rational creation will share in the restoration wrought by Christ:

> All natures which [God] has made to flow out of him to work his will, they will be restored and brought back into him by the salvation of humanity through the operation of grace. For all natures which [God] has put separately in different creatures are all in the human being, wholly, in fulness and power, in beauty and in goodness, in kingliness and in nobility, in every manner of stateliness, preciousness and honor (62:302–3).

In considering rational creation, Julian follows Augustine by placing no other being between the human soul and God:

> When God was to make [the human] body, God took the slime of the earth, which is matter mixed and gathered from all bodily things, and of that [God] made [the human] body. But to the making of [the human] soul God would accept nothing at all, but made it. And so is created nature rightfully united to the maker, who is substantial uncreated nature, that is God. And so it is that *there may and will be nothing at all between God and [the human} soul* (53:284; emphasis mine).

Unlike Aquinas, who developed Pseudo-Dionysius on this point, Augustine did not place angelic nature higher or closer to God than human rational creation.[16] Nor does Julian formally consider the angels. Her only mention of them occurs with respect to their ministerial function: "I believe and understand the ministration of holy angels, as scholars tell, but it was not revealed to me; for God himself is nearest" (80:336).

God's loving activity extends to the whole of creation, the small as well as the great:

> [God] wants us to know that he takes heed not only of things which are noble and great, but also of those which are little and small, of [the humble] and simple, of this [one] and that [one]. And this is what God means when God says: Every kind of thing will be well. For God wants us to know that the smallest thing will not be forgotten (32:231).

Julian insists that "our Lord God wishes us to have great regard for all the deeds which he has performed in the most noble work of creating all things" (1:176). Her sense of the value of creation is enhanced by the fact that we find virtually nothing in her text advocating withdrawal from the world or custody of the senses, a fact that distinguishes her from the majority of medieval spiritual writers.[17] Instead, Julian is convinced that the created universe is good and reveals the trinitarian God. In the first revelation Julian saw three "properties" in the little thing representing all creation: "The first is that God made it, the second is that God loves it, the third is that God [keeps] it. But what did I see in it? It is that God is the creator and the [keeper] and the lover" (5:183). Julian is again in continuity with the Augustinian tradition which saw vestiges of the trinity everywhere in the created universe.[18]

Julian returns to the *exemplum* of the lord to make the revelatory nature of creation clear:

> Everything which God has made shows [God's lordship], as understanding was given at the same time by the example of a creature who is led to see the great nobility and the rulership which is fitting to a lord, and when it had seen all the nobility beneath, then in wonder it was moved to seek up above for that high place where the lord dwells, knowing by reason that his dwelling is in the most honorable place. And thus I understood truly that our soul may never have rest in anything which is beneath itself. And when it comes above all creatures into itself, still it cannot remain contemplating itself; but all its contemplation is blessedly set in God, who is the creator, dwelling there, for in [the human] soul is [God's] true dwelling (68:313–14).

Julian is utilizing here the popular medieval theme, again with Augustinian roots, of the soul's gradual ascent through contemplation of material creation and the human soul to God's own self.[19] Everything created reveals God and leads the soul to a greater understanding of God. Julian's only caution is that one does not attempt to find rest or fulfillment in the created world:

> Our hearts and souls are not in perfect ease, because here we seek rest in this thing which is so little, in which there is no rest, and we do not know our God who is almighty, all wise and all good, for [God] is true rest. . . . Everything which is beneath [God] is not sufficient for us (5:183–84).[20]

Once we realize that God "made us only for himself" and seek our rest only there, it is possible to regard the created world positively, "for [God's] goodness fills all creatures and all his blessed works full, and endlessly overflows in them" (5:184).[21] All this blessedness can be ours in God, a sentiment beautifully expressed in the following prayer:

> God, of your goodness give me yourself, for you are enough for me, and I can ask for nothing which is less which can pay you full worship. And if I ask anything which is less, always I am in want; but only in you do I have everything (5:184).[22]

Once the heart is set on God, the proper Christian attitude towards the world can be described as "endlessly marvelling at the greatness of God, the creator, and at the smallest part of all that is created" (75:327). This passage is found in the context of Julian's description of the awe which the blessed will experience before the face of God. Material creation, even the smallest part thereof, finds an inclusion there.

Human Nature: The Image of God

Julian's anthropology is the most difficult part of her theology to understand. Her descriptions of the "substance and sensuality" of the human soul, their dual creation, and their relationship to Christ are not without ambiguity. I have found it necessary to move behind her statements to what I consider to be their source, the Augustinian notion of the image of God. Within the interpretative framework provided by the notion of image, some of Julian's most puzzling statements about the human being begin to gain clarity.

The *imago Dei* was one of the dominant themes of medieval anthropology in the Western Church. Based upon Gen 1:26–27, it is the idea that the human being, specifically the human soul, was created in the image and likeness of God. The theme was first developed by the Eastern patristic writers and creatively modified by Augustine.[23] Countless medieval theologians reflected upon it in a variety of ways, especially on its meaning for the spiritual life.[24] Julian was influenced by this theme, especially as it developed in the West under Augustine's influence, and it forms the background to her own anthropology.

Certain aspects of the *imago Dei* tradition considered women, because of their closer ties to physicality, as less perfect or deficient images of God. While Julian was probably aware of this, she chose to ignore it.[25] In doing so, she exhibits a consistency with most medieval women, who were generally less self-conscious about gender distinctions and roles than men were. Creation in and restoration to God's image were prominent themes in their spirituality.[26] Thus Julian drew heavily upon the Augustinian notion of image, assuming it to be inclusive of all humanity.

Julian follows Augustine in seeing the human soul as an image of the trinity: "the blessed trinity made [humankind] in their image and their likeness" (10:194). More specifically, "God is endless supreme truth, endless supreme wisdom, endless supreme love uncreated; and a [human] soul is a creature in God which has the same properties created" (44:256). God's image resides in the human intellectual faculties: in the mind or memory, which reflects God's truth or might; in the reason or understanding which reflects God's wisdom; in the will which reflects God's love. In her own development of this pattern, Julian most often uses the triad of human might, wisdom, and love. By might she means the inner strength and ability to accomplish what one desires;[27] by wisdom, true sight or knowledge of what one desires, and by love, the desire for God.

This image is humanity's true nature and substance, a sharing in the nature and substance of God. It is more than simply participating in God's being, which all creatures do. It means that there is nothing more like God than the human soul in the hierarchy of being. This point is essential to the Augustinian notion of image,[28] and in her search for a way to express this truth, Julian makes statements like the following:

> Our soul, which is created, dwells in God in substance, of which substance, through God, we are what we are. And I saw no difference between God and our substance, but, as it were, all God; and still my understanding accepted that our substance is in God, that is to say that God is God, and our substance is a creature in God (54:285).[29]

Being image of God means that there is nothing between the human soul and God on the ladder of creation and that the human soul mirrors God's might, wisdom, and love in its own faculties. But it also means that there is an eternal union of love between the image and the creator so close that nothing can destroy it:

> For before [God] made us he loved us, and when we were made we loved him; and this [love] is made only of the natural substantial goodness of the Holy Spirit, mighty by reason of the might of the Father, wise in mind of the wisdom of the Son. And so is [the human] soul made by God, and in the same moment joined to God (53:283–84).

And again:

> Our soul is united to [God] who is unchangeable goodness. And between God and our soul there is neither wrath nor forgiveness in God's sight. For our soul is so wholly united to God, through his own goodness, that between God and our soul *nothing can interpose* (46:259; emphasis mine).

Julian's stress upon God as Love is all important here. The fact that the human soul is next to God in the chain of being designates not only a static ontological reality, but also a relational one; it means being united to God in love: "And in this endless love [the human] soul is kept whole" (53:284).

Again Julian follows Augustine who saw the image as related to its exemplar not only in origin and likeness, but also in a dynamic tendency to return to it. This last is based upon Augustine's theology of creation, which, for the spiritual creature, involves an immediate recall and conversion to God, simultaneous with the act of creation, both of which take place before time.[30] When Julian says that the substance of the human soul is eternally united to or grounded in God's love "from without beginning" she is expressing this Augustinian concept in her own words.[31] The soul, by virtue of being God's image, is drawn back to God and held in a unity of love that transcends time.[32] The term Julian uses to designate this notion of image, "substance of the soul," includes an ontological understanding, but it primarily designates a relation, the eternal union of the soul to God through love.

Julian makes this point repeatedly: "God judges us in our natural substance, which is always kept one in [God], whole and safe, without end" (45:256); "Our natural substance is now full of blessedness in God, and has been since it was made, and will be without end" (45:258); "In our creating [God] joined and united us to himself and through this union we are kept as pure and as noble as we were created" (58:293). This union is not due to any effort on the part of human nature, but to the eternal love of God which is ever active in the preservation of God's image in the human soul: "Just as we were to be without end, so we were treasured and hidden in God, known and loved from without beginning" (53:284).[33] Because this union is eternal, it is permanent and unchanging. It is the source of God's promise that, in spite of what seem to us to be the endless fluctuations and confusions of human life in time, all will be well.

What does Julian mean, precisely, by statements like these? Does she mean that the essence of the soul literally exists united to God from all eternity and descends to earth at a point in time? Or does she mean that the soul exists as an idea in the mind or intention of God, eventually to come into actual existence? My sense is that Julian continues to speak here, as she does with respect to evil, from God's eternal perspective as opposed to our temporal one. God sees things as already accomplished. The distinction between what is in God's mind as an intention or idea and what actually has existence is a useless one in such a perspective. Furthermore, Julian is convinced that God's loving will is strong to effect what it desires. To be an idea in God's mind or intention is, in effect, to be.

Another part of the *imago Dei* tradition stressed the place of Christ. Here the primary and only perfect image of God is the Logos, the second person of the trinity, in whose image the human soul is made image of God.[34] Julian draws upon this tradition when she says that our true natural substance (God's image in us) is preserved eternally in God by being united to the human soul of Christ. This union has its origins in the eternal purpose of God:

> God the blessed trinity, who is everlasting being, just as he is eternal from without beginning, just so was it in his eternal purpose to create human nature, which fair nature was first prepared for his own Son, the second person; and when he wished, by full agreement of the whole trinity he created us all at once (58:293).

The specific role of Christ is described as follows:

> By the endless intent and assent and the full accord of all the trinity, the mediator wanted to be the foundation and the head of this fair nature, out of whom we have all come, in whom we are all enclosed, into whom we shall all go (53:283).[35]

Thus Christ is the beginning and end of the human soul, its efficient, exemplary and final cause.[36]

The parable of the lord and the servant clarified humanity's relation to Christ for Julian: "our good Lord showed his own Son and Adam as only one" (51:275); "because of the true union which was made in heaven, God's Son could not be separated from Adam" (51:274). Therefore,

> [God] makes no distinction in love between the blessed soul of Christ and the least soul that will be saved. . . . Where the blessed soul of Christ is, there is the substance of all the souls which will be saved by Christ (54:285).

Where is the blessed soul of Christ? It is eternally with God through its union with the second person of the trinity. There it is eternally loved by God; there too, the person of the Son eternally loves the Father, which love is the Holy Spirit. Humanity's eternal union with God in love is thus mediated by the love God has for Christ, and it is also through Christ that humanity can be said to love God eternally. This is why God loves us; when God sees us, God sees Christ. And Christ's human soul includes not only the individual soul of Jesus of Nazareth, but all humanity: "Christ, having joined in himself [everyone] who will be saved, is perfect [humanity]" (57:292).

So far we have spoken only of the substance of the human soul, wherein alone lies the image of God.[37] What of the body? How is it united to the soul? Julian shared the difficulty of all Western theology in coming to a satisfactory answer to this question.[38] The Christian doctrines of incarnation and bodily resurrection were not readily compatible with the neoplatonic notion of a spiritual, immutable, and eternal soul, free from bodily influences. Augustine himself always asserted the unity of the human body and spirit, and, although he struggled to give this a satisfactory philosophical solution, his efforts were never free from ambiguity.[39] While in general the problem of the unity between soul and body could lead to a devaluation of the body, important qualifications to this tendency were introduced. This is certainly true of Augustine himself, in spite of the fact that he is grossly misunderstood today in this area.[40] Among the twelfth century Cistercians, efforts to reconcile the unity of soul and body resulted in a concentration on medicine and physiology as important to human self-knowledge, the theme of the human as microcosm of the universe, and the use of analogies between body and soul as a way of mediating the dichotomy between the two.[41] Of all the theologians before Julian's time, Aquinas probably achieved the most favorable solution to the unity between body and soul available to the Middle Ages.[42] However, Julian exhibits no indebtedness to Aquinas in this area.

Though Julian does not consider the body as such in any systematic way, she is generally free from statements which devalue the body. In fact, her only description of the body finds God directing even the lowliest bodily function of the elimination of waste:

> A man walks upright, and the food in his body is shut in as if in a well-made purse. When the time of his necessity comes, the purse is opened and then shut again, in most seemly fashion. And it is God who does this, as it is shown when he says that he comes down to us in our humblest needs. For [God] does not despise what he has made, nor does he disdain to serve us in the simplest natural functions of our body, for love of the soul which he created in his own likeness. For as the body is clad in the cloth, and the flesh in the skin, and the bones in the flesh, and the heart in the trunk, so are we, soul and body, clad and enclosed in the goodness of God (6:186).

The value of human bodiliness in God's eyes was made even more explicit by God's actually assuming human flesh in the incarnation. Julian exhibits a comfort with human bodiliness consistent with a truly incarnational spirituality.[43]

One of the ways classical and medieval authors maintained the unity between soul and body was through the tradition of the bipartite soul. Augustine used the term "mens" to designate the spiritual, intellectual soul, untouched and unaffected by the body, and the inferior "spiritus" to designate the soul in its contact with the body and with external material reality. The lower faculty of the soul acted as a mediator between the purely intellectual soul and the physical body.[44] This tradition was dominant throughout the Middle Ages, and various terms were introduced to designate the dual soul: higher and lower, internal and external, spirit and soul.[45] One strand of the tradition even distinguished the two as animus and amina, identifying the higher faculty as male and the lower as female, but Julian makes no use of this distinction.

The terms Julian uses for the dual soul are "substance," indicating the higher power of the soul that is always united to God, and "sensuality," indicating the lower power of the soul united directly to the body. And, insofar as the "sensual soul" is linked to the body, Julian's use of the term "sensuality" can at times be interpreted to include the body itself. It is important to remember that there is only one soul, and that these words designate the soul as related to God and to the body, and are not disjointed "parts" as such (56:289; 55:288).

As far as I can tell, the pairing of the words "substance and sensuality" in this context is unique to Julian. It is not hard to speculate where she may have acquired the term "substance" because the soul was generally called a "spiritual substance." What Julian means by "substance" sounds very like what is described in the anonymous twelfth century Cistercian treatise, *The Spirit and the Soul*: "The intellectual soul is a certain substance. . . . God is its proper element and dwelling place, deriving from the fact that it was made in God's likeness."[46] Later in the same treatise, we find: "Sensuality is the power of the soul which makes the body grow, and by the bodily senses it knows and discerns what is outside itself."[47] However, the terms this treatise generally uses for the dual soul are "spirit and soul," not "substance and sensuality."

In Julian's theology, unlike the soul's substance which is eternally united to God, sensuality is changeable, seeming to be "now one thing and now another, as it derives from parts and presents an external appearance" (45:256). It is affected by the changeableness of this "passing life" which can confuse us; we often do not know "in our sensuality what our self is," and need faith to help us see this (46:258). While we are full and complete in our substance, "in our sensuality we are lacking," unfinished, incomplete (57:291). We need God's mercy and grace to bring our sensuality to completion.

Julian separates the creation of the substance of the soul and its becoming sensual. Human substance was created "all at once" when the human soul of Christ was created (58:293). The body, on the other hand, came from "the slime of the earth" (53:284). When the substance of the soul "is breathed into our body" then "we are made sensual" (55:286). Again Julian is indebted to Augustine, for whom the sequence of creation as described in the six-day cycle of Genesis 1, although causal, was not a temporal succession, but occurred before time in its entirety.[48] The human soul, as image and likeness of God, was created *actually* within this a-temporal work, but the body was created then only in its "seminal reasons" and would make its actual appearance, corresponding to its formation from the earth, only in time.[49] Thus, what Julian calls the "substance" of the human soul exists with God before time, while its "sensuality" begins only with its insertion into the body in the course of time.

Julian solves the problem of the union between substance and sensuality by situating it in God, "the mean which keeps the substance and the sensuality together" (56:289). More specifically, this union is due to the incarnation of the Wisdom of God in human history:

> In the same time that God joined himself to our body in the maiden's womb, he took our soul, which is sensual, and in taking it, having enclosed us all in himself, he united it to our substance. In this union he was perfect [humanity] (57:292).[50]

"Perfect humanity" means that the whole human race is the full human nature of Christ. But it also means the union of human sensuality with the image of God that is the substance of the soul. This is what Julian calls the "increase" of human nature which is effected by the incarnation, and it is something permanent: substance and sensuality "will never separate" (56:289).

This solution, as stated by Julian, is not without ambiguity. Let me interpret what I think she means. The substance of the human soul of Christ, the created reality most like the Logos, the one true image of God, was the highest being created before time and eternally joined to the Logos. The substance of all human souls was created at the same time and made one with the substance of Christ's human soul, thereby eternally united with God. The sensuality of human souls appears only in time as their bodies gradually develop from the seminal reasons. In the human being, the same soul, whose substance is eternally united to God, becomes related to corporeal nature, but the unity between substance and sensuality is a fragile one, incomplete, partial. Full unity between human substance and sensuality was not achieved until the substance of Christ's soul united itself to a human body in time. Thus the incarnation, God's work of mercy in time, completes human nature by bringing sensuality into complete union with the soul's substance.

As suggested above in Chapter 3, there is an incipient "evolutionary" perspective to Julian's thought here. She cannot speak of human nature in its entirety except in light of the incarnation. As a result of the incarnation, humanity's increase, that is, the assumption of human sensuality into union with its substance, is made possible by Christ. But it is only by a gradual process of growth in the life of grace, through the presence of the Holy Spirit, that this increase occurs:

> All the gifts which God can give to the creature he has given to his Son Jesus for us, which gifts he, dwelling in us, has enclosed in him until the time that we are fully grown, our soul together with our body and our body together with our soul. Let either of them take help from the other, until we have grown to full stature as creative nature brings about; and then in the foundation of creative nature with the operation of mercy, the Holy Spirit by grace breathes into us gifts leading to endless life (55:287).[51]

Here we see again the growth of the soul as imaging the trinity's acts in human history. As the first person of the trinity is the principle and foundation of the others, so is substantial human nature, which is always held in God, the foundation upon which the works of mercy and grace build in order to bring human sensuality into union with its substance:

Our faith comes from the natural love of our soul, and from the clear light of our reason, and from the steadfast memory which we have from God in our first creation. And when our soul is breathed into our body, at which time we are made sensual, at once mercy and grace begin to work, having care of us and protecting us with pity and love, in which operation the Holy Spirit forms in our faith the hope that we shall return up above to our substance, into the power of Christ, increased and fulfilled through the Holy Spirit (55:286).

By substance or nature, humanity is created in the image of the trinity's might, wisdom, and love, a task appropriated to the Father's creative power. But that image is meant to be increased by the action of God's Wisdom and perfected by the action of God's Spirit in human history, through the union of human sensuality and substance. Thus it is true to say that human sensuality, too, though not the image of God as such, "is founded in nature, in mercy and in grace, and this foundation enables us to receive gifts which lead us to endless life" (55:287).

Sensual human life, fleshly existence in the world of time, is, from a human perspective, gradually lifted up and included in the eternity of God. In the process the image of God's might, wisdom, and love in the human being is increased and fulfilled. Made in God's image, the human is meant to become even more like God through earthly existence. The neoplatonic *exitus et reditus* theme is here, to be sure, but without the denigration of earthly existence that can often accompany it. We are meant to be with God in eternity, and cannot be entirely happy until we are there, but when we do arrive there, we bring our sensuality with us, increased and fulfilled by our earthly sojourn. Again, the root of Julian's thought is Augustinian: "that reform of the inner man which was made possible by Incarnation and Redemption was not a return only to the spiritual aspect of creation, but the completion and elevation of a spiritual-corporeal compound."[52] According to Gerhard Ladner, the Western tradition differs essentially from the East in its emphasis upon the corporeality of what is brought back to God and upon the eternal value of time and history. Julian is squarely in the Western tradition here.[53]

Human sensuality is something very precious; in fact, Julian calls it the city of God, "that honorable city in which our Lord Jesus sits." He is enclosed therein, together with human substance which is enclosed in Christ (56:289). This has been true from the moment the soul entered the body:

In the same instant and place in which our soul is made sensual, in that same instant and place exists the city of God, ordained for [God] from without beginning. He comes into this city and will never depart from it, for God is never out of the soul, in which he will dwell blessedly without end (55:287).

The phrase "city of God" is loaded with allusions, first of all to the church, sign of the kingdom of God on earth, obviously dependent upon Augustine's classical work in which the church's historical and corporeal character is developed. Further, calling the individual soul the "city of God" was common among medieval spiritual writers.[54] While Julian sometimes calls the soul without qualification the city of God, the fact that she often specifically designates sensuality as God's city shows that she was conscious of the historical and bodily implications of the term as employed by Augustine. For Julian, human bodiliness is important to both humans and to God. It is not to be dismissed as useless or detrimental to human spiritual growth. In fact, its development over the course of human life in time contributes to that increase of God's image in the human which God predestined "from before beginning" and in which humanity and God will eternally rejoice in heaven.

It is clear that Julian knows nothing of a human nature that is untouched by God's grace. Yet she is precise in distinguishing between God's "natural goodness," which is "uncreated nature" from which mercy and grace flow (63:303), and human "natural goodness" which is able to receive mercy and grace:

In our substance we are full and in our sensuality we are lacking, and this lack God will restore and fill by the operation of mercy and grace, plentifully flowing into us from God's own natural goodness. And so this natural goodness makes mercy and grace to work in us, and the natural goodness that we have from [God] enables us to receive the operation of mercy and grace (57:291).

Nonetheless, the presence of God's grace to that created natural goodness is constant. Julian would agree with Karl Rahner that there is no such thing, practically speaking, as "pure nature" untouched and unaffected by God's grace, although it is necessary to distinguish the two conceptually.[55]

With such an optimistic picture of human nature united eternally to God through the bond of love, it is no wonder that Julian asked the question, "What is sin?" For Julian, God's image is not lost by sin, but damaged.[56] Retained in the soul's eternal substance, God's image is distorted in human sensuality: "though the soul may be always like God in nature and in substance . . . , it is often unlike [God] in condition, through sin" (43:253).[57] Of the three faculties by which the sensual soul images God, might and wisdom are hurt by sin, but the will seems to be relatively unaffected. As a result of his fall, the servant of the parable "was injured in his powers and made most feeble, and in his understanding he was amazed, because he was diverted from looking on his lord, but his will was preserved in God's sight" (51:270).

Julian could be indebted for the root of this idea to Bernard's treatise *On Grace and Free Choice*, where the image of God which remains constant in the human being after sin is situated in the will, in the power of free choice, mirroring God's freedom. As originally created, the human being also had two "likenesses" to God: free pleasure which mirrored God's might, and free counsel which mirrored God's wisdom. These two were completely lost as a result of sin.[58] Julian does not distinguish image from likeness as Bernard does. For her the image of God resides in all three faculties and remains constant in the substance of the soul which is always held united to God. But in sensual human life, what mirrors God's might and wisdom is weakened and blinded, while the desire of the will to love God remains constant. For both Bernard and Julian, the ability to mirror God's might and wisdom, that is, the ability to effect and understand what one wills, is damaged by sin, while the image remains in the will, although Julian means something more by this than mere free choice.

For Julian, the damage done by sin to the soul's might and wisdom prevents the realization in sensual existence of who one truly is in God's sight. This damage also prevents a knowledge of the will to some extent, but the will continues to assert itself: "Our natural will is to have God, and God's good will is to have us, and we can never stop willing or loving until we possess [God] in the fulness of joy" (6:186). The way the image is discernible in the will is in its desire for God, which remains so strong that it can never fully assent to sin:

> In each soul which will be saved there is a godly will which never assented to sin nor ever will, which will is so good that it cannot ever will evil, but always constantly it wills good and it does good in the sight of God (53:283).[59]

Hatred of sin is natural to the human: "our self is opposed to our sin and to our weakness" (72:321). When humans sin, they paradoxically go against their own deepest desire.

This constancy of will is the result of God's love, which is so strong that it draws the soul like a magnet, holding it always in union with God. Because "we are they whom [God] loves . . . eternally we do what [God] delights in" (37:242). The bond of love which unites the soul to God is so strong that it can never be broken, and the soul is always aware of this on some level, though that awareness be dimmed. It is felt in the longing "to be filled with endless joy and bliss" (45:258), which remains in spite of the weakness and blindness that cause one to be distracted by other desires:

> For the natural desire of our soul is so great and so immeasurable that if all the nobility which God ever created in heaven and on earth were given to us for our joy and our comfort, if we did not see [God's] own fair blessed face, still we should never cease to mourn and to weep in the spirit, because, that is, of our painful longing, until we might see our creator's fair blessed face (72:321).

The deepest need of the human soul is to have God; thus "in our intention we wait for God" (52:279). This is Julian's way of expressing what Augustine called the human restless search for God and what we might today call the constant drive of human transcendence toward what lies beyond the world of space and time. The image cannot refrain from seeking full and complete union with the Love that created it. This is the central theme of Julian's anthropology.

One might well ask at this point what part freedom plays in the life and destiny of the human being. Being eternally united to God in a bond of love that nothing, not even sin, can destroy seems deterministic. Unfortunately, Julian does not treat the question of human freedom formally. We can only draw implications from her discussion of other issues to speculate about how she understood the role of human freedom in the Christian life.

An important clue is found in the parable of the lord and the servant, where the servant stood eager to do the lord's will. As this was spelled out in Chapter 3 above in reference to the suffering Christ, we saw that Christ "voluntarily" went to his death because he wanted the same thing the Father did, the salvation of those he loved. But the servant also represents all humanity, and we can come to a similar conclusion about the relationship of God's will to human free will.

Humans are made in such a way that they freely desire union with God. The more the human will becomes conformed to what God wills, the more free human beings are to become who they truly desire to be.[60] God's will for humanity and humanity's own deepest desire are the same: ultimate union with God. It is when humans resist God and the desire of their true self (human "substance") that they experience a lack of freedom. Thus, Julian says that "reluctance and deliberate choice are in opposition" within the human self (19:212). The reluctance to move in the direction of God, which humans experience within the self as a result of sin, prevents them on occasion from freely and fully choosing what they most deeply desire. Freedom is hindered, not increased, by choosing other than what God wills. The fact that God holds human beings in an eternal bond of love thus enables the exercise of human freedom, allowing the "deliberate choice" of God and God's will, which is also consistent with the deepest desire of the human heart.

Thus it is logical to Julian that God should reward those who have "voluntarily served God" (14:203), especially those who have "voluntarily and freely" offered their youth to God (14:204). Humans are not automatons mechanically doing what God wills, but "partners in [God's] good will and work" (43:253), exercising free will in cooperation with God. Christ is working in us, but "we are by grace according with him" (54:286). Christ "wants us to be his helpers, giving all our intention to him" (57:292) and "[keeping] ourselves faithfully in him" (71:318). All of these sayings indicate Julian's belief in the free cooperation of the human will with God's grace.

6

The Work of Mercy

The Problem of Sin

The late fourteenth century was an age preoccupied with sin, guilt, and eternal punishment.[1] This preoccupation was due in part to the influence of the Fourth Lateran Council of 1215 which had tried to stimulate an awareness of the inner motivations for sin and the workings of the human conscience, so as to help the faithful to a life of virtue.[2] It had therefore set down detailed instructions for educating both clergy and laity in the method of hearing and making a proper confession. New penitential manuals were prepared to aid the confessor in this process of instruction.[3] Above all, since pastors were to ensure that those in their care knew the sins against the commandments and the "seven deadly sins" and their progeny, the manuals described and categorized these sins in elaborate detail.[4] Throughout the thirteenth and fourteenth centuries, the English bishops were thorough in making sure such instruction was carried out,[5] especially through detailed, prescribed preaching.[6] As a result, by Julian's day, the material descriptive of sin and its remedies found in the penitential manuals was familiar to the general populace, and is clearly discernible in the literature, both religious and secular, of the period.[7] The Council had also made mandatory the annual confession of sins. In England this mandate was interpreted even more rigorously; the faithful were to confess their sins three times annually: at Easter, at Christmas, and during Pentecost. The penalty for noncompliance was excommunication, which meant the denial of the eucharist and of Christian burial and the prospect of eternal damnation.[8]

In addition to a general emphasis upon confession and the cataloguing of particular sins, the episodes of the Black Death had exacerbated feelings of guilt and fear of eternal punishment.[9] Thousands had gone to their graves unshriven for lack of confessors willing or able to hear their final confessions. It was thought that such a catastrophe must indicate divine punishment for some terrible sin. The result was an overly scrupulous fascination with the description of particular sins and the degree of guilt attached to each, along with attempts to erase the punishment due to such sins, leading eventually to the abuse of indulgences which would so incense Luther a century and a half later. [10]

Julian's amazement at the message of God's unconditional love that was the substance of her revelations indicates that she herself had experienced some of the fearful fascination that accompanied reflection on the meaning of sin in her day. Thus, when she gazes at the "hazelnut" representing all that is, and realizes that God does everything that is done, it is not surprising that the question "What is sin?" immediately occurs to her (11:197). Since God does no sin, and since sin was not shown in her vision of "everything that is," she concludes that "sin is no deed, . . . no kind of substance, no share in being" (27:225). [11] In short, as the absence of good, sin is nothing.

Yet Julian is acutely aware of how much human beings suffer from sin. Sin may be nothing, but the pain resulting from it certainly is "something for a time." While agreeing with its logic, Julian is not totally satisfied with the notion of sin as nothing; it seems to dismiss too easily the harm caused by sin. Indeed she had "often wondered why, through the great prescient wisdom of God, the beginning of sin was not prevented," for then "all would have been well." The answer Christ gives is that "sin is necessary, but all will be well," and that God shows "no kind of blame to . . . anyone who will be saved." This is scarcely a direct reply to the question Julian had posed, and she can only submit her understanding to "an exalted and wonderful mystery" hidden in God "which God will make plain and we shall know in heaven" (27:224–26).

But Julian's doubts persist and she continues to address her objection to God:

> Ah, good Lord, how could all things be well, because of the great harm which has come through sin to your creatures? And here I wished, so far as I dared, for some plainer explanation through which I might be at ease about this matter (29:227).

This time she realizes that, although "Adam's sin was the greatest harm ever done or ever to be done," the "glorious atonement" is greater, "without comparison, than ever Adam's sin was harmful." Furthermore, since God "has set right the greatest of harms," God will "set right everything which is less" (29:228). Julian is told to stop wondering why sin came to be. Instead of mourning the harm caused by sin, she should rejoice and take comfort in the act of salvation that overcame sin. She is invited to share in God's eternal perspective which always sees fall and incarnation together and thus attributes no blame to humanity for sin. She is advised, in other words, not to consider sin apart from God's work of mercy.

Throughout her revelations, Julian tries to understand this viewpoint, but the nagging questions persist. Isn't the human race responsible for the introduction of sin into the world? Don't all human beings share in the guilt of this and deserve punishment as a result? Don't all compound this guilt by committing personal sins? These are all teachings of the Church, which God encouraged Julian to respect. However, God's attitude, as revealed in her revelations, seems to oppose these. Contrary to the whole spirit of her age, and perhaps to her own experience of sin, guilt, and fear, God seems to Julian to dismiss sin far too easily. She prays for further light, and is given in answer the parable of the lord and the servant. Her final teaching which follows here, informed by her understanding of the parable, stands out in stark contrast to the general attitude towards sin characteristic of the latter fourteenth century.

Through her experience and long years of reflection upon an eternally loving God who does not look with wrath upon sinners, Julian became convinced that her revelations were given as a remedy for the excessive preoccupation with sin characteristic of her age. Her God is a God of relationality, a God in love with the human race, and the power of that God's love will simply not allow sin to be finally triumphant. Such a picture of God challenged the more prevalent picture of God the judge, who keeps a detailed record of human sinfulness, demanding exact payment for every sin committed, standing forever in judgment, waiting to punish the sinner. Furthermore, Julian was not content with a purely logical argument for sin which did not take into account the human suffering resulting from it. Her pastoral motivation is most clearly visible in her discussion of sin, since she viewed her theology as words of comfort for those who suffer from fear and scrupulosity regarding sin. Although the influence of traditional theology continues to be evident in Julian's treatment of sin, this is the most original area of her theological reflections. Sin and the suffering it causes are neither denied nor ignored, but they are always seen only in light of the eternal love of God.

The Origin of Sin

The thing that initially puzzled Julian about the parable was that the servant, whom she took to represent Adam, did not seem to be responsible for the fall:

> I looked carefully to know if I could detect any fault in him, or if the lord would impute to him any kind of blame; and truly none was seen, for the only cause of his falling was his good will and his great desire. And in spirit he was as prompt and as good as he was when he stood before his lord, ready to do his will (51:268).

The fall appears to be nothing more than an unhappy accident, from which the human race suffers. [12] Why, then, did God not prevent it? Is God responsible in some way for sin's origin? Julian knows that God did not cause sin, for God cannot do evil. But for some reason which is hidden from us, God does tolerate evil; there is a "property in God which opposes good to evil" (59:295), [13] allowing sin to arise in opposition to goodness but subsuming it into God's plan to do good:

> Everything which our Lord God does is righteous, and all which God tolerates is honorable; and in these two are good and evil comprehended. For our Lord does everything which is good, and our Lord tolerates what is evil. I do not say that evil is honorable, but I say that our Lord God's toleration is honorable, through which God's goodness will be known eternally (35:237).

The way by which sin is subsumed into good is through the incarnation. From an eternal vantage point, God never sees sin apart from its having been overcome by Christ. This is why no blame is attributed to those who will be saved. The sin which they experience has already been nullified by Christ's act of salvation, and God knows this from all eternity.

The question of how or why sin came to be remains shrouded in mist. [14] Whatever Adam's motivation might have been, whatever degree of guilt might belong to him, questions like these are not as important as the fact that wickedness has been overcome by the goodness of God. Julian eventually abandons such questions. She gives no detailed account of the fall, nor does she speculate about what human nature might have been like before sin, beyond saying "if there had been no sin, we should all have been pure and as like our Lord as [God] created us" (27:224). [15] The one point she makes unequivocally is that however sin entered the world, it was against the true inner will of human nature. Adam may have chosen evil on some level of his will, but in doing so, he opposed what he truly desired for himself, to do the will of God. Furthermore, the bond of love by which God holds humanity united to God is not loosened, only obscured, by sin:

> [God] wants us to know that he takes the falling of any creature who will be saved no harder than he took the falling of Adam, who, we know, was endlessly loved and safely protected in the time of all his need (53:282). [16]

Like the writer of Genesis, Julian knows of no primal "fall" in which humanity experiences the total absence of God's grace. [17]

The Effects of Adam's Sin

Following her revelations, Julian regards sin as "necessary." She does not mean ontological necessity, in the sense that God alone is necessary being; she means that sin is a fact of human temporal existence, universally affecting the whole human race, that must be accepted and endured. When God told Julian she would sin, she saw that God meant "everyone who is sinful and will be until the last day." As a "member" of this one humanity, Julian participates in the universal tragedy of sin (79:333).

While sin might be regarded as nothing on the ontological level, the pain it causes is something that theology must consider. For all practical purposes, "suffering" is the most accurate definition of sin for Julian:

> Sin is the sharpest scourge with which any chosen soul can be struck, which scourge belabors man or woman, and breaks a man and purges him in his own sight so much that at times he thinks himself that he is not fit for anything but as it were to sink into hell (39:244). [18]

In fact, sin is the greatest pain that can afflict humankind:

> If it were laid in front of us, all the pain there is in hell and in purgatory and on earth, death and all the rest, we should choose all that pain rather than sin. For sin is so vile and so much to be hated that it can be compared with no pain which is not itself sin. And no more cruel hell than sin was revealed to me, for a loving soul hates no pain but sin; for everything is good except sin, and nothing is evil except sin (40:247).

The word "sin" in Julian's theology thus embraces everything that is not good, including "the passions, spiritual and bodily, of all God's creatures" that result from sin, and the pains and sufferings of Christ (27:225). Julian usually makes no distinction between physical and moral evil. Her concern is primarily with sin, and she regards physical evil as an effect of sin, including it in the general meaning of the word "sin."[19]

The main effect of sin is that the image of God in human nature is weakened and obscured, causing humanity to enter into what Bernard called the "region of unlikeness,"[20] where one can no longer see God or see things from God's perspective, including the self as God's image. Most damaging of all, one loses sight of God's love, a point graphically made by the picture of the fallen servant of the parable:

> He cannot rise or help himself in any way. And of all this, the greatest hurt which I saw him in was lack of consolation, for he could not turn his face to look on his loving lord, who was very close to him, in whom is all consolation; but like a man who was for the time extremely feeble and foolish, he paid heed to his feelings and his continuing distress. . . . He was blinded in his reason and perplexed in his mind, so much so that he had almost forgotten his own love (51:267–68).

The chief effect of the sinful condition in which all humanity finds itself is the harm done to the image of God in human sensual existence: loss of might and wisdom, preoccupation with suffering, and confusion of will.

Loss of Might

Because of sin, one loses the strength that comes from the memory of who human beings are in God's sight; the truth or might of the soul which images God's might is enfeebled, making one unable to do the desired good. Thus the servant, hurt and injured in the ditch, cannot rise to pull himself out in order to fulfill his and the lord's desire. Humanity is trapped by the hurt and injuries caused by sin. The resulting weakness is experienced in various ways, through "our frailty and our falling, our trespasses and our humiliations, our chagrins and our burdens and all our woe" and we find we can do nothing but sin on our own power (62:302). Here Julian links "original" and "actual" sin.[21] One of the effects of Adam's sin is that it is impossible to avoid personal sin in this life: "in ourselves we are nothing at all but sin and wretchedness," unable to do the good we desire (78:332). There is no way to restore human might "except through God who created humanity" (10:194). The "deed" which God will perform to make all well will be done by God alone, while "humankind will do nothing at all but sin" (36:239).[22]

Loss of Wisdom

Julian makes much of the difference between the divine and human viewpoint, a difference partly due to God's incomprehensibility (34:235), but compounded by sin.[23] As a result of sin, the wisdom of the human soul which mirrors God's wisdom is obscured; one becomes "unwise," no longer able to see God or the self as they truly are. Blindness to God's way of looking at evil is especially detrimental, because it can lead to despair:

> There are many deeds which in our eyes are so evilly done and lead to such great harms that it seems to us impossible that any good result could ever come of them. And we contemplate this and sorrow and mourn for it so that we cannot rest in the blessed contemplation of God as we ought to do. And the cause is this: that the reason which we use is now so blind, so abject and so stupid that we cannot recognize God's exalted, wonderful wisdom, or the [might] and the goodness of the blessed trinity (32:232).

Inability to see sin from God's viewpoint is only a symptom of a deeper "ignorance which most hinders God's lovers" (73:323), the inability to see God's true nature as love. This is why people sin personally, because "if [we] saw God continually, [we] would have no harmful feelings nor any kind of prompting, no sorrowing which is conducive to sin" (47:260). The absence of a true knowledge of God as love causes an unhealthy preoccupation with the self:

> We fall back upon ourselves, and then we find that we feel nothing at all but the opposition that is in ourselves, and that comes from the old root of our first sin, with all that follows from our own persistence; and in this we are belabored and tempted with the feeling of sin and of pain in many different ways (47:261).[24]

One no longer sees the image of God in the self, as God does, but becomes preoccupied and saddened by one's own sinfulness, experienced within as "opposition" or "contrariness" (49:264). This leads to despair:

> Our spiritual eye is so blind, and we are so burdened with the weight of our mortal flesh and the darkness of sin that we cannot see clearly the blessed face of our Lord God. No, and because of this darkness, we can scarcely believe or have faith in [God's] great love and faithfulness (72:321).

Through sin's vicious cycle humanity experiences itself as alienated from God. Though "peace and love are always in us" because we are held secure in the eternal love of God, we do not experience ourselves this way

(39:245). Instead we feel wrath, "a perversity and an opposition to peace and to love," caused by the injury to God's image in us (48:262). The most pernicious effect of sin is that we no longer believe in God's love.

Temptation and Preoccupation with Suffering

Because of the damage to the image of God, human beings are afflicted by constant temptation to personal sin. Julian recognizes the three classic sources of temptation: the world, the flesh, and the devil, but she discusses them with respect to one form of temptation that she emphasizes above all others: the temptation to become preoccupied with one's own suffering.

Under the influence of sin, the world, created good by God, becomes burdensome. Because of sin, the place where the servant of the parable found himself was "narrow and comfortless and distressful" (51:268), and the place where the lord sat "was unadorned . . . barren and waste" (51:271).[25] Because of sin, Julian calls the earth "the valley of this wretched world" (51:274) which is experienced as "prison" and "penance" (77:331).[26]

Under the influence of sin, the body becomes a hindrance to the workings of grace. One of the seven pains suffered by the servant was "the heaviness of his body" (51:267). Julian draws upon her own experience to illustrate this. Once she began to suffer the physical pain of her illness, she regretted having prayed to share Jesus' pains. She attributes this to "the reluctance and domination of the flesh" which opposes the true desire of the soul:

> Reluctance and deliberate choice are in opposition to one another, and I experienced them both at the same time; and these are two parts, one exterior, the other interior. The exterior part is our mortal flesh, which is sometimes in pain, sometimes in sorrow, and will be so during this life, and I felt it very much at this time; and it was in that part of me that I felt regret. The interior part is an exalted and blessed life which is all peace and love; and this is more secretly experienced (19:212).[27]

As a result of sin, one can become so preoccupied with bodily suffering that one cannot concentrate on one's relationship with God. This preoccupation with suffering is detrimental, for it can give rise to "harmful feelings" which are "conducive to sin" (47:260).

Julian refers to the body under the influence of sin as "our foul mortal flesh, . . . Adam's old tunic, tight-fitting, threadbare and short" (51:278). In a particularly graphic passage she describes it as a body of pain from which one needs to be rescued:

I saw a body lying on the earth, which appeared oppressive and fearsome and without shape and form, as it were a devouring pit of stinking mud, and suddenly out of this body there sprang a most beautiful creature, a little child, fully shaped and formed, swift and lively and whiter than the lily, which quickly glided up to heaven. The pit which was the body signifies the great wretchedness of our mortal flesh; and the smallness of the child signifies the cleanness and the purity of our soul. And I thought: In this body there remains none of this child's beauty, and in this child there remains none of the body's foulness. It is most blessed for [us] to be taken from pain, more than for pain to be taken from [us] (64:306–7).[28]

The body as described here represents human bodily pain, which in Julian's theological construction is ultimately related to sin. Thus this passage does not make a distinction between soul and body as such. The body itself is good; united to the soul it is meant to be God's dwelling place. But, in a way similar to Paul's "spirit and flesh," Julian is marking the difference between the human being as influenced by grace and sin respectively.[29] The opposition created by this dual influence is experienced especially in the reluctance of the body to follow the inner impulses of grace, a reluctance the tradition named concupiscence.[30] Just as Paul feels the opposition to grace particularly "in his members," so Julian feels the influence of sin in her body, making her unwilling or unable to perform the good she desires.[31]

Julian records her own experiences of the third source of temptation, the devil. Thinking she was on her deathbed, she fully expected to be tempted by devils (4:182). Everything around the cross which her curate had set before her face "was ugly and terrifying to me, as if it were occupied by a great crowd of devils" (3:180).[32] After the fifteenth revelation Julian has a nightmare about the devil:

And as soon as I fell asleep, it seemed to me that the devil set himself at my throat, thrusting his face, like that of a young man, long and strangely lean, close to mine. I never saw anything like him; his color was red, like a newly baked tile, with black spots like freckles, uglier than a tile. His hair was red as rust, not cut short in front, with sidelocks hanging at his temples. He grinned at me with a vicious look, showing me white teeth so big that it all seemed the uglier to me. His body and his hands were misshapen, but he held me by the throat with his paws, and wanted to stop my breath and kill me, but he could not (67:311–12).

The gruesome detail of this description shows that Julian shared in the fear and fascination with the powers of evil that permeated her age.[33] One of the strongest messages of her revelations is that these forces of evil have been overcome by Christ's passion. Nonetheless, the devil continues to harass human beings, with God's permission, with "the same malice as he had before the incarnation" (13:201). Julian reminds us that God did not promise: "You will not be troubled, you will not be belabored, you will not be disquieted," but only "you will not be overcome" (68:315). Temptation to sin is part of the mystery of evil which continues to be something humans suffer, as long as earthly life lasts.

Conflict of Will

Although the true will continues to be fastened on God, all of the above sufferings can cause the will to be "overpowered in the time when we are assailed and in sorrow and woe" (47:260), "blinded and hindered from knowing" what it truly desires (51:270). The weakness of the body and its sufferings begin to affect the will, and one experiences "a beastly will in the lower part which cannot will any good" (37:242). One is influenced by what sensuality or the "exterior part" desires, and loses sight momentarily of the will of the soul's substance, which is always drawn towards God. Thus one experiences a conflict of wills within the self.[34]

Because of sin, human sensuality does not always "induce agreement" with the true will of the soul's substance, but must be drawn into harmony with it through grace. However, human sensuality as weakened by sin does not pull the substance of the soul down to its level; Julian distinctly says this was not shown to her. What God revealed was how the substance of the soul, always united to God and made powerful through grace, draws sensuality up to its level (19:212–13).[35]

In spite of the conflict of wills, sin is always experienced as what ought not to be, the opposite of the true will of the soul. Sin is unnatural to humans:

> [Sin] . . . is in opposition to our fair nature; for as truly as sin is unclean, so truly is sin unnatural. All this is a horrible thing to see for the loving soul which would wish to be all fair and shining in the sight of God as nature and grace teach (63:304).

Since the will is always united to God in some sense, whenever human beings sin they do so, paradoxically, against their true will.

Personal Sin

As we have seen, one of the effects of the sin of Adam is the fact that human beings choose and are guilty of personal sin: "we cannot in this life keep ourselves completely from sin, in the perfect purity that we shall have in heaven" (52:281). No one is exempt from this: "If there be any such liver on earth, who is continually protected from falling, I do not know, for it was not revealed to me" (82:339).[36]

Julian usually talks about sin only in a general way, inclusive of both original and actual sin and their effects; nor are her distinctions between temptation and actual sin always clearcut. She does distinguish in one place between "mortal" and "venial" sin: while no one can avoid sin completely, it is possible for those growing in the life of grace to avoid "the sins which would lead us to endless torment," and also "to eschew venial sin, reasonably, to the extent of our power" (52:281).

In direct contrast to the widespread popular fear of mortal sin, Julian carefully qualifies her own treatment of it. For those who will be saved, this sin is never "deadly" in actual fact, for God never departs from them (72:265). Indeed, "in the sight of God the soul which will be saved was never dead, and never will be" (50:265). Yet sin can appear deadly to the sinner for a time, and legitimately so. Sin is the greatest opposition to the human ability to see God; therefore, "the more horrible and grievous our sins may be" the farther we fall away from this sight. And this is experienced as a kind of death:

> It often seems to us as if we were in danger of death and in some part of hell, because of the sorrow and the pain which sin is to us, and so for that time we are dead to the true sight of our blessed life (72:320).

However, Julian completely ignores the practice common in her day to catalogue personal sins, such as the sins against the commandments and the seven deadly sins, evaluating their degree of guilt and the punishment due to each. While she acknowledges pride and presumption as dangerous sinful tendencies,[37] and recognizes the tension involved in avoiding both presumption and despair,[38] there are only two particular sins that she discusses in any kind of detail:

> God showed two kinds of sickness that we have. One is impatience or sloth, because we bear our labor and our pain heavily. The other is despair or doubtful fear. . . . [God] showed sin generally, in which all sin is comprehended; but showed no sins in particular but these two, and it is these two which most belabor and assail us, by what our Lord showed me, of which he wants us to be amended (73:322).

These are the sins that most afflict those who are consciously attempting to make progress in the Christian life of grace, and they are interrelated.

Impatience with suffering causes an apathy that leads to "wasting of time," which Julian considers "the beginning of sin" (64:306). This leads to despair, since the sinner becomes ashamed and guilt-ridden, "afraid to appear before our courteous Lord" (76:329).[39]

Despair, for Julian, is the most deadly and destructive of sins. This idea is in contrast to that of most fourteenth century spiritual writers, who considered pride the root of all evil and treated it extensively.[40] Julian's emphasis upon despair comes directly from her revelations and is consistent with her whole theological view. Given her emphasis upon God's love, it is logical that the most heinous sin in her eyes should be despair, which essentially denies God's love. But this need not prevent us from wondering to what extent Julian's experience as a woman had an effect upon her understanding of sin. Feminist scholars point out that unhealthy self-denial and self-loathing, rather than the self-aggrandizement of pride, are the sins to which women are particularly prone.[41] Julian's emphasis upon depression and doubtful fear of one's self-worth lends support, from a distant century, to this view. Her analysis of the experience of despair exhibits a wise and healthy understanding of the workings of the human, and particularly of the female, psyche.

As Julian understands it, the temptation to despair stems from the ignorance of God's love that is the result of the fall and it remains even when sinners begin to hate sin and amend their lives:

> There still persists a fear which hinders us, by looking at ourselves and at our sins committed in the past, and some of us because of our everyday sins, because we do not keep our promise or keep the purity which God has established us in, but often fall into so much wretchedness that it is shameful to say it. And the perception of this makes us so woebegone and so depressed that we can scarcely see any consolation (73:323).

Such a condition makes the sinner an easy target for the devil:

> Because of our own inconstancy, we often fall into sin. Then by the prompting of our enemy and by our own folly and blindness we come to this. For they say: You know well that you are a wretch, a sinner and also unfaithful, because you do not keep your covenant. Often you promise our Lord that you will do better, and then you fall again into the same state (76:329).[42]

The devil's purpose is "to make us so depressed and so sad in this matter that we should forget the blessed contemplation of our everlasting friend" (76:329).

Despair or doubtful fear is a dangerous and subtle sin, because it can be mistaken for virtue:

> Sometimes we take this fear for humility, but it is a reprehensible blindness and weakness; and we do not know how to despise it like any other sin which we recognize, and this comes through lack of true judgment, and it is contrary to truth (73:323).

Julian was surely aware that women, traditionally taught to be modest and self-effacing, are particularly susceptible to such deception. Such feelings of depression need to be recognized as sinful and confessed, so that the sinner may return to the consolation of God's love:

> [God] wants us to see our wretchedness and meekly to acknowledge it; but he does not want us to remain there, or to be much occupied in self-accusation, nor does he want us to be too full of our own misery. But he wants us quickly to attend to him, for he stands all alone, and waits for us continually (79:334).

Julian speaks of despair as the sin that most affects contemplatives, but writing for contemplatives did not keep others from uttering dire warnings about the deadly sins.[43] Julian's lack of attention to sins other than despair is highly unusual for her day. While she struggled with the problem of sin at the beginning of her revelations, she learned to see sin from God's perspective, in relation to God's work of mercy. She was only too aware that undue preoccupation with sin could result in scrupulosity and loss of self-worth, only exacerbating the experience of separation from God. Her revelations taught her that God loves and values humanity and will not permit those chosen for salvation to be lost. This is attributed especially to God's work of mercy, and it is within this context that Julian begins to see that sin, from which humanity suffers so greatly, can actually become beneficial.

The First Work of Mercy: Deriving Benefit from Sin

Sin is called "necessary" by Julian because it is a fact of human life that must be dealt with. But "necessary" is the nearest modern equivalent for the actual word Julian used, "behovely," which also carried with it the notion of being beneficial. Sin is beneficial not because there is any good to sin itself, but because God is powerful enough to bring good out of it.

Since sin has been subsumed into God's plan for good, God permits human beings to be afflicted by it and even rejoices over this:

> Our Lord rejoices with pity and compassion over the tribulations of his servants; and he imposes on every person whom he loves . . . something that is no defect in his sight, through which souls are humiliated and despised in this world, scorned and mocked and rejected (28:226).

When God showed her sin and said "all will be well," Julian realized that, just as God was able to create the world from nothing, so God will be able to "make well" everything affected by the nothingness of evil (32:233). God's first work of mercy, then, the work of God's Wisdom, our Mother, is directed against sin, allowing it to become beneficial for us.

The only way to understand the beneficial aspect of sin is to understand that God does not leave sinners alone in the experience. While humanity certainly suffers intensely from sin, God continues to be present in love and grace. In this life, sin and grace are always experienced together:

> During our lifetime here we have in us a marvellous mixture of both well-being and woe. We have in us our risen Lord Jesus Christ, and we have in us the wretchedness and the harm of Adam's falling. Dying, we are constantly protected by Christ, and by the touching of his grace we are raised to true trust in salvation. And we are so afflicted in our feelings by Adam's falling in various ways, by sin and by different pains, and in this we are made dark and so blind that we can scarcely accept any comfort. But in our intention we wait for God, and trust faithfully to have mercy and grace (52:279).

It is important to acknowledge both the divine and human perspective on sin, important to acknowledge both the constancy of God's protective love and humanity's existential awareness of the pain and horror of sin. Thus, "we do not fall in the sight of God, and we do not stand in our own sight."[44] Attempting to have God's perspective is the "higher truth," but human experience cannot be denied. Indeed, Julian sees it as "most profitable" that we see the two together: "for the higher contemplation keeps us in spiritual joy" and the other "keeps us in fear" of our own weakness (82:339).

The primary effect of God's work of mercy is that it enables the sinner to recognize sin for what it is. One of the most dangerous effects of sin is that, because of human blindness, it can remain hidden from one's consciousness, and even masquerade as virtue.[45] God alone can reveal sin for what it is:

Our Lord in his mercy reveals our sin and our feebleness to us by the sweet gracious light of his own self, for our sin is so foul and so horrible that he in his courtesy will not reveal it to us except by the light of his mercy (78:332).

It is only in the protection of God's love that the sinner can "see . . . sin, profitably, without despair." Indeed, God "measures" the sight of sin, "for it is so foul and so horrible that we should not endure to see it as it is." God knows how much the sinner can endure, and takes care of the rest: "by the sight of the less which our Lord reveals to us, the more which we do not see is dispelled" (78:332). In short, God reveals sin so that the proper balance can be maintained to avoid both presumption and despair.

A true knowledge of sin is crucial for Julian: we need to "see truly and know our falling, and all the harms which come from it" (52:281). The reason for this is not because of the danger of damnation, for Julian is speaking only about those who will be saved. Rather, the reason has to do with the love that exists between God and humanity. Julian's revelations were meant to be a word of comfort and consolation for all who would be God's lovers. Horrible as sin is, seeing it from God's perspective can provide comfort and courage in the face of it. Julian knew that those who do not recognize sin for what it is, only heap more suffering upon themselves. In publishing her revelations, she shares in the love and compassion which God has for all, allowing herself to be the intermediary of the message that God does not want sinners to suffer more than is necessary.

This sentiment is expressed repeatedly throughout Julian's text: "If we well contemplate [God's] will in this, it keeps us from lamenting and despairing as we experience our pains" (28:227); "our courteous Lord does not want his servants to despair because they fall often and grievously; for our falling does not hinder [God] in loving us" (39:245); "when we fall back into ourselves, through depression and spiritual blindness . . . it is God's will that we know that he has not forgotten us" (64:307); God wishes us "to forget our sin with regard to our unreasonable depression and our doubtful fears" (73:323). Note, once again, Julian's strong warning against the sin of despair, which, for women especially, can all too easily be confused with the virtue of humility.

Another reason why a true perspective on sin is important to Julian is that without it one becomes so self-absorbed and bogged down in depression that one leaves Christ alone:

When we fall into sin, and neglect recollection of him and the protection of our own soul, then Christ bears all alone the burden of us. And so he remains, moaning and mourning. Then it is for us in reverence and kindness to turn quickly to our Lord, and not to leave him alone. He is here alone with us all; that is to say, he is here only for us. And when I am distant towards him through sin, despair or sloth, then I leave my Lord to remain alone, inasmuch as he is in me. And this is the case with us all who are sinners (80:336).

This is the opposite of the true desire of one who would be Christ's lover, who consciously longs to share Christ's desires and longings for the salvation of all.

Once viewed in the presence of God's love, sin can begin to be profitable for sinners, and Julian spells out sin's benefits in some detail. Sin gives the sinner a proper sense of shame and guilt, preventing one from falling into presumption or pride (78:332).[46] This is especially important for contemplatives like Julian herself:

Though we may be lifted up high into contemplation by the special gift of our Lord, still, together with this, we must necessarily have knowledge and sight of our sin and of our feebleness; for without this knowledge we may not have true meekness, and without this we cannot be safe (78:333).

Sinfulness thus creates a legitimate fear in the sinner, not the doubtful fear which denies God's love, but a healthy awareness of one's own weakness:

I was taught to be fearful because of my own uncertainty, because I do not know how I may fall, nor do I know the measure or the greatness of my sin. For in my fearfulness I wanted to know that, and I had no answer to it (79:334).

If we did not fall into sin, "we should not know how feeble and how wretched we are in ourselves" (61:300). Sin also teaches sinners to endure suffering, including their own sinfulness, with patience. God tells Julian, "do not be too much aggrieved by the sin which comes to you against your will" (82:338). Seeing sin from God's perspective helps sinners to understand and accept the suffering they are in, allowing it to become "profitable penance" (77:331).

Sharing God's viewpoint enables true love of self and others in spite of sin. Julian especially warns against being unduly concerned or judgmental about the sins of others:

The soul which wants to be in rest should, when other [people's] sins come to mind, flee that as the pain of hell, seeking from God help against it. For the contemplation of [others'] sins makes as it were a thick mist before the soul's eye, and during that time we cannot see the beauty of God, unless we can contemplate [another's sins] with contrition with [the sinner], with compassion on him, and with holy desires to God for him. For without this it harasses and troubles and hinders the soul which contemplates them (76:328).[47]

Julian was taught to see her own sin and not those of others, unless it may be for their "comfort and help" (79:334). The awareness of her own sinfulness enables her to give that comfort and help with God's compassion.

The more sinners see their sin for what it is, in the light of God's love, the more they hate and try to avoid it:

The soul which truly accepts the teaching of the Holy Spirit hates sin more, for its vileness and horribleness, than it does all the pain which is in hell. For the soul which contemplates the gentleness of Jesus does not hate any hell, but the sin of hell, as I see it. And therefore it is God's will that we recognize sin, and pray busily and labor willingly and seek meekly for teaching, so that we do not fall blindly into it, and if we fall, so that we quickly rise (76:328).

Under the influence of God's love sin actually "purges us and makes us know ourselves and ask for mercy" (27:225). Awareness of sin and guilt can result in profound sorrow, causing the sinner to seek God's help through sacramental confession (39:244). Sin can thus become the means that leads the sinner to God.

Above all, sin increases understanding of the great love of God which never leaves human beings alone in their sin: "[hard] and [marvelous] is that love which cannot and will not be broken because of offences."[48] If one never fell into sin, one would not "know so completely the wonderful love of our creator" (61:300).

Because sin has been overcome by the sufferings of Christ, God wants only to reward sinners for the pains they have endured. In fact, the more they suffer from sin in this life, the greater will be their reward:

Just as there is indeed a corresponding pain for every sin, just so love gives to the same soul a bliss for every sin. Just as various sins are punished with various pains, the more grievous are the sins, so will they be rewarded with various joys in heaven to reward the victories over them, to the degree to which the sin may have been painful and sorrowful to the soul on earth (38:242).

Julian thus shares Paul's perspective that sin increased so that grace might abound all the more. And, like Paul, she finds it necessary to utter a warning:

> Now, because of all this spiritual consolation which has been described, if any man or woman be moved by folly to say or to think 'If this be true, then it would be well to sin so as to have the greater reward, or else to think sin less important,' beware of this impulse, for truly, should it come, it is untrue and from the fiend (40:247).[49]

Throughout this work I have consistently noted Julian's debt to the Augustinian synthesis. Yet her treatment of sin is certainly a significant departure from Augustine's thought. The most obvious difference is that, unlike the author of the traditional doctrine of original sin, Julian shows little interest in sin's origin, nor does she spell out any specific link between original sin and human propagation. It is sufficient for her to take for granted the existential fact that all share in humanity's universal tragedy.

Julian emphasizes the fact that those to be saved are kept eternally in the love of God. God permits the devil to try to snatch them from God, and they painfully experience that, but the devil's efforts are to no avail, since they continue to retain God's image in their substance, and this is evident most clearly in the will, which always longs for God. Augustine would not disagree with this. He admits that a vestige of God's image always remains in the human will, even if only as some vague dissatisfaction or longing which is actually the desire for God. Thus human nature is not totally corrupted by sin. However, Augustine also makes it very clear that sin resides in the will, the result of the misuse of human freedom. He would certainly question Julian's conclusion that Adam was not responsible for the fall.

Augustine emphasizes much more emphatically humanity's enslavement to evil. For example, in his treatise on original sin, he writes:

> The entire mass of our nature was ruined beyond doubt, and fell into the possession of its destroyer. And from him no one—no, not one—has been delivered, or is being delivered, or ever will be delivered, except by the grace of the Redeemer.[50]

Julian would not disagree with this, but she stresses the deliverance which has been accomplished as a result of the incarnation, as part of the eternal plan of God. Augustine emphasizes the harm done by sin and the need for deliverance. Neither would dispute the actual points made by the other, but each would certainly question the other's emphases.

One reason for the difference between the two can be found in the existential situation each was attempting to address. Augustine was defending the necessity of God's grace against those who seemed to deny it in the midst of the Pelagian controversy. In doing so, he drew upon his early personal experience where he had found it impossible to do good without God's help, and upon the many years he had spent as bishop grappling with the evils that threatened the unity of the church. Hence Augustine emphasizes the all-pervasiveness of sin's domination over human nature.

By contrast, Julian was attempting to override the extreme demoralization, scrupulosity, and despair that was the Black Death's legacy to her age. She saw that trust in God was degenerating into the superstitious use of various intermediaries (relics, indulgences, pilgrimages, and so on) to placate God and to ensure eternal salvation. Over against this tendency, Julian stresses the ever constant and abiding love of God as humankind's one sure haven of peace against the ravages of sin and suffering. This eventually results in a description of sin and salvation that calls into question Augustine's more pessimistic view, and that certainly disagrees entirely with his conclusions about predestination, as will be made evident in the next chapter.

The Second Work of Mercy: The Restoration and Increase of the Image of God

God's work of mercy does more than reveal and heal sinfulness. It removes the weakness and blindness which prevent the full flowering of the image of God, thus restoring that image. In the process it also provides gifts to increase that image beyond its original splendor.

The incarnation makes this possible. The work Christ accomplished in his earthly sojourn provided an example for a life of love and virtue that was not available to humanity's original perfection. The imitation of Christ, particularly through the virtues that came to light through his lowering of self to earth and through his passion and death, forms the focal point for the restoration and increase of the image of God in human nature: "Just as we were made like the trinity in our first making, our creator wished us to be like Jesus Christ our savior in heaven forever, through the power of our making again" (10:194–95).

However, the Christian life is far more than the mere imitation of an extrinsic model. Human restoration and increase in likeness to Christ is accomplished because Christ dwells in the soul through grace:

> Our good Lord revealed himself to his creature in various ways, both in heaven and on earth; but I saw him take no place except in [the human] soul. . . . He has taken there his resting place and his honorable city. Out of this honorable throne he will never rise or depart without end. Marvellous and splendid is the place where the Lord dwells; and therefore he wants us promptly to attend to the touching of his grace, rejoicing more in his unbroken love than sorrowing over our frequent fallings (81:336–37).

Julian's image of Christ dwelling in his city can be understood in two ways. She certainly means Christ's dwelling in the individual soul, but she also means Christ's dwelling in the church. Indeed, it is through Christ's presence in individual Christians that they are all knit together into the one body of Christ, the church:

> We are all enclosed in him, and he is enclosed in us. . . . He sits in our soul, for it is his delight to reign blessedly in our understanding, and sit restfully in our soul, and to dwell endlessly in our soul, *working us all into him* [i.e., into his body, the church] (57:292; my emphasis).

To "go into our own soul, where our Lord dwells" is equivalent to going "to holy church, into our Mother's breast" (62:303). This is because God dwells in God's city the church by dwelling in the individual souls which make up the body of Christ. It is only within the context of the church's life of grace that Julian examines the restorative effects of God's mercy on the life of the soul. Hers is no purely individual mystical spirituality, but an ecclesial one. She knows of no life of holiness apart from the one body of Christ.[51]

God's indwelling effects in humanity the works of both mercy and grace. Both operations comprise what is traditionally known as grace; Julian simply uses the term "mercy" to describe the graces more obviously connected with the salvation accomplished by Christ, the discussion of which will comprise the rest of this chapter. It involves the increase of love and the restoration and increase of wisdom and might in the image of God, which Julian links to the traditional "theological virtues" of love, hope, and faith, respectively. The work of grace, which brings eschatological fulfillment, will be discussed in the next chapter.

Love's Increase

The starting point for the increase of God's image in the soul is the natural love or desire for God that remains in spite of sin. Though that desire may be obscured because of the weakness and blindness of the soul's other faculties, it is securely held in God's love. God's work of nature thus becomes the foundation for the restoration and increase of the image of God:

> [God] made us so noble and so rich that always we achieve his will and glory. . . . For truly I saw that we are that which [God] loves, and that we do what is pleasing to him, constantly, without any stinting. And from this great richness and this high nobility, commensurate powers come into our soul, whilst it is joined to our body. . . . The natural goodness that we have from him enables us to receive the operation of mercy and grace (57:290–91).

Longing for God is constant in the life of the soul, present even in the midst of the ravages wrought by sin, and mirroring God's longing for humanity:

> I saw three kinds of longing in God, and all to the same end, and we have the same in us, and from the same power, and for the same end. The first is because he longs to teach us to know him and to love him always more and more, as is suitable and profitable to us. The second is that he longs to bring us up into bliss, as souls are when they are taken out of pain into heaven. The third is to fill us with bliss, and that will be fulfilled on the last day, to last forever (75:326).[52]

In the beginning stages of spiritual growth, this longing may not be a conscious seeking for God, but may exhibit itself as a vague dissatisfaction with earthly pleasures and achievements. But as the life of grace grows, love and longing for God increase in intensity even as one becomes more explicitly aware of what one desires. Julian says of herself at the very beginning of her revelations: "I wanted to live to love God better and longer, so that I might through the grace of that living have more knowledge and love of God in the bliss of heaven" (3:179). The spiritual life for Julian is this constant effort to see more of God, through which one's love for God is continually increased. The desire for God is never sated in this life: "it must necessarily be that the nearer that we are to our bliss, the more we shall long, both by nature and by grace" (46:258). One of the effects of the work of mercy, therefore, is the increase of the natural desire of the soul for God.

Restoration and Increase of Wisdom

In the beginning of growth in the spiritual life, the longing for God is often expressed as the desire for true self-knowledge. But because the human soul is the image of God, knowledge of self inevitably leads to the knowledge of God: "When we know and see, truly and clearly, what our self is, then we shall truly and clearly see and know our Lord God" (46:258).[53] On the other hand, we can come to know ourselves only because deep in our substance we already know God:

> For our soul sits in God in true rest, and our soul stands in God in sure strength, and our soul is naturally rooted in God in endless love. And therefore if we want to have knowledge of our soul, and communion and discourse with it, we must seek in our Lord God in whom it is enclosed (56:289).[54]

The search for true self-knowledge, then, inevitably leads into the search for God. Like human longing for God, this search continues and intensifies throughout the course of the Christian life: "When by grace we see something of [God], then we are moved by the same grace to seek with great desire to see him for our greater joy." Thus Julian concludes, "I saw him and sought him, and I had him and lacked him; and this is and should be our ordinary undertaking in life, as I see it" (10:193).

The "loving yearning" and active search of the soul for God is the beginning of prayer (5:184), through which one begins to see with God's eyes. In the process the image of God's wisdom is restored to the soul through which one gains a threefold knowledge:

> The first is that we know our Lord God. The second is that we know ourselves, what we are through [God] in nature and in grace. The third is that we know humbly that our self is opposed to our sin and to our weakness (72:321).

Perseverence in prayer enables conversion from the region of unlikeness, where one is guided by the "blind judgments" of human beings, to the "contemplation of God and of all God's works," where one is guided by "the judgments, lovely and sweet, of our Lord God" (11:198). Through prayer, "our precious lover helps us with spiritual light and true teaching, in various ways, from within and from without" through which we learn "to perceive him wisely, and sweetly receive him, and to keep ourselves faithfully in him" (71:318). Thus the image of God's wisdom is restored, and the soul which contemplates God becomes "like to [God] who is contemplated," united to God in rest and peace (68:314).

The life of prayer is a gradual process, and its beginning point, for Julian, is the contemplation of Christ's passion:

> We pray to God for his holy flesh and for his precious blood, his holy passion, his precious death and his glorious wounds, for all the blessings of nature and the endless life that we have of all this, it is of the goodness of God. . . . And we pray for his holy cross on which he died, and all the help and the strength that we have of that cross, it is of his goodness (6:185).[55]

This is the surest way to discover the love and goodness of God, and the "mind of Christ," upon which human restoration and increase is based.

Julian learned three ways of contemplating the passion. First, one ought to "contemplate with contrition and compassion the cruel pain he suffered" (20:214). This reveals sin's horror, and enables one to see sin for what it truly is, meekly to accuse oneself of it, and to turn to God for mercy and help. Second, one moves beyond contemplation of Christ's suffering to the eternal love which motivated it. This enables one to see God as Love, which in turn enables one to to see oneself from God's perspective, not as a sinner deserving of punishment, but as a beloved servant who suffers from sin (22:217). Third, one eventually understands "the joy and the bliss which make God delight in [the passion]" (23:218).[56] This provides an entirely new perspective, not only on Christ's sufferings, but on the sufferings humans endure in union with him. Contemplation of the painful details of Christ's passion, therefore, is only the beginning. Though that form of meditation has its value, one ought not to remain there, but to move beyond it to the contemplation of the eternal love and joy of the trinity which it reveals.

Meditation on the life, passion, and death of Christ instills the virtue of hope, the trust that one has been saved from one's mortal enemies and will be brought into final union with God in eternal bliss. Christian hope is evidence, in this life, of the restoration of wisdom to the image of God through God's work of mercy. Through it one sees oneself with God's eyes, as eternally saved and destined for a life of bliss. It is the virtue Julian learned most about in her revelations and which she stresses above all others as the necessary foundation for living the Christian life profitably.

Christian hope is an absolute confidence that the love of God guarantees future salvation:

> I understood that any man or woman who voluntarily chooses God in this lifetime for love, . . . may be sure that he is endlessly loved with an endless

love which makes that grace in him. For [God] wants us to pay true heed to this, that we are as certain in our hope to have the bliss of heaven whilst we are here as we shall be certain of it when we are there (65:308).

This virtue pleases God above all others: "the more delight and joy that we accept from this certainty, with reverence and humility, the more pleasing it is to God" (65:308).

Confidence in salvation provides the Christian with a strong stance against the powers of evil. Since they have been overcome by Christ's passion, one has no reason to be afraid of them. God wants us to realize that "all the power of our enemy is shut in the hand of our friend," and has no control over us (65:309). The love of God which was revealed in the passion is a strong fortress against the fear of evil. This confidence in salvation engendered by the virtue of hope is not to be confused with presumption. It is only legitimate when it is accompanied by the "reverent fear and meek love" which mark the truly humble (74:326).

Restoration and Increase of Might

The soul's natural desire for God is also the beginning of faith, which is a dynamic virtue for Julian, rather than merely a form of knowledge or trust. Faith is the rudimentary virtue for the living of the Christian life:

> Our faith is a power which comes from our natural substance into our sensual soul by the Holy Spirit, in which [might] all our powers come to us, for without that [no one] can receive [might], for it is nothing else than right understanding with true belief and certain trust in our being, that we are in God and [God] in us, which we do not see. And this power with all the others which God has ordained for us, entering there, works great things in us; for Christ is mercifully working in us, and we are by grace according with him, through the gift and the power of the Holy Spirit (54:285–86).

The working of faith in us "makes it so that we are Christ's children and live Christian lives" (54:286).

Faith enables the restoration and increase of human might, which images God's Might, that is, the ability to do what one desires, initiating the life of Christian virtue:

> From [faith] comes all our good, by which we are led and saved. For in that come the commandments of God, of which we ought to have two kinds of understanding. One is that we ought to understand and know what things

[God] commands, to love them and to keep them. The other is that we ought to know what things [God] forbids, to hate them and refuse them.[57] For in these two is all our activity comprehended. . . . For the same virtues which we have received from our substance, given to us in nature by the goodness of God, the same virtues by the operation of mercy are given to us in grace, renewed through the Holy Spirit (57:291–92).

These commandments and virtues are "treasured" in Christ (57:292), who, through the example of his life, has become "our way, safely leading us in his laws" (55:286).[58] It is Christ, dwelling in the soul through the Spirit, who effects the growth of the life of virtue in Christians. But he "wants us to be his helpers, giving all our intention to him, learning his laws, observing his teaching, desiring everything to be done which he does, truly trusting in him" (57:292).

The surest way to learn Christ's way of life is to contemplate his passion, thereby acquiring Christ's own "mind," the inner vitality which animated his life on earth. Under the power of God's indwelling, the Christian reproduces in his or her own life the pattern of Christ's life, thus restoring and increasing the image of God's might, the ability to accomplish what one desires, in the soul. The virtues which Julian emphasizes in this process are humility, patience in suffering, and compassionate love for others.[59]

Humility

The virtue of humility was strongly emphasized in Julian's day, since it was viewed as the antidote for pride, root of the seven deadly sins.[60] Julian's own treatment of it is rooted in scripture: the servant of the parable mirrors the attitude of Christ as described in Philippians 2:5–8. Leaving the privileges of divinity behind and taking upon himself willingly the lowest aspects of human life, including the indignities and sufferings resulting from sin, Christ exemplifies for Julian the perfection of humility. Growing in this virtue is part of what it means to acquire the "mind" of Christ.

Christ's humility allowed him to "become sin" for us; thus Christian growth in humility is associated with one's attitude towards sin. The acknowledgment of sinfulness is the primary act of humility upon which further progress is absolutely dependent, for it opens one up to seek God's mercy and realize God's love:

So this is the remedy [for sin], that we acknowledge our wretchedness and flee to our Lord; for always, the more abased we are, the more profitable it is for us to touch him. And let us then in intention say this: I know well that I have deserved pain; but our Lord is almighty, and may punish me greatly, and he is all wisdom, and can punish me wisely, and he is all goodness, and loves me tenderly. And it is profitable for us to remain in this contemplation; for it is a most lovely humility in a sinful soul, made by the mercy and grace of the Holy Spirit (77:330).

Humility is the virtue of spiritual childhood, expressing total dependence upon God for rescue from sin:

When our falling and our wretchedness are shown to us, we are so much afraid. . . . But then our courteous Mother does not wish us to flee away, . . . but he then wants us to behave like a child. For when it is distressed and frightened, it runs quickly to its mother; and if it can do no more, it calls to the mother for help with all its might. So he wants us to act as a meek child, saying: My kind Mother, my gracious Mother, my beloved Mother, have mercy on me. I have made myself filthy and unlike you, and I may not and cannot make it right except with your help and grace (61:301).[61]

In fact, Julian understood "no greater stature in this life than childhood, with its feebleness and lack of might and intelligence," for that stature recognizes the creature's dependence upon God: "the child does not naturally rely upon itself, naturally the child loves the mother." This is a lowliness very different from the false humility of despair, for "the child does not naturally despair of the mother's love" (63:304–5).

The contemplation of God's majesty also "makes the creature marvellously meek and mild" (75:327), reminding one that, compared to God, all creation is actually almost nothing. True humility means that "a creature should see the lord marvellously great and herself marvellously little" (65:308). This is the same attitude that Julian describes as the "reverent fear" or awe before God which will last into eternity. Indeed, humility is the way to the rest one seeks in God: "When [the soul] by its will has become nothing for love, to have God who is everything, then is it able to receive spiritual rest" (5:184).

Because of Christ's act of humility God "highly exalted him" (Phil 2:9); so because of humble acts God raises human beings high. Paradoxically, "where the soul is highest, noblest, most honorable, still it is lowest, meekest and mildest" (59:296). Through the humility obtained through the sight of one's littleness before God's majesty, "we shall be raised high in heaven, to which raising we might never have come without that meekness" (61:300).[62]

Patience in Suffering

Patience was a prominent virtue in the later Middle Ages, understood primarily as the endurance of evil with equanimity. Its corresponding vice, impatience, was understood as the disintegration of the personality into two of the seven deadly sins: either anger or sloth, the latter of which was interpreted as either *accidia*, spiritual apathy, or *tristitia*, undue melancholy. [63] Julian was aware of this tradition. We have seen that in her discussion of sin, impatience is connected with sloth as that apathy or "wasting of time" which can lead to despair. [64] She also connects impatience in suffering with that wrath or "contrariness" which impedes the enjoyment of the peace and rest that God desires for the soul. It is no surprise, then, that patience in suffering is a principle virtue for Julian.

Contemplation of Christ's passion teaches the proper attitude one ought to adopt toward one's own suffering:

> Our Lord showed what patience he had in his cruel passion, and also the joy and delight that he has in that passion, because of love. And he showed me this as an example of how we ought gladly and easily to bear our pains, for that is very pleasing to him and an endless profit to us (73:322–23).

God knows and humans experience the fact that this life is always a life of penance. For one thing, "the substantial and natural longing in us for [God] is a lasting penance in us" which will not end "until the time when we are fulfilled, when we shall have [God] for our reward." But this is a penance which God causes and "mercifully . . . helps us to bear" (81:337). This life is a constant waiting for God, and one ought to endure it "steadfastly, out of love for [God], without grumbling and contending against [God]" (10:196). Sin is another source of earthly suffering, but one ought to endure this patiently, resisting the temptation to fall into despair because of it. As we have seen, God's work of mercy helps with this by teaching God's perspective on sin.

In all human suffering one is helped by the realization that in it one suffers with Christ, experiencing the three wounds for which Julian had prayed: "the wound of true contrition, the wound of loving compassion and the wound of longing with [the] will for God" (2:179). Insofar as suffering can bring one closer to God, the desire to suffer with Christ can itself be a mark of the life of virtue. Julian's own desire had been "to suffer with him" (3:181), but once she received a taste of suffering, she confesses honestly, "if I had known what it had been, I should have been reluctant to ask for it" (17:209).

However, Julian is very cautious about recommending acts of asceticism voluntarily assumed, even out of the desire to suffer with Christ. She does not condemn them explicitly, but neither does she recommend them: "As to the penance which one takes upon oneself, that was not revealed to me." This distinguishes Julian clearly from the majority of medieval women visionaries, for whom rigid acts of asceticism were part of their daily routine.[65] Julian deems it far more important to accept the penance which God sends into the ordinary course of one's life:

> What was revealed . . . is that we ought meekly and patiently to bear and suffer the penance which God himself gives us, with recollection of his blessed passion. For when we recall his blessed passion, with pity and love, then we suffer with him as his friends did who saw it (77:330).[66]

Life itself provides suffering which is hard enough to endure patiently; there is little need to look for additional suffering. What one must learn to do is see life's daily trials as a way of sharing in the sufferings of Christ.

Another fruitful way of viewing suffering in relation to Christ is to see it in light of the resurrection. While Julian regarded the face of the suffering Christ from her sickbed, suddenly "he changed to an appearance of joy." This change immediately affected her:

> The change in his blessed appearance changed mine, and I was as glad and joyful as I could possibly be. And then cheerfully our Lord suggested to my mind: Where is there now any instant of your pain or of your grief? And I was very joyful (21:215).[67]

Julian realized that Christ was teaching her about the fleeting and temporary nature of all earthly suffering, however terrible it might be.

Yet this realization does not take away the reality of earthly suffering. Humans still suffer, and must deal with that as an important part of earthly life, since this is not yet the life of glory. Indeed, "if [Christ] revealed to us now his countenance of joy, there is no pain on earth or anywhere else which could trouble us." But Christ does not do this, except, perhaps, fleetingly in moments of privileged prayer. Instead, "he shows us his suffering countenance, as he was in this life as he carried his cross." In fact, Christ himself continues to suffer on earth through human suffering, and "we are therefore in suffering and labor with him as our nature requires" (21:215). We are one humanity with Christ, the servant. If he suffered, we too will suffer.

The remembrance of the resurrection, though, provides patience to wait in hope for the future joy which will come as a result of suffering:

The reason why [Christ] suffers is because in his goodness he wishes to make us heirs with him of his joy. And for this little pain which we suffer here we shall have an exalted and eternal knowledge in God which we could never have without it. And the harder our pains have been with him on his cross, the greater will our glory be with him in his kingdom (21:215).

God's promise is that humanity will be taken from pain. God wants Christians to remember this in order to receive consolation in the midst of suffering:

It is God's will that we focus our thought on this blissful contemplation, as often as we can and for as long as we can continue in it. . . . It is God's will that we accept his commands and his consolations as generously and as fully as we are able; and [God] also wants us to accept our tarrying and our sufferings as lightly as we are able, and to count them as nothing. For the more lightly that we accept them, the less importance we ascribe to them because of our love, the less pain shall we experience from them and the more thanks and reward shall we have for them (64:307).

God does not want humans to suffer more than is necessary; therefore, out of mercy, God helps them to look upon suffering with God's eyes, so they might be able to suffer with patience. Acceptance of suffering will then be "very tender and very easy, if we will only keep ourselves content with [God] and with all [God's] works" (77:330).[68]

Love and Compassion for Others

Christ's acts of humility and patient suffering were done out of love for all who will be saved. Christ is thus the personification of the "cheerful giver" who longs only to please those he loves (23:219). Julian wrote her *Showings* in the same spirit. She realized from the beginning that what God had revealed to her was meant to be given "generally, to the comfort of us all." Indeed all during the time of the revelations Julian tells us "I was greatly moved in love towards my fellow Christians, that they might all see and know the same as I saw, for I wished it to be a comfort to them" (8, 9:190–91). Great as the grace was which God showed to her in these revelations, "it was not revealed to me that God loves me better than the humblest soul who is in a state of grace." This is because "we are all one in love" (9:191).[69]

The unity of all Christians in love is a constant theme throughout Julian's work. Loving one's fellow Christians is the only way to love God, since God has united self with humanity:

[Whoever] has general love for all [one's] fellow Christians in God has love towards everything that is. For in [humankind] which will be saved is comprehended all, that is to say all that is made and the maker of all. For God is in [humanity] and in God is all. And [whoever] loves thus loves all (9:192).

God's love for all is the motivating force behind human love for others, revealing humanity's fundamental goodness:

What can make me love my fellow Christians more than to see in God that he loves all who will be saved, all of them as it were one soul? For in every soul which will be saved there is a godly will which never assents to sin (37:241).

The model for this love is Christ:

Christ himself is the foundation of all the laws of Christian [people], and he taught us to do good in return for evil. Here we may see that he is himself this love, and does to us as he teaches us to do: for he wishes us to be like him in undiminished, everlasting love towards ourselves and our fellow Christians (40:247).

Furthermore, since this love was given freely and compassionately to humans while still in their sin, one who would imitate Christ's love, must compassionately love the sinner:

No more than his love is withdrawn because of our sin does he wish our love to be withdrawn from ourselves or from our fellow Christians; but we must unreservedly hate sin and endlessly love the soul as God loves it (40:247).

Julian felt this compassion herself in the midst of her experience of sharing the suffering of Christ:

I saw how Christ has compassion on us because of sin; and just as I was before filled full of pain and compassion on account of Christ's passion, so I was now in part filled with compassion for all my fellow Christians, because he loves very dearly the people who will be saved, that is to say God's servants (28:226).

The unity in love of all Christians is another way of talking about the church as the body of Christ. Julian realized that in her compassion for her fellow Christians she was experiencing Christ loving through her:

I saw that every natural compassion which one has for one's fellow Christians in love is Christ in us, and that every kind of self-humiliation which he manifested in his passion was manifested again in this compassion (28:227).

Christ continues to love through the love of Christians for one another. And this love has two aspects to it, as does the church itself, corresponding to the twofold gaze of joy and compassion with which the lord looked upon the servant in the parable.

The love within Christ's body reveals the harmony that follows when Christians are "loving and content with ourselves and with our fellow Christians and with everything which God loves," which is a foretaste of the joy, peace, and love of heaven (49:265). But the love within Christ's body also provides "consolation in our pain," the knowledge that no one suffers alone but together with each other in Christ (28:227). Both of these aspects of Christian love, the anticipation of bliss and the need for consolation, break down any boundaries that may exist within Christ's body between the high and the low, the good and the bad:

> [Someone] who is highest and closest to God may see himself sinful and needy along with me. And I who am the least and the lowest of those who will be saved may be comforted along with [the one] who is highest. So has our Lord united us in charity (78:333).[70]

All Christians are one in God's eyes, the faithful servant of the parable through union with Christ, deserving of God's compassion and pity, awaiting the joy of eschatological fulfillment.

7

The Work of Grace

Although the Spirit of God is active with the whole trinity in the works of nature and mercy already described, the particular work attributed to the Spirit by Julian is eschatological fulfillment, which she calls the work of grace:

> Grace works with mercy, and especially in two properties, . . . which working belongs to the third person, the Holy Spirit. He works, rewarding and giving. Rewarding is a gift of trust which the Lord makes to those who have labored; and giving is a courteous act which he does freely, by grace, fulfilling and surpassing all that creatures deserve (58:294).

The ultimate gift and reward of the Spirit is heaven, that state of union with God which the blessed will enjoy for all eternity. Julian's strong emphasis upon heaven is proof of her indebtedness to the monastic tradition, where the longing for heaven was the fundamental atmosphere within which monastic culture flourished, an atmosphere that was predominantly eschatological and transcendent.[1] The message of Julian's revelations which urged her to live within the divine perspective with respect to sin and salvation is consistent with such an eschatological tradition.

Future Eschatology: The Bliss of Heaven

In the sixth revelation, Julian's understanding is "lifted up into heaven" where she sees God as the lord of a great feast, "gladdening and consoling" all his friends.[2] As she contemplates this image, she is led to understand that anyone "who has voluntarily served God in any degree on earth" will enjoy "three degrees of bliss" in heaven. The person will experience "honor and thanks from our Lord God," a thanks "so exalted and so honorable" that it is indescribable joy. Furthermore, God will make this thanks public so that "all the blessed in heaven will see the honor of the thanks," increasing the joy and honor experienced by the saved person. Finally, this joy and honor "will last forevermore."[3] Although Julian makes the point that joy will be especially great for those who "voluntarily and freely offer their youth to God," all three degrees of bliss belong to all the saved, whether their service lasted a lifetime or a day (14:203–4).[4]

Later, in the ninth revelation, Julian's understanding is lifted up into heaven again, where she sees "three heavens" reflecting the three persons of the trinity, all in relation to the humanity of Christ. The first heaven reveals the pleasure the Father takes in rewarding the Son for "all the deeds that Jesus has done for our salvation" (22:216). The second heaven is the bliss the Son experiences through the honor he receives from the Father by being awarded the gift of all the saved. The third heaven is the "endless delight" the Holy Spirit takes in the work of salvation (23:218).

The three degrees of bliss experienced by the blessed in heaven correspond to the three heavens of the trinity. Heaven is essentially a sharing in the pleasure and joy of the Father, the honor and bliss of the Son, and the endless delight of the Holy Spirit over the great deed of salvation which has enabled the human race, made in God's image, to become the bliss, the reward, the honor, and the crown of God. Heaven is thus the final fulfillment of the work of the incarnation, through which temporal and earthly reality has been raised up into the mystery of God.

There is a parallel between God's joy, honor, and endless delight and the qualities of might, wisdom, and love by which Julian usually describes the trinity. The Father's joy represents the triumph of God's might, the Son's honor the vindication of God's wisdom, and the Spirit's endless delight the eternity of the love which has guided all to fulfillment. When the blessed in heaven share in the joy, honor, and delight of the trinity over their salvation, they are, in effect, sharing, insofar as it is possible for creatures, in the triumphant might, wisdom, and love of God. They are sharing this through the perfection of those qualities in themselves by which they have always imaged God, the qualities of human might, wisdom, and love, which were blemished by sin but restored and increased by Christ and fulfilled by the Holy Spirit. Heaven means the fulfillment of God's desire "to have the blessed creatures who will be in heaven with him without end like himself in all things" (77:331).

The end of the parable of the lord and the servant crystallizes Julian's understanding of the bliss of heaven. There the servant is no longer dressed in an old, tight-fitting, threadbare, and short tunic, representing the blemished image of God, but in clothing "made lovely by our savior, new, white and bright and forever clean," fairer, even, than the clothing on the lord. Restored human nature, symbolized by Christ's clothing, is "now of a fair and seemly mixture," so marvellous that it is beyond description (51:278).[5] The fact that it is fairer than the original clothing of the lord seems to imply that the works of mercy and grace have added something to God's glory, not to the essence of God, but to the glory given to God through God's works in time.

It is customary to think of heaven as a state of joy for human beings. What is unique about Julian's presentation is her stress on the joy which God experiences there, when all the saved are given to Christ as his reward for suffering on their behalf. The saved are given to Christ as his crown, and the entire trinity rejoices in this: "For it was revealed that we are his crown, which crown is the Father's joy, the Son's honor, the Holy Spirit's delight, and endless marvellous bliss to all who are in heaven" (51:278).[6] Christ takes up his permanent residence in the city prepared for him by the Father, the souls of all the faithful which together comprise the heavenly kingdom, where there is eternal peace, joy, and love.[7] There all the saved enter into the inner life of the trinity, sharing in the very attributes of God.

Heaven means that God's promise, "all will be well," will be fulfilled and understood by all the blessed. Julian is told that this promise includes the fact that "you will see yourself that every kind of thing will be well." She understood this phrase to indicate the "union of all who will be saved in the blessed trinity" (31:229).[8] The nature of this union is more precisely described in the following passage:

> We shall all come into our Lord, knowing ourselves clearly and wholly possessing God, and we shall all be endlessly hidden in God, truly seeing and wholly feeling, and hearing him spiritually and delectably smelling him and sweetly tasting him. And there we shall see God face to face, familiarly and wholly. The creature which is made will see and endlessly contemplate God who is the maker (43:255).[9]

In heaven the blessed will finally see with God's wisdom and will with God's love. Full union with the mind and will of God and the true knowledge of self which accompanies it will be finally achieved.

Jesus promises Julian that heaven also means the cessation of all suffering:

> Suddenly you will be taken out of all your pain, all your sickness, all your unrest and all your woe. And you will come up above, and you will have me for your reward, and you will be filled full of joy and bliss, and you will

never again have any kind of pain, any kind of sickness, any kind of
displeasure, no lack of will, but always joy and bliss without end
(64:306). [10]

But the labor spent on earth dealing with the suffering caused by sin will
endure eternally, transformed into honor:

> As we are punished here with sorrow and penance . . . we shall be rewarded
> in heaven by the courteous love of our almighty God, who does not wish
> anyone who comes there to lose his labors in any degree. . . . The reward
> which we shall receive will not be small, but it will be great, glorious and
> honorable. And so all shame will be turned into honor and joy (39:245).

Julian looks forward to having her most perplexing problems about sin
and salvation solved in heaven: "when the judgment is given, and we are
all brought up above, we shall then clearly see in God the mysteries which
are now hidden from us" (85:341). However, this will cause a bliss "so
deep and so high" that, "out of wonder and marvelling" the blessed will be
filled with a reverent fear of God, so far surpassing what they have
experienced before, "that the pillars of heaven will tremble and quake"
(75:327). [11] This is the proper attitude of the creature before God, even in
heaven. Although the creature experiences union with the wisdom and
love of God, the essential difference between creature and Creator is not
dissolved. Indeed, the awareness of this difference, with the reverent fear
that accompanies it, increases in heaven with greater knowledge of God:

> For this reverent fear is the fairer courtesy which is in heaven before God's
> face; and by as much as he will be known and loved, surpassing how he now
> is, by so much will he be feared, surpassing how he now is. Therefore it
> must necessarily be that all heaven, all earth will tremble and quake
> (75:327–28).

God will remain for all eternity the totally other, holy, Incomprehensible
Mystery before whom creatures can only bow in adoration.

Realized Eschatology: Anticipation of Heaven

In the monastic tradition, heaven was not solely a future reality to be
awaited, but one experienced partially in the present through the life of
grace, which was greatly aided by the practice of contemplative prayer.
Julian follows this tradition, and is particularly interested in showing how

this present anticipation of heaven, this realized eschatology, can provide comfort and solace in the midst of earthly suffering.

While Julian emphasizes particular virtues of the Christian life closely associated with God's work of mercy (as outlined in the last chapter), she also treats those gifts of the Spirit through which all who will be saved receive a foretaste on earth of the sharing in the life of God which they will enjoy in heaven. Once again, the notion of the *imago Dei* dominates Julian's study of growth in the life of grace. The gifts she describes correspond to the attributes of God discussed in Chapter 4: God's immutability finds a parallel in the gift of peace, God's joy in the gift of joy, and God's love in the further increase of love, accompanied by the reverent fear which reflects God's incomprehensibility.

The surest entrance into the enjoyment of these gifts is through contemplative prayer, wherein one is afforded a sight of God suited to one's present need and condition:

> And so we shall by his sweet grace in our own meek continual prayer come into [God] now in this life by many secret touchings of sweet spiritual sights and feelings, measured out to us as our simplicity may bear it. And this is done and will be done by the grace of the Holy Spirit, until the day that we die, still longing for love. . . . But when [God] of his special grace wishes to show himself here, he gives the creature more than its own strength, and measures the revelation according to his own will, and it is profitable for that time (43:255).

The effect of this sight is to fill the soul with peace, joy, and love.

The Gift of Peace and Rest

For Julian, "God is true rest," and desires "that we should rest in him" (5:184). Therefore God bestows the gift of peace on the willing soul:

> Our good Lord the Holy Spirit, who is endless life dwelling in our soul . . . produces in the soul a peace, and brings it to ease through grace, and makes it obedient and reconciles it to God. And this is . . . the way on which our good Lord constantly leads us, so long as we are in this changeable life (48:261–62).

Julian often describes peace as the absence of the wrath or "contrariness" caused by sin.[12] When filled with God's peace, "we find no contrariness in any kind of hindrance," not even in the things that at other times greatly afflict us (49:265).

The gift of peace and rest in God is a foretaste of the eternity of heaven, a sharing in the immutability of God, for God "will make us as unchangeable as he is when we are there" (49:265). When one contemplates God and God's works under the influence of this gift, one realizes that "all [God's] judgments are easy and sweet," and learns to prefer them to the "blind judgments" of human beings (11:198). [13] One glimpses the "blessed harmony" that always exists between God and God's works, seeing that God "is always fully pleased with himself and with all his works" (35:237). One becomes, in short, as one shall be in heaven: "wholly contented with God and with all his works and with all his judgments, and loving and content with ourselves and with our fellow Christians and with everything which God loves" (49:265).

Resting in the peace of God is an experience of the assurance of salvation, and Julian describes her personal realization of this:

> I was filled full of everlasting surety, powerfully secured without any painful fear. This sensation was so welcome and so spiritual that I was wholly at peace, at ease and at rest, so that there was nothing upon earth which could have afflicted me. . . . And then presently God gave me again comfort and rest for my soul, delight and security so blessedly and so powerfully that there was no fear, no sorrow, no pain, physical or spiritual, that one could suffer which might have disturbed me (15:204–5).

However, this consoling experience was a fleeting one for Julian, alternating with the experience of desolation. She realized that peace is the unearned, free gift of the Spirit, yet she also learned that God wants human beings to dispose themselves to receive and retain it:

> For it is God's will that we do all in our power to preserve our consolation, for bliss lasts forevermore, and pain is passing, and will be reduced to nothing for those who will be saved. Therefore it is not God's will that when we feel pain we should pursue it in sorrow and mourning for it, but that suddenly we should pass it over, and preserve ourselves in the endless delight which is God (15:205).

The Gift of Joy

In the first revelation, while Julian is contemplating the suffering Christ, she tells us of her sudden experience of joy: "Suddenly the trinity filled my heart full of the greatest joy, and I understood that it will be so in heaven without end to all who will come there" (4:181). In heaven the blessed share in "the delight which the blessed trinity has in the cruel

passion of Christ, once his sorrowful death was accomplished." But it is
God's will that this, too, be experienced on earth: "[God] wishes that joy
and delight to be our solace and happiness, as it is [God's], until we come
to glory in heaven" (1:176). One ought to seek for this gift from God, for
God is eager to give it (10:196). Julian records her own prayer:

> Ah, Jesus, let us pay heed to this bliss over our salvation which is in the
> blessed trinity, and let us desire to have as much spiritual delight by his
> grace. . . . Let our delight in our salvation be like the joy which Christ has
> in our salvation, as much as that may be whilst we are here (23:219).

It is especially through contemplation that the soul enters into this joy
of God. One first learns to understand God's joy over human salvation:

> Our courteous Lord shows himself to the soul, happily and with the
> gladdest countenance, welcoming it as a friend. . . . Our soul is honorably
> received in joy, as it will be when it comes into heaven, as often as it comes
> by the operation of grace of the Holy Spirit and the power of Christ's
> passion (40:246). [14]

Then the contemplative begins to share in God's joy, and to recognize it as
the gift beyond all others that God wants human beings to possess:

> What can make us to rejoice more in God than to see in him that in us, of
> all his greatest works, God has joy? . . . . [God] wants our hearts to be
> powerfully lifted above the depths of the earth and all empty sorrows, and
> to rejoice in him (68:314). [15]

We are invited, in other words, to rejoice in God's joy in us. We can love
ourselves, find joy in ourselves, because God loves and rejoices in us. This
joy can be ours even in the midst of pain and suffering. While throughout
our lives we always have "matter for mourning, because our sin is the cause
of Christ's pains," *even more* do we have "constantly matter for joy, because
endless love made [Christ] suffer" (52:280; my emphasis). Once again we
are reminded of the "much more" of Romans 5. [16]

Contemplative prayer is actually "a right understanding of that fulness
of joy which is to come, with true longing and trust" (42:252). As such, it
initiates in the contemplative a foretaste of the bliss of heaven, which is "to
possess God in the clarity of endless light, truly seeing him, sweetly
feeling him, peacefully possessing him in the fulness of joy" (72:320). In
the union thus created, "God rejoices in the creature and the creature in
God, endlessly marvelling" (44:256).

The joy received as gift from the Spirit overflows into thanksgiving and praise:

> Thanksgiving is a true inward acknowledgment, we applying ourselves with great reverence and loving fear and with all our powers to the work that our Lord moved us to, rejoicing and giving thanks inwardly. And sometimes the soul is so full of this that it breaks out in words and says: Good Lord, great thanks, blessed may you be (41:250). [17]

This is what the saved experience in the bliss of heaven, "praising and thanking God," saying "with one voice: Lord, blessed may you be."[18] In spite of human foolishness and blindness, this is how God constantly regards humanity, rejoicing in the work of creation which praises God. One can, even now, please God best "by wisely and truly believing it, and rejoicing with him and in him" (85:341).

The Perfection of Love

Julian describes every aspect of the Christian life in terms of its grounding in love. There is a permanence about humanity's love for God, even when one is separated from God through sin, because human creation is always held united to God in the substance of the soul; but that love is also increased and perfected through sensual life in time. Julian uses three terms to describe this love: Uncreated Charity, created charity, and given charity. God is Uncreated Charity, the source of the soul's love for God, in distinction to created charity which is the human soul in God, that is, the natural love by which the human always longs for God, the ineradicable image of God seated in the human will. But given charity is a gift of the Spirit over and above created charity; it perfects and increases the soul's natural love and desire for God. It is "a gift of grace in deeds, in which we love God for himself, and ourselves in God, and all that God loves for God" (84:341). [19] It is the gradual bringing of the whole self, including one's sensuality, into the union with God's will which has been eternally present in one's substance.

It is especially through prayer that the Spirit brings to perfection the union of wills that exists between God and the creature. Eventually, the human will is so much in tune with God's that one can pray for what one desires, confident that it is also pleasing to God: "we may with reverence ask from our lover all that we will, for our natural will is to have God, and God's good will is to have us" (6:186). Consequently, one can have a certain confidence that God will do what one desires. As Christ told Julian:

> How could it now be that you would pray to me for anything pleasing to me which I would not very gladly grant to you? For my delight is in your holiness and in your endless joy and bliss in me (24:221).

Prayer is, then, in essence, "a true and gracious, enduring will of the soul, united and joined to our Lord's will by the sweet, secret operation of the Holy Spirit." Through it, God gradually "makes us like to himself in condition as we are in nature" (41:249). This is a foretaste of the union with God's will in love that one will enjoy in heaven. The Christian is made like the servant of the parable, "loving to do his lord's will" (51:267). Like the servant, the Christian realizes deep within the self "a foundation of love, the love which he had for the lord, which was equal to the love which the lord had for him" (51:273). And this love is the presence of the Spirit, who is "Uncreated Charity," bringing into fulfillment the potential of the human to image the love of God.

We have already discussed the emphasis Julian places upon love for others in her theology. Hers is no "private mysticism." Growth into union with the will of God finds expression in love for others. In this union Christians experience "a great and marvellous knowledge of love in God without end," which "makes us to love everything which [God] loves for love of him, and to be well satisfied with him and with all his works" (61:300). This love is what prompted Julian to insist so strongly that the privileges granted her in prayer were meant for all her fellow Christians: "For of all things, contemplating and loving the creator makes the soul to seem less in its own sight, and fills it full with reverent fear and true meekness, and with much love for its fellow Christians" (6:187).

Love and Reverent Fear

The gradual perfection of love drives out fear, especially the fear destructive of trust in God which Julian calls despair or "doubtful fear."[20] In the seventh revelation, Julian experienced a security in God's love which was completely "without any painful fear" (15:204). When a person opens self to God in love to receive God's "sweet gracious teaching," and knows the comforting presence of God, doubtful fear disappears, and one learns to resist any movement which encourages it (79:334).

The perfection of love in human nature has the same qualities as God's love for humanity, namely courtesy and homeliness.[21] The absence of doubtful fear and the assurance of salvation, which come as the gifts of prayer, allow one to enter into a certain intimacy with God: "For our courteous Lord wants us to be as [homely] with him as heart may think or soul may desire." Yet this homeliness does not wipe out courtesy: "let us beware that we do not accept this [homeliness] so carelessly as to forsake courtesy. For our Lord himself is supreme [homeliness], and he is as courteous as he is [homely]" (77:331). True love for God never degenerates into presumptive familiarity, but the courtesy that the creature owes the majesty of God is expressed in an attitude of awe which Julian calls "reverent fear."

Though all other forms of fear are driven out by love, reverent fear is increased. It is gentle, like God's attitude of courtesy, but it honors the reality of who God is in all God's transcendent, mysterious otherness. It always accompanies the perfection of love:

> Love and fear are brothers, and they are rooted in us by the goodness of our Creator, and they will never be taken from us without end. It is our nature to love, and we are given grace to love; and it is our nature to fear, and we are given grace to fear. . . . And yet this reverent fear and love are not the same, but they are different in kind and in effect, and neither of them may be obtained without the other (74:324–25).[22]

Love and reverent fear are human responses to different attributes in God:

> It is proper to God's lordship and his fatherhood to be feared, as it is proper to his goodness to be loved; and it is proper to us who are his servants and his children to fear him, for his lordship and fatherhood, as it is proper to us to love him for his goodness (74:325).

Whoever loves God also fears God, and the experience of this on earth is a foreshadowing of the life of heaven:

> The natural attribute of fear which we have in this life by the grace-giving operation of the Holy Spirit will be the same in heaven before God, gentle, courteous, most sweet; and thus in love we shall be [homely] and close to God, and in fear we shall be gentle and courteous to God, and both the same, in the same way (74:325).[23]

Julian's notion that reverent fear increases with the perfection of love allows her to describe mystical union with God in a way that forbids any identification between the soul and God. The sense of the essential difference between creature and Creator is enhanced, not diminished, by the perfection of love.

The Saints in Heaven

Julian's description of heaven includes the community of the saints, that "blessed company" completely united in mind and will with God, who rejoice in the salvation of each other as much as they do in their own salvation. They also long, with Christ's love-longing, for the coming to bliss of those still on their earthly sojourn. Therefore Christians receive help from them, and "holy, endless friendship" (6:185).

Julian lived in an age well aware of the companionship of love and concern provided by the blessed in heaven to the church on earth. The intercession of the saints, the veneration of relics, and pilgrimage to sacred shrines were hallmarks of the late Middle Ages.[24] However, undoubtedly aware of the extremes to which such devotions could go, Julian exhibits a cautious attitude towards them.[25] It was much more important for her to enter into companionship with God in prayer than to pray to many saints. In speaking of the purpose of her first revelation, Julian makes the following comment:

> This revelation was given to my understanding to teach our souls wisely to adhere to the goodness of God; and in that same time our habits of prayer were brought to my mind, how in our ignorance of love we are accustomed to employ many intermediaries. Then I saw truly that it is more honor to God and more true delight if we faithfully pray to him for his goodness, and adhere to this by grace, with true understanding and steadfast belief, than if we employed all the intermediaries of which a heart may think. For if we employ all these intermediaries, this is too little and it is not complete honor to God; but his goodness is full and complete, and in it is nothing lacking (6:184–85).

Julian intimates that, for many in her day, devotion to the saints had replaced prayer to God, chiefly because God's goodness and love were poorly understood. Through the publication of her revelations, which emphasize God's love so strongly, she hopes to help rectify this.

There is a place for devotion to the saints: "the intermediaries which the goodness of God has ordained to help us are very lovely and many," and it pleases God "that we seek him and honor him through intermediaries," as long as we understand that God is "the goodness of everything." The proper attitude towards the saints is the same that holds for everything else in Julian's understanding of reality. One cannot find rest in anything created, but only in God. Though it may be good and beneficial on occasion to pray to the saints, "the highest form of prayer is to the goodness of God, which comes down to us to our humblest needs." Furthermore, one must always remember that "the chief and principal intermediary is the blessed nature which [Christ] took of the virgin" (6:185). It is through the mediation of Jesus, especially the suffering Jesus, that one is put in touch with the inner life of the trinity.

Julian does consider the saints, however, as concrete evidence for the triumph of God's mercy and grace over sin. With the exception of Mary, the only saints she mentions are those whose sinfulness is well documented, such as David, Mary Magdalen, Peter and Paul, Thomas of India, and John of Beverly (38:242–43).[26] Since the saints once shared human weakness yet now enjoy honor in heaven, sinners can take courage that the same honor will come to them.

Mary: Prototype of the Perfect Christian

Mary is the only saint whom Julian "saw" in her revelations; she gained an inward understanding of "the virtues of her blessed soul, her truth, her wisdom, her love" through which Julian was taught to know herself and reverently to fear God (25:222). Mary functions in Julian's theology as a prototype for human nature. She is the true image of God, one whose own truth [or might], wisdom, and love luminously reflect the trinity.

Julian saw Mary on three occasions: "as she conceived, . . . as she had been under the cross, and . . . as she is now, in delight, honor and joy" (25:223). The first sight emphasizes Mary as the perfect example of human nature as created by God, the second reveals the way she shared in Christ's work of mercy, suffering compassionately with him and for him, and the third presents Mary as the human being perfected by grace, sharing in the three "heavens" of the trinity. All three works of God, nature, mercy, and grace, are seen in their effects upon Mary, the perfect Christian.

At the time of the Incarnation, Mary's attitude towards God's messenger reveals those virtues basic to the creature who realizes the Creator's greatness:

I saw her . . . [as] a simple, humble maiden, young in years, grown a little taller than a child, of the stature which she had when she conceived. Also God showed me part of the wisdom and the truth of her soul, and in this I understood the reverent contemplation with which she beheld her God, who is her creator, marvelling with great reverence that he was willing to be born of her who was a simple creature created by him. And this wisdom and truth, this knowledge of her creator's greatness and of her own created littleness, made her say very meekly to Gabriel: Behold me here, God's handmaiden (4:182).[27]

Mary is thus the perfection of creaturehood, the true image of God, "greater, more worthy, and more fulfilled, than everything else which God has created," except for the humanity of Christ (4:182).

When Julian saw Mary at the time of Christ's passion, she was given to understand the nature of her compassion for Christ:

Christ and she were so united in love that the greatness of her love was the cause of the greatness of her pain. For in this I saw a substance of natural love, which is developed by grace, which his creatures have for him, and this natural love was most perfectly and surpassingly revealed in his sweet mother; for as much as she loved him more than all others, her pain surpassed that of all others. For always, the higher, the stronger, the sweeter that love is, the more sorrow it is to the lover to see the body which he loved in pain (18:210).

Mary represents for Julian the perfection of the quality of compassion which she herself had prayed to attain: the grace of being able to "have the mind of Christ" in order to suffer with him. She represents the realism of Julian's approach to suffering. Though suffering is temporary, and will be cause for joy in heaven, it is nevertheless real and painful. It becomes even more painful, not less so, when one grows in love of Christ, because then one sorrows over the sufferings of Christ, whom one loves.

Finally, Julian saw Mary's glorification in heaven:

Just as before I had seen her small and simple, now [Christ] showed her high and noble and glorious and more pleasing to him than all creatures. And so he wishes it to be known that all who take delight in him should take delight in her, and in the delight that he has in her and she in him (25:222–23).

Julian makes an explicit link between Mary in glory and Mary at the foot of the cross. She sees the exalted Mary immediately after the countenance of the Crucified has turned to joy, and he has revealed to her the "three heavens" by which the trinity rejoice over Christ's sufferings, and the joy he takes in his side opened up for love. Then he "looked down on his right, and brought to . . . mind where our Lady stood at the time of his passion" (25:221). Julian does not see the sorrowing mother, but Mary glorious in heaven. Her glory, however, is intimately connected to the suffering she endured in union with the suffering and death of Christ. So it shall be for all the saved.

Julian understood her vision of Mary in glory as a revelation not only of Mary, but of the love God has for her:

> Because of the wonderful, exalted and singular love that he has for this sweet maiden, his blessed mother, our Lady St. Mary, he reveals her bliss and joy through the sense of these sweet words, as if he said, do you wish to see how I love her, so that you could rejoice with me in the love which I have in her and she has in me? (25:222).

Mary is therefore the model for the unity of love that exists between creature and God in heaven.

Furthermore, through the love Christ showed towards Mary, Julian understood an even deeper message of love for all who will be saved:

> And for greater understanding of these sweet words our good Lord speaks in love to all [humankind] who will be saved, addressing them all as one person, as if he said, do you wish to see in her how you are loved? It is for love of you that I have made her so exalted, so noble, so honorable; and this delights me. And I wish it to delight you (25:222).

Christ's love for all the saved motivated him to enter into Mary's womb, so that he might become "our mother in all things" (60:297). Julian therefore understands the motherhood of Mary towards humanity in terms of the motherhood of Christ:

> So our Lady is our mother, in whom we are all enclosed and born of her in Christ, for she who is mother of our savior is mother of all who are saved in our savior; and our savior is our true Mother, in whom we are endlessly born and out of whom we shall never come (57:292).

Mary is the mother of the whole Christ, "perfect humanity," which includes all the saved united to Christ in one renewed human nature (57:292).

Like all those on the path to salvation, Mary enjoyed in her earthly life the intimations of the life of heaven which are the fruits of the Spirit's work. These gifts come most easily and abundantly through prayer, and Mary is the model of the true contemplative:

Our good Lord showed our Lady St. Mary . . . to signify the exalted
wisdom and truth which were hers as she contemplated her creator. This
wisdom and truth showed her in contemplation how great, how exalted,
how mighty and how good was her God. The greatness and nobility of her
contemplation of God filled her full of reverent fear; and with this she saw
herself so small and so humble, so simple and so poor in comparison with
her God that this reverent fear filled her with humility. And founded on
this, she was filled with grace and with every kind of virtue, and she
surpasses all creatures (7:187).[28]

Except for Christ himself, there is no better example of the fully graced
image of God than Mary.

The Possibility of Universal Salvation

Throughout her revelations, Julian reminds us that she is speaking only
of those destined for salvation because "God showed me no one else"
(9:192). Yet this also causes her some perplexity concerning damnation,
about which nothing was revealed. In fact, her revelations seem to come
close to preaching *apocatastasis*, or universal salvation, and Julian sees this
as being in conflict with official Church teaching.[29] Though no clear
revelation about eternal damnation is ever given to her, Julian eventually
comes to some conclusions about it.

From the beginning to the end of her revelations, Julian had "two kinds
of contemplation," two points of view, from which to consider what was
revealed to her. The one supplied by her revelations was "endless continuing love, with certainty of protection and blessed salvation," the
notion summed up so often in the phrase "all will be well," and which
certainly tended towards *apocatastasis*. The other was "the common teaching of Holy Church" in which, until the time of her revelations, Julian
"had been instructed and grounded" and which she had "practiced and
understood" (46:258). Julian insists that the new insight supplied by her
revelations did not replace the teaching of the church:

And the contemplation of this [church teaching] did not leave me, for by
the revelation I was not moved or led away from it in any way at all; but I
was taught in the revelation to love it and rejoice in it, so that I might with
the help of our Lord and his grace increase and rise to more heavenly
knowledge and a higher loving (44:258–59).

Since both her revelations and church teaching come from God, they cannot contradict one another, but only contextualize and deepen each other.

Nonetheless, church teaching, as Julian understands it, seems incompatible with the tendency towards *apocatastasis* she sees in her revelations:

> And one article of our faith is that many creatures will be damned, such as the angels who fell out of heaven because of pride, who now are devils, and many . . . upon earth who die out of the faith of Holy Church, that is to say those who are pagans and many who have received baptism and who live unchristian lives and so die out of God's love. All these will be eternally condemned to hell, as Holy Church teaches me to believe (32:233).[30]

Julian believes that this teaching is "founded on God's word" which "will be preserved in all things." Indeed, Christ explicitly promises Julian, "I shall preserve my word in everything," but in the same breath also promises, "I shall make everything well." Julian understands this dual promise to mean that she must believe firmly in both church teaching and the more universally salvific promise of her revelations (32:233), and at first she views this as an irreconcilable contradiction. If church teaching were indeed true, it seems to her "impossible that every kind of thing should be well." The only answer she receives to her perplexity is Christ's statement that "what is impossible to you is not impossible to me" (32:233).[31]

But Julian's speculative mind will not let her rest with this, and she seeks greater clarity. She desires "some sight of hell and of purgatory," not because she wants confirmation of church teaching, but so that she might better understand it. This sight is never granted to her (33:234). Instead, she is reminded of God's attitude towards the devil which had already been revealed in the fifth revelation:

> In God there can be no anger . . . and it is with power and justice, to the profit of all who will be saved, that [God] opposes the damned, who in malice and malignity work to frustrate and oppose God's will. Also I saw our Lord scorn [the devil's] malice and despise him as nothing . . . . For in this God revealed that the devil is damned. . . . I saw that on Judgment Day he will be generally scorned by all who will be saved, of whose salvation he has had great envy. For then he will see that all the woe and tribulation which he has caused them will be changed into the increase of their eternal joy. And all the pain and the sorrow that he wanted to bring them into will go forever with him to hell (13:201–2).

God's making all well could conceivably include the ultimate destruction of the devil along with all the evils he attempted to inflict upon the human race. Julian speculates that the same might be true of people who become enslaved to Satan:

> I understand that every creature who is of the devil's condition in this life and so dies is no more mentioned before God and all his saints than is the devil, notwithstanding that they belong to the human race, whether they have been baptized or not (33:234).[32]

It is not clear what Julian means here. Perhaps God and the saints simply overlook the damned, not taking them seriously since they pose no threat to them. She could, however, be implying that the damned will fall into oblivion, into nothingness, rather than suffer some eternal torment.[33] She certainly receives no pictures of eternal hell-fire. Elsewhere, she equates the pain of hell with despair (17:209). Her revelations remain silent on the subject: "the revelation was shown to reveal goodness, and little mention was made in it of evil" (33:234).

While Julian seems able to entertain the possibility of damnation for certain persons who are truly evil, she questions its application towards the multitudes which seem to be condemned by church teaching. She singles out the Jews for special mention:

> But I saw nothing so exactly specified concerning the Jews who put [Christ] to death; and nonetheless I knew in my faith that they were eternally accursed and condemned, except those who were converted by grace (33:234).

"All will be well" continues to seem irreconcilable with the church's judgment on this issue.

Another possible way out of the contradiction between her revelations and church teaching is through the subordination of the particular to the general. At one point Julian asks whether someone she loves will be saved, and she is given no reply. Instead, she is counseled to accept "generally" the lessons she learns about salvation, "for it is more honor to God to contemplate him in all things than in any one special thing" (35:236). If she can learn to act in accordance with this, Julian thinks, "I should not be glad because of any special thing or be greatly distressed by anything at all, for all will be well; for the fulness of joy is to contemplate God in everything" (35:237). By viewing the whole picture, in which God has ordained everything "for the best" and always leads it to that end, one might conceivably be able to include the eternal damnation of particular persons as part of that process.

However, Julian is also taught that the promise "all will be well" specifically includes the particular: "every kind of thing." God takes heed not only of "the noble and great" but also of the "little and small," and God wants us to know "that the smallest thing will not be forgotten" (32:231–32). Contemplating God's activity on behalf of humanity "in general" does not exclude particular individuals (36:240), as is evident in the following passage reminiscent of the gospel parable of the lost sheep:[34]

> [Christ] dwells here in us, and rules us, and cares for us in this life, and brings us to his bliss. And so he will do as long as any soul is on earth who will come to heaven; and so much so that if there were no such soul on earth except one, he would be with it, all alone, until he had brought it up into his bliss (80:335–36).

Julian's revelations strongly suggest that the "all" that will be well in God's promise includes "every particular" human being, although this is never stated absolutely.

In further support of this conclusion, the stress throughout Julian's revelations on the goodness of creation, situated within the eternal goodness and power of God, tends towards the absolute:

> I saw most truly that [God] never changed his purpose *in any kind of thing*, nor ever will eternally. For there was nothing unknown to him in his just ordinance before time began, and therefore *all things were set in order*, before anything was made, as it would endure eternally. And *no kind of thing will fail* in that respect, for he has made *everything totally good* (11:198–99; emphasis mine).

This is why sin is ultimately powerless against God's eternal might, wisdom, and goodness.[35]

Julian's revelations lead to the conclusion that it is at least much more probable that everyone will be saved than that some will be damned. Their emphasis upon trust in salvation is so strong, and the absence of anything to the contrary so glaring, that this is likely the conclusion that Julian herself reached, though she does not say so explicitly.

This conclusion is further supported by two other insights which Julian received. First, the full reality of God and God's purposes are finally beyond human understanding in this world, even beyond the teachings of the church, though those are truly God's word. Julian talks about this insight by contrasting God's viewpoint with that of the church in terms of two "portions," two mysteries, and two judgments.

God's will for humanity is contained in two portions, one open and revealed, the other hidden. The open portion contains everything related to "our savior and our salvation." It includes "all who are of good will," that is, all the just who live the sacramental life, and follow the teachings of the church and the inner inspirations of the Holy Spirit:

> We are bound to this [open portion] by God, and drawn and counselled and taught, inwardly by the Holy Spirit, and outwardly through the same grace by Holy Church. Our Lord wants us to be occupied in this, rejoicing in him, for he rejoices in us. And the more plentifully we accept from this with reverence and humility, the more do we deserve thanks from him, and the more profit do we win for ourselves (30:228).

The other portion includes "all which is additional to our salvation," which I take to mean God's will for those outside the pale of Christianity and unacquainted with the gospel message of salvation, along with all the aspects of human history that do not appear consistent with Christian doctrine. This is hidden from human understanding in this life:

> For this is our Lord's privy counsel, and it is fitting to God's royal dominion to keep his privy counsel in peace, and it is fitting to his servants out of obedience and respect not to wish to know his counsel (30:228).[36]

Julian speaks in a similar fashion of two kinds of mystery:

> One is this great mystery, with all the individual mysteries pertaining to it, and these [God] wishes us to know as hidden until the time that he wishes to reveal them to us plainly. The other is the mysteries which he himself plainly showed in this revelation, for these are mysteries which he wishes to make open and known to us (34:235).

Here Julian's "private" revelations are included with the teachings of the church as part of the open revelation which God wants humans to know.

Julian also speaks of two "judgments," in which her revelations are distinguished from church teaching: the first is "that fair, sweet judgment" which was shown in her revelations, wherein God always looks upon sinners with love; the second is "mixed" human judgment, sometimes "good and lenient," and sometimes "hard and painful." Julian calls the latter the "lower judgment" and equates it with the judgment of the church: "The lower judgment had previously been taught me in Holy

Church, and therefore I could not in any way ignore the lower judgment" (45:256–57). The higher judgment, however, comes from God's eternal viewpoint, and while stated as general fact in Julian's revelations, still contains many mysteries hidden within it. The full realization of its meaning will not be available until the end of time.

In all three cases, God's activity towards the world is not limited by the church's understanding and interpretation of God's revelation, even though church teaching is truly God's word. There remains a profound mystery surrounding God's dealings with humanity.

The second insight Julian received in support of universal salvation deals with a mysterious deed which God will perform at the end of time:

> There is a deed which the blessed trinity will perform on the last day, as I see it, and what the deed will be and how it will be performed is unknown to every creature who is inferior to Christ, and it will be until the deed is done. . . . This is the great deed ordained by our Lord God from without beginning, treasured and hidden in his blessed breast, known only to himself, through which deed he will make all things well. For just as the blessed trinity created all things from nothing, just so will the same blessed trinity make everything well which is not well (32:232–33).

Julian must mean some further salvific act on the part of God whereby all those presently unconnected with Christianity will somehow be saved at the end of time.[37] She refuses to speculate more specifically about it, because God does not wish her to do so (33:235). God's love wants human beings to know it will occur, and it is summarized in the promise, "all will be well." Trusting in this promise will allow Christians "to be at ease in our souls and at peace in love, disregarding every disturbance which could hinder our true rejoicing." But God's power and wisdom, also out of love for humanity, "want to conceal it and hide it from us, what it will be and how it will be done" (32:232).

These two insights, working together, allow Julian to make an eventual reconciliation between church teaching and the message of her revelations. Church teaching is the open portion of God's revelation. God allows the possibility of damnation to be one of the teachings which can lead to salvation. Eternal damnation is understood in a way similar to Julian's reflection on mortal sin, which can be interpreted as "deadly" for us, though it is not actually so in God's sight.[38] Church teachings about damnation, like those about mortal sin, are legitimate and necessary; without them human beings would not realize the horror of sin, nor the value of the sacramental life of grace within the church, and they would be tempted to presumption.

But Julian's revelations provide a corrective to this teaching, which she sees as even more important. The fear engendered by any unmitigated teaching about eternal damnation could, in fact, lead many away from salvation and into despair.[39] God's promise that "all will be well," points beyond specific church doctrine to a God utterly more loving and mysterious than humans can understand. The promise that such a loving and generous God will indeed "make all well" allows God's lovers to take courage and find comfort in the midst of their struggle with evil. The way to salvation is through trust and love, not through painful fear.

Julian eventually came to the conclusion that both ways of looking at salvation are needed:

> It seemed to me that it was necessary to see and to know that we are sinners and commit many evil deeds which we ought to forsake, and leave many good deeds undone which we ought to do, so that we deserve pain, blame and wrath. And despite all this, I saw truly that our Lord was never angry, and never will be. . . . I saw in the same revelation that there are many hidden mysteries which can never be known until the time when God in his goodness has made us worthy to see them (46:259).

With this realization she found a resolution to the apparent contradictions between her revelations and church teaching. She tells us, "I am well satisfied, waiting upon our Lord's will in this great marvel. And now I submit myself to my mother, Holy Church, as a simple child should" (46:259).

Julian does not, strictly speaking, teach a doctrine of universal salvation. For one thing, she allows the possibility that the devil and those enslaved to the powers of evil will sink into nothingness at the end of time. She keeps eternal damnation as a possibility, and admits that church teaching on this subject is legitimate. But she finds it far more important to stress the power of God's love to conquer evil in all its forms and to bring "every kind of thing" into the perfection for which it was created. Since God's love is infinitely more powerful than diabolical or human efforts to perpetrate evil, we can hope that God will effect the salvation even of those whom human judgment deems irrevocably lost.[40] Since God's might, wisdom, and love exceed by far human ability to know, one ought to submit one's understanding to the greater judgment of God. Finally, Julian expresses faith in some eschatological deed, presently beyond human knowledge and understanding, through which God will bring everything into the fulfillment established as God's will from the beginning.

If Julian's teaching can be summed up in one word, that word is love. Her whole effort is to present to her troubled times the picture of a God who loves absolutely the whole creation which is itself an expression of divine love. Eschatological hope is not misplaced when it trusts that this love can bring all into eternal fulfillment. No more fitting conclusion to a discussion of Julian's eschatology can be found than the words with which she herself ends *Showings*, words summing up the meaning of her whole revelatory experience:

And from the time that it [the showing] was revealed, I desired many times to know in what was our Lord's meaning. And fifteen years after and more, I was answered in spiritual understanding, and it was said: What, do you wish to know your Lord's meaning in this thing? Know it well, love was his meaning. Who reveals it to you? Love. What did he reveal to you? Love. Why does he reveal it to you? For love. Remain in this, and you will know more of the same. But you will never know different, without end.

So I was taught that love is our Lord's meaning. And I saw very certainly in this and in everything that before God made us he loved us, which love was never abated and never will be. And in this love he has done all his works, and in this love he has made all things profitable to us, and in this love our life is everlasting. In our creation we had beginning, but the love in which he created us was in him from without beginning. In this love we have our beginning, and all this shall we see in God without end (86:342–43).

Notes

Introduction

1. Virginia Woolf, *A Room of One's Own* (New York: Harcourt Brace Jovanovich, 1957), 93.

2. Women's silence in the whole history of religion, especially in the West, is similarly noted by Valerie Saiving, "Androcentrism in Religious Studies," *The Journal of Religion* 56:2 (1976): 177–97.

3. Woolf, 4, 110, 117.

4. Elizabeth Alvilda Petroff, ed., *Medieval Women's Visionary Literature* (New York/ Oxford: Oxford University Press, 1986), 4.

5. Gerda Lerner, *The Majority Finds Its Past: Placing Women in History* (Oxford: Oxford University Press, 1979); Anne E. Carr, *Transforming Grace: Christian Tradition and Women's Experience* (San Francisco: Harper & Row, 1988), 63–76.

6. This is the view of many contemporary theologians, not only feminists. Karl Rahner, for one, has strongly urged consulting the experiences of mystics and saints as authentic sources of theology, in order to repair the rift between "lived piety and abstract theology," and the entire sixteenth volume of *Theological Investigations* is devoted to this subject (New York: Crossroad, 1983); all further references to *Theological Investigations* are abbreviated *TI* and are from the edition published by Crossroad in 1982–83. See also Harvey D. Egan, S.J., *Christian Mysticism: The Future of a Tradition* (New York: Pueblo Publishing Company, 1984), 374–81; William M. Thompson, *Fire and Light: The Saints and Theology* (New York: Paulist Press, 1987).

7. There is a considerable variety of feminist theologies. I situate myself among those known as Christian reformist or revisionist feminists, and am especially indebted to Roman Catholic feminist scholars such as Rosemary Radford Ruether, Elisabeth Schüssler Fiorenza, Anne Carr, and Elizabeth Johnson.

8. Jean Leclercq makes this point in his preface to *Showings*, translated by Edmund Colledge and James Walsh from the critical text (New York: Paulist Press, 1978), 6.

9. Recently, Julian's text has begun to be studied as theology, spurred in part by the publication of its critical edition: Edmund Colledge and James Walsh, *A Book of Showings to the Anchoress Julian of Norwich*, 2 vols. (Toronto: Pontifical Institute of Mediaeval Studies, 1978). In their introduction, the editors laid out sequentially the theological content of each revelation, but made no attempt to analyze the work from a systematic viewpoint. (NB: All future references to this volume will be cited with the abbreviation "C&W.") Since then, three authors have produced extended studies of Julian's theology: John P. H. Clark, "*Fiducia* in Julian of Norwich," *Downside Review* 99 (1981): 97–108, 214–29, "Predestination in Christ according to Julian of Norwich" and "Nature, Grace and the Trinity in Julian of Norwich," *Downside Review* 100 (1982): 79–91 and 203–20 respectively; Brant Pelphrey, *Love Was His Meaning: The Theology and Mysticism of Julian of Norwich* (Salzburg: Institut für Anglistik und Amerikanistik, 1982); and Grace M. Jantzen, *Julian of Norwich: Mystic and Theologian* (New York: Paulist Press, 1988).

10. Of first importance is Thomas Merton, who called Julian "one of the greatest

English theologians" who has produced "a coherent and indeed systematically constructed corpus of doctrine" (*Mystics and Zen Masters* [New York: Ferrar, Straus & Giroux, 1961], 140–41), and "with greater clarity, depth and order than St. Theresa" (*Conjectures of a Guilty Bystander* [Garden City: Doubleday, 1966], 191–92). George Tyrell saw Julian's work as "a doctrinal system" ahead of its time, "prescient of . . . views that had not yet appeared above the theological horizon" (*XVI Revelations of Divine Love Shewed to Mother Juliana of Norwich* [London: Kegan Paul, Trench, Trübner, 1902], ix and xv).

Others who noted Julian's speculative nature include Grace Warrack, ed., *Revelations of Divine Love* (London: Methuen, 1901), xliv, l; Roger Hudleston, ed., *Revelations of Divine Love Shewed to a Devout Ankress by Name Julian of Norwich* (London: Burns & Oates, 1927), x; Thomas W. Coleman, *English Mystics of the Fourteenth Century* (London: Epworth Press, 1938), 148; Clifton Wolters, ed., *Revelations of Divine Love* (Harmondsworth: Penguin Books, 1966), 19–20; P. Franklin Chambers, *Juliana of Norwich: An Introductory Appreciation and An Interpretive Anthology* (New York: Harper & Bros., 1953), 18–22, 42; Evelyn Underhill, *The Mystics of the Church* (New York: Schocken Books, 1964, reprint 1971), 128; Paul Molinari, *Julian of Norwich: The Teaching of a 14th Century English Mystic* (London: Longmans, Green, 1958, reprint 1979), v; Conrad Pepler, *The English Religious Heritage* (St. Louis: B. Herder Book Co., 1958), 306–7; David Knowles, *The English Mystical Tradition* (London: Burns & Oates, 1961), 129–30; Wolfgang Riehle, *The Middle English Mystics* (London: Routledge & Kegan Paul, 1981), 10–11.

11. Ann Oakley, *Sex, Gender and Society* (New York: Harper & Row, 1972), 158–72; John Archer and Barbara Lloyd, *Sex and Gender* (Cambridge: Cambridge University Press, 1985); Carr, 76–84.

12. See Saiving's similar analysis, and the questions this suggests for the student of religion ("Androcentrism," 177–80, and n. 4).

13. The phrase is Paul Ricoeur's. See his *Interpretation Theory: Discourse and the Surplus of Meaning* (Ft. Worth: Texas Christian University Press, 1976), especially 45–69.

14. Carolyn Walker Bynum, "Introduction: The Complexity of Symbols" in Bynum, Stevan Harrell, and Paula Richman, eds., *Gender and Religion: On the Complexity of Symbols* (Boston: Beacon Press, 1986), 1–16.

15. For the notion of "passing over," see John Dunne, *A Search for God in Time and Memory* (Notre Dame: University of Notre Dame Press, 1977), vii–xi, 1–8.

Chapter 1: Historical Background

1. My discussion of Julian's historical context is intentionally brief; it has been treated extensively elsewhere (Jantzen, pp. 3–50; C&W, 33–59).

2. It was common practice for an anchoress to take the saint's name of the church to which the anchorhold was attached (Pelphrey, 9, n. 11).

3. ii:127, 2:177, 3:179. While the year is undisputed, the actual date of the revelations is not certain. Some manuscript versions of the text read "May viii" rather than "xiii" (Jantzen, 13, n. 10; Pelphrey, 1, n. 1).

4. ii:127–28, xx:162, xxii:163, 165, 3:179, 65:309–10, 66:310.

5. The only extant copy of the Short Text is a manuscript which does not date back to Julian herself, but is a copy in a mid-fifteenth century hand. Thus we have no absolute guarantee that it is an exact replica, without contamination from the already extant Long Text, of what Julian herself wrote as her initial reflections. For textual and historical information about this manuscript, see C&W, 1–5, 10–12, 18–19. For the origin of the

theory that the Short Text was written twenty years earlier than the other, rather than being a summary of the Long Text, see Molinari, 4–6.

6. There are three complete extant manuscripts of the Long Text and one complete early printed edition, none of which can be dated before 1650. There are also two short collections of extracts, one of which is circa 1500, the other 1650. For complete textual and historical information about these, see C&W, 6–10, 12–18 and their "Editing Julian of Norwich's *Revelations*: A Progress Report," *Mediaeval Studies* 38 (1976): 404–7.

7. C&W, 25.

8. Ibid., 33.

9. Ibid., 33–35. Actually, there are bequests to an unnamed anchoress at St. Julian's Church, who could have been Julian, up until 1429; see Norman Tanner, *The Church in Late Medieval Norwich, 1370–1532* (Toronto: Pontifical Institute of Mediaeval Studies, 1984), 200, n. 29.

10. However, Colledge and Walsh do not think Julian entered the anchorhold until after she had completed the Long Text ("Editing Julian," 417–18).

11. *The Book of Margery Kempe*, ed. and trans. W. Butler-Bowdon (New York: The Devin-Adair Company, 1944). The description of Margery's visit with Julian is found on 33–34, from whence the following quotations are cited. For the Middle English version, see *The Book of Margery Kempe*, EETS 212, ed. Sanford Brown Meech and Hope Emily Allen (London: Oxford University Press, 1940), 42–43.

12. Tanner, 200, n. 29; C&W, 35. For the latter's full account of the evidence from Margery Kempe, see 35–38.

13. The source for this may have been a gloss on one of the psalms; see Meech and Allen, 257, n. 3/2 and 279, n. 43/11–12. It could also be a conflation of several scriptural texts (C&W, 37).

14. "Editing Julian," 407–23; C&W, 43–59. For a complete list of what Colledge and Walsh have discovered as the possible sources for Julian's work, see C&W, 775–78.

15. There were many compilations of theological writings translated into English in Julian's day, most often for nuns who could not read Latin. For example, *The Chastising of God's Children* (written sometime between 1373 and 1401) contains translations of excerpts from Augustine as well as Gregory, Cassian, Isidore, Anselm, Bernard, and Aelred of Rievaulx. See Colledge's Introduction to *The Chastising of God's Children and The Treatise of Perfection of the Sons of God*, ed. Joyce Bazire and Eric Colledge (Oxford: Basil Blackwell, 1957), 34–46.

16. Jaroslav Pelikan has demonstrated the primacy of Augustine in the early Middle Ages, which, although challenged, interpreted, and revised, continued as the dominant influence throughout the medieval period (*The Christian Tradition: A History of the Development of Doctrine*, Vol. 3: *The Growth of Medieval Theology (600–1300)* [Chicago: University of Chicago Press, 1978], 16–50).

17. A thorough study of the influence of twelfth century spiritual writings upon Julian's theology would be instructive. Giles Constable has shown that these writings became increasingly popular in the late Middle Ages. See his "Twelfth-Century Spirituality and the Late Middle Ages," *Medieval and Renaissance Studies* 5, ed. O. B. Hardison, Jr. (Chapel Hill: University of North Carolina Press, 1972), 27–60, and "The Popularity of Twelfth-Century Spiritual Writers in the Late Middle Ages" in *Renaissance Studies in Honor of Hans Baron*, ed. Anthony Molho and John A. Tedeschi (DeKalb, IL: Northern Illinois University Press, 1971), 5–28.

18. It is impossible to prove this absolutely, but I think their arguments convincing, as does Clark ("*Fiducia*," 97).

19. The editors note incidences of this throughout their critical version. A complete list of scriptural passages alluded to by Julian is found in C&W, 779–88. For some examples of how Julian cited scripture, see "Editing Julian," 408–9 and C&W, 45–47.

20. Henry Hargreaves of St. Andrew's University, the leading expert in medieval English biblical translations, could find no vernacular version which matched Julian's scriptural citations. In every case Julian never used the same English words for crucial Latin words, but always synonyms. While this does not rule out the possibility that she had an English bible no longer extant, or that someone else translated the passages for her, or that she may have known French and used an Anglo-Norman bible, the editors conclude that the more likely possibility is that she knew Latin herself ("Editing Julian," 409–10). For English translations of the bible extant in Julian's time, see Margaret Deanesly, *The Lollard Bible and Other Medieval Biblical Versions* (Cambridge: Cambridge University Press, 1920), 140–55, 174–80, 220–21, 252–88, 298–318.

21. They include an appendix listing forty-seven such figures, with a definition and an example of each from Julian's text (C&W, 735–48). Most of the definitions are from Harry Caplan's translation of the pseudo-Ciceronian *Rhetorica Ad Herennium* (Cambridge: Harvard University Press, 1954). For a discussion of Julian's rhetorical skills, see C&W, 47–52 and "Editing Julian," 422–23. On medieval rhetoric in general, see James J. Murphy, *Rhetoric in the Middle Ages: A History of Rhetorical Theory from Saint Augustine to the Renaissance* (Berkeley: University of California Press, 1974).

22. C&W, 50.

23. Colledge and Walsh's rhetorical analysis of Julian's text has convinced me of the inadequacy of the amanuensis theory to explain its writing. The theological truths being expressed are so closely bound to their rhetorical expressions, that to consider Julian the author of the ideas without being the author of the rhetorical constructions makes no sense. Unless we want to deny any form of authorship to Julian, I think we must accept the fact that she wrote *Showings* herself. This opinion differs from earlier interpreters of Julian such as David Knowles (121) and Marion Glasscoe (see the introduction to her edition of Julian, *A Revelation of Love* [Exeter: Exeter University Press, 1976], xv–xvi).

24. C&W, 48.

25. For information about the English anchoress, see Ann K. Warren, "The Nun as Anchoress: England 1100–1500" in *Distant Echoes: Medieval Religious Women*, Vol. 1, ed. John A. Nichols and Lillian Thomas Shank (Kalamazoo: Cistercian Publications, 1984); Linda Georgianna, *The Solitary Self: Individuality in the "Ancrene Wisse"* (Cambridge: Harvard University Press, 1981); Francis D. S. Darwin, *The English Medieval Recluse* (London: SPCK, 1944); Rotha Mary Clay, *The Hermits and Anchorites of England* (London: Methuen, 1914; reprint, Detroit: Singing Tree Press, 1968); Tanner, 57–64; Jantzen, 28–48.

26. Colledge and Walsh think it probable that Julian was a nun, although it cannot be proven ("Editing Julian," 417–20). If Julian had been a nun before she became an anchoress, she probably belonged to Carrow Abbey, a Benedictine house just outside Norwich (the only nunnery in the vicinity). St. Julian's Church, where Julian had her anchorhold, was under the patronage of Carrow Abbey (C&W, 43–44; Tanner, 23, 27, 60). See Eileen Power, *Medieval English Nunneries c. 1275 to 1535* (Cambridge: Cambridge University Press, 1922), 12 and 268 for evidence that Carrow Abbey had a school for girls, although the quality of education it provided was probably quite limited.

27. "By the thirteenth century the institutional church had pretty well closed off the possibility of convent life for any except the most aristocratic women," Elizabeth Petroff, *Consolation of the Blessed* (New York: Alta Gaia Society, 1979), 21; Eileen Power, *Medieval Women*, ed. M. M. Postan (Cambridge: Cambridge University Press, 1975), 89–90; idem., *Medieval Nunneries*, 4–24.

28. Janet Coleman, *English Literature in History, 1350–1400: Medieval Readers and Writers* (London: Hutchinson, 1981), 18–57; Margaret Aston, *Lollards and Reformers: Images and Literacy in Late Medieval Religion* (London: Hambledon Press, 1984), 101–3; Power, *Medieval Women*, 86; Nicholas Orme, *English Schools in the Middle Ages* (London: Methuen, 1973), 52–55.

29. Power, *Medieval Nunneries*, 237–55; Orme, 52–55. After the Norman conquest, French had become the language generally used at the English court and in all public offices, except for the university and the church where Latin was the official language.

30. J. Coleman, 18–57.

31. On the movement to make spiritual writings accessible to the laity, see David Lyle Jeffrey, ed., *The Law of Love: English Spirituality in the Age of Wyclif* (Grand Rapids: William B. Eerdmans, 1988), 28–47.

32. C&W, 39–42; Tanner, 18–42, 191–97.

33. For example, see Pelphrey, 18–28.

34. Petroff points out that the transfer of the central seats of learning from the monasteries to the universities effectively closed the door to women's access to any advanced formal education (*Consolation*, 19).

35. C&W, 47; Molinari, 10–11; Jean Leclercq, *The Love of Learning and the Desire for God*, 2nd ed., trans. Catharine Misrahi (New York: Fordham University Press, 1974), 162–64. For a few other interpretations of Julian's disclaimer, see Jantzen, 15–16.

36. Underhill, 127. Julian's formative effect upon the English language has long been studied by English literature scholars. See, for example, Robert Karl Stone, *Middle English Prose Style: Margery Kempe and Julian of Norwich* (The Hague: Mouton, 1970) and Sr. Mary Arthur Knowlton, *The Influence of Richard Rolle and Julian of Norwich on the Middle English Lyrics* (The Hague: Mouton, 1973).

37. For the development of the medieval devotion to the passion see Richard W. Southern, *The Making of the Middle Ages* (New Haven: Yale University Press, 1959), 231–38.

38. See the Modern English translation by Mary B. Salu, *The Ancrene Riwle* (London: Burns & Oates, 1955), 46–52, 80.

39. Caroline Walker Bynum, *Holy Feast and Holy Fast: The Religious Significance of Food to Medieval Women* (Berkeley: University of California Press, 1987), 120, 199–200, 209; Riehle, 28–29; Petroff, *Visionary Literature*, 9–14.

40. Contrition, compassion, and longing for God comprise a concise description of compunction, the Benedictine ideal virtue for the development of the contemplative life (Leclercq, *The Love of Learning*, 37–41; C&W, 72).

41. This is consistent with the Western mystical tradition, which has always viewed psycho-physical phenomena as secondary and nonessential to the mystical experience itself; see Cuthbert Butler, *Western Mysticism: The Teaching of Ss. Augustine, Gregory and Bernard on Contemplation and the Contemplative Life*, 2nd ed. (London: Constable, 1926), 50–55, 83–87, 115–19; Egan, 303–5; Molinari, 49–59.

42. Julian describes the course of her illness in graphic detail (ii:127–29, 3:179–81), from which one author has attempted to diagnose the actual disease afflicting her: James T.

McIlwain, "The 'Bodelye syeknes' of Julian of Norwich," *Journal of Medieval History* 10 (1984): 167–80. Julian's illness and its possible causes have also been analyzed by Molinari (21–31); his effort to prove her illness had a divine rather than an organic or psychosomatic cause seems to me unnecessary. What is important is how Julian viewed her illness (as coming from God), a view that could easily have accompanied what medical science would consider of organic or psychosomatic origin (McIlwain, 171–72). I do, however, agree with Molinari's conclusion that Julian does not exhibit the signs of a neurotic or hysterical personality, based upon the good sense evidenced in her text (cf. C&W, 67–69). See also Robert H. Thouless, *The Lady Julian: A Psychological Study* (London: SPCK, 1924).

43. One of the common meanings of the *imitatio Christi* in the latter Middle Ages was the literal participation in the physical sufferings of Christ's passion (Bynum, *Holy Feast*, 207, 211–12).

44. Julian probably makes this remark to stress that what happened subsequently was not due to her own wishful thinking or delusion, but was a true gift from God. She herself has a moment of doubt about this (xxi:162).

45. Julian's analysis bears some similarity to the Augustinian classification of visions as corporeal, imaginative, and intellectual, corresponding to the faculty affected by the sight: the external senses, the imagination, and the intellect, respectively (Butler, 36, 52; Egan, 307–9). One text which Julian may have known, *The Chastising of God's Children*, in a passage dependent upon Augustine's *De genesi ad litteram* 12.6–11, 32 and upon Gregory's *Moralia* 28, has a lengthy description of these three kinds of visions (Bazire and Colledge, 169–72). Molinari has analyzed Julian's visions in terms of this classification. He doubts that her bodily sights are corporeal visions, but are better explained as imaginative, a conclusion with which I am in agreement (60–67; cf. C&W, 74–75). This is corroborated by Julian herself; when she describes the blood pouring from Christ's body as a result of the scourging, she says, "I saw this blood run so plentifully that it seemed to me that if it had in fact been happening there, the bed and everything around it would have been soaked in blood" (viii:137; cf. 12:199–200; C&W, 87).

46. She is also precise about the way she has transmitted her revelations in the text: "About the bodily [sight] I have said as I saw, as truly as I am able. And about the words formed, I have repeated them just as our Lord revealed them to me. And about the spiritual [sight], I have told a part, but I can never tell it in full; and therefore I am moved to say more about this spiritual [sight], as God will give me grace" (xxiii:167).

47. Women visionaries who either wrote or dictated accounts of their revelations include Hildegard of Bingen (d. 1179), Elizabeth of Schönau (d. 1165), Mechtild of Magdeburg (d. c. 1282), Mechtild of Hackeborn (d. 1298), Gertrude the Great (d. c. 1302), Angela of Foligno (d. 1309), Christina of Stommeln (d. 1312), Margaret Ebner (d. 1351), Christine Ebner (d. 1356), Bridget of Sweden (d. 1373), Adelheid Langmann (d. 1375), Catherine of Siena (d. 1380), Katherine of Sweden (d. 1391), Dorothea of Prussia (d. 1394), listed in Hope Allen's "Prefatory Note" to *The Book of Margery Kempe*, lx. For a study of the flowering of this tradition, see Caroline Walker Bynum, "Women Mystics in the Thirteenth Century: The Case of the Nuns of Helfta" in *Jesus as Mother: Studies in the Spirituality of the High Middle Ages* (Berkeley: University of California Press, 1982), 170–262. For a sampling of the writings of these women, see Katharina M. Wilson, ed., *Medieval Women Writers* (Athens: University of Georgia Press, 1984) and Petroff, *Visionary Literature*.

48. Hope Emily Allen's promise to do so was never fulfilled. For the beginning of her efforts in this direction, see her Prefatory Note to *The Book of Margery Kempe*, liii-lxviii.

Wolfgang Riehle has continued her investigation in his comparative study of the imagery used by continental and English mystics (especially 24–33, 165–68). We know that Mechtild of Hackeborn's *Book of Special Grace* was translated into English in Julian's day, and Colledge and Walsh make frequent comparisons between this and Julian's text (C&W, 153). Marguerite Porete's *Mirror of Simple Souls* was also in circulation in a Middle English translation. The cult of St. Brigid of Sweden was extremely popular in England in the early fifteenth century, when an English translation of her *Revelations* circulated widely and when the Birgittine Order was established at the famous Syon Abbey, but these events are too late to establish a connection with Julian's text; however, there was a Latin version of Brigid's *Revelations* extant in England around 1373, and it is conceivable that Julian may have had access to it (W. P. Cumming, ed., *The Revelations of Saint Birgitta*, EETS 178 [London: Oxford University Press, 1929], xxix–xxxix). A portion of Catherine of Siena's *Dialogue*, entitled *The Orcherd of Syon*, was translated into English for the Birgittine Order in the early fifteenth century, but again too late to have influenced Julian (Jeffrey, 18, 197–206).

49. Norman Tanner establishes the link between Norwich and these regions as an important one, and explicitly links Julian with their influences (xvii, 58, 64–66).

50. Petroff's effort is to expand the common tripartite division of the mystical life (the purgative, illuminative and unitive phases) "which applies primarily to the experiences of male mystics trained in an abstract intellectual tradition" into a schemata more adequately descriptive of the more affective form of meditation practiced by most medieval women (*Consolation*, 39–82). Bynum thinks Petroff "overinterprets the evidence," but has "brilliant insights" into women's mystical experience (*Holy Feast*, 317, n. 47).

51. Petroff, *Visionary Literature*, 6–7; note the severe ascetical practices of Marie D'Oignies (179–83), Christina of St. Trond (184–88), and Catherine of Siena (239, 267–68).

52. Ibid., 7–8; such visions predominate in the experiences of Elisabeth of Schönau (161–68), Marie d'Oignies (181), and Christina of St. Trond (187–88).

53. Ibid., 8–9; of the selections in Petroff's anthology, only Hildegard of Bingen (151–58) and Elisabeth of Schönau (159–60, 169–70) provide examples of doctrinal visions.

54. There are exceptions, of course, and Hildegard of Bingen, who lived several centuries before Julian, is perhaps the most notable one.

55. Petroff, *Visionary Literature*, 9–11; these meditative visions were often full of tender, intimate detail. See, for example, Christina of Markyate's vision of Mary (144–45), Marie d'Oignies' experience of Joseph, Mary, and the Child Jesus (181–82), and Margery Kempe's imaginative sharing in Mary's life experiences (318–20).

56. iii:129, iv:131, vii:136, viii:137, x:141, xii:144, and the corresponding places in the Long Text, especially the elaboration upon Christ's dying in 16:206–7.

57. Elisabeth of Schönau, for example, frequently had visions of Sts. John the Baptist, Peter and Paul, Benedict, and John the Evangelist (Petroff, *Visionary Literature*, 160, 162–64, 168–69).

58. Ibid., 11–14.

59. Ibid., 14–19; the most highly developed examples of this in Petroff's anthology are Hadewijch of Brabant (195–200), Mechthild of Magdeburg (212–20), and Gertrude the Great (222–30). See also Bynum, *Jesus as Mother*, 170–262; Riehle, 29, 44–47; Jantzen, 61–70.

60. i:127, 51:278, 52:279, 58:293.

61. Petroff, *Visionary Literature*, pp. 19–20.

62. Ibid., 3–53; Petroff, *Consolation*, 39–40.

63. Petroff, *Consolation*, 3–4, 12.

64. Karl Rahner, "Mystical Experience and Mystical Theology," *TI* XVII, 90–99.

65. Colledge and Walsh note that, between the writing of the two texts, Julian had grown in confidence of the truth of her revelations, in her understanding of them and in her consequent ability to convey their meaning (C&W, 222.40n).

66. On Julian's intended audience, see C&W, 71 and 77. In the Short Text, Julian had written about the teaching of the first revelation: "Every man and woman who wishes to live contemplatively needs to know of this," but she omitted this phrase from the Long Text, along with the comment that "those who deliberately occupy themselves with earthly business, constantly seeking worldly well-being" will not easily find God (iv:131–32). Between the writing of the Short and Long Texts, Julian must have come to the realization that her revelations were for all Christians, not only contemplatives (cf. C&W, 215.42n).

67. For a vivid picture of the disasters of the fourteenth century, see Barbara W. Tuchman, *A Distant Mirror: The Calamitous 14th Century* (New York: Ballantine Books, 1978). For English history, see May McKisack, *The Fourteenth Century: 1307–1399* (Oxford: Clarendon Press, 1959).

68. 2:178, 3:179, 12:200, 39:244, 52:281. For an additional reference to confession not in the Short Text, see 73:323.

69. 30:228, 33:234, 46:259. While the specific references to the paintings of crucifixes and the legend of St. Cecilia are omitted in the Long Text, they are replaced with Julian's general assertion that her desire to receive the three wounds grew out of her understanding of the teaching of the church (2:178–79). Christ's identification of himself as the one whom the church preaches is repeated verbatim in the Long Text (26:223) as are the ideas that Adam's sin is the greatest harm (29:228) and that God is Holy Church, its ground and substance (34:235–36).

70. 13:201, 38:242–43, 39:245, 46:259, 49:264.

71. 27:225, 31:229, 32:231–33, 34:236, 85:341.

72. We will examine this parable extensively in the chapters to follow.

73. See M. D. Lambert, *Medieval Heresy: Popular Movements from Bogomil to Hus* (London: Edward Arnold Publishers, 1977), 217–19. For a list of isolated instances of heresy prosecution in England before this time, see H. G. Richardson, "Heresy and the Lay Power under Richard II," *English Historical Review* 201 (1936): 1–4. The absence of overt heresy, however, does not mean there were no theological or ecclesiological controversies. For a brief, helpful discussion of such, see W. A. Pantin, *The English Church in the Fourteenth Century* (Cambridge: Cambridge University Press, 1955), 123–35.

74. The inquisition as such, as directed by the papacy, was never established in England. But the methods employed by the local church and government were exactly similar to the European inquisition by the early fifteenth century. See Gordon Leff, *Heresy in the Later Middle Ages: The Relation of Heterodoxy to Dissent c. 1250–c. 1450*, vol. II (Manchester: Manchester University Press/ New York: Barnes & Noble, 1967), 595–98.

75. For the history of Wyclif and the Lollards, see K. B. McFarlane, *John Wycliffe and the Beginnings of English Nonconformity* (London: English Universities Press, 1952); John Stacey, *John Wyclif and Reform* (London: Lutterworth Press, 1964); Lambert, 217–71; Leff, 494–605.

76. Lambert, 247–49; Richardson, 5–25. The penalty of death by burning for heresy was not written into English law until 1401 and the first Lollard was burned in that year. It was only after Oldcastle's rebellion in 1414 that Lollardy came out into the open and was

persecuted so vehemently that it was dead as a political force by 1431, although it continued to exist clandestinely until the eve of the Reformation (Leff, 595–605; Lambert, 249–56).

77. The standard work on the Free Spirit heresy is by Robert E. Lerner, *The Heresy of the Free Spirit in the Later Middle Ages* (Berkeley: University of California Press, 1972), whose conclusions are tellingly summarized in the following statement: "As if their history had been plotted by the Red Queen, heretics of the Free Spirit were condemned before very many of them can be proved to have existed" (61). For a discussion of the particular predicament of the mystics, see 182–99. A similar position is taken by Eleanor McLaughlin, "The Heresy of the Free Spirit and Late Medieval Mysticism," *Medievialia et Humanistica* n.s. 4 (1973): 37–51. See also Richard Kieckhefer, *Repression of Heresy in Medieval Germany* (Philadelphia: University of Pennsylvania Press, 1979), 19–51, and Petroff, *Visionary Literature*, 276–98.

78. For the beguines and beghards, see H. Grundmann, *Religiöse Bewegungen im Mittelalter*, 2nd ed. (Hildesheim, 1961) and Ernest W. McDonnell, *The Beguines and Beghards in Medieval Culture* (New Brunswick: Rutgers University Press, 1954). Shorter accounts are found in Richard W. Southern, *Western Society and the Church in the Middle Ages* (Harmondsworth: Penguin Books, 1970), 318–31; Brenda M. Bolton, "Mulieres Sanctae," *Sanctity and Secularity: The Church and the World*, Studies in Church History X, ed. Derek Baker (Oxford: Basil Blackwell, 1973), 77–95; Petroff, *Visionary Literature*, 171–78.

79. Perhaps the most famous beguine burned as a Free Spirit heretic is Marguerite Porete, who was executed in 1310 (Petroff, *Visionary Literature*, 276–82; Lerner, 67–78, 200–8). Her "heretical" book, *The Mirror of Simple Souls*, was translated into Middle English, and had wide circulation, either under anonymous or pseudonymous authorship; see Romana Guarnieri, "Il Movimento del Libero Spirito," in *Archivio Italiano per la storia della pieta* 4 (1965), 351–708. Colledge and Walsh note some comparisons between *The Mirror* and Julian's text, but always with the intent to show Julian as orthodox where Marguerite was not (C&W, 471.39n, 41n, and 720.27n).

80. Colledge and Walsh say that Julian "shows no interest in Continental heretical movements" ("Editing Julian," 426). Jantzen also dismisses the notion that Julian was concerned about heresy, implying that such a motive would compromise the sincerity of her assertions of loyalty to the church (101); however, it does not seem to me that fear of being accused of heresy and sincere loyalty to the church are mutually exclusive. Lerner comments that the English may not have known much about the details of the Free Spirit heresy (195, n. 46). However, it is unlikely that they were unaware of the prosecution of heresy in general: "Everyone knew that across the channel death by burning awaited the impenitent heretic" (Richardson, 20).

81. The actual Free Spirit heresy as described in the Council of Vienne (1312) can be linked only to Cologne in the Rhineland and Hainaut in the Low Countries (Lerner, 61–78). After the Council these areas continued to be investigated for heresy regularly throughout the fourteenth century. As example, see Lerner's treatment of one city, Strassburg (85–105).

82. Ibid., 131–43; McDonnell, 557–74.

83. The impropriety of women aspiring to be teachers is abundantly attested to in the *Ancrene Riwle*, which reads: "Some anchoresses are so learned or can talk with such wisdom that they would like their visitors to know it, and when a priest talks to them, they are always ready with a reply. In this way a woman who ought to be an anchoress sometimes

sets up as a scholar, teaching those who have come to teach her, and wishes to be soon recognized and known among the wise. Known she is, for by those same sayings by which she wants to be considered wise, he sees that she is foolish, for she is looking for esteem and instead she incurs blame; at the very least, when he has gone he will say, 'this anchoress talks a great deal.' In Paradise Eve talked a great deal to the serpent . . . and so the devil soon learned her weakness. . . . Our Lady behaved in an altogether different way. She did not speak words of information to the angel. . . . You, my dear sisters, are following Our Lady and not the cackling Eve; therefore an anchoress, whatever she is, should be as silent as possible. She should not have the characteristics of a hen, which when it has laid, can do nothing but cackle" (Pt. 2; Salu, 28–29).

84. Deanesly, 18–88; Petroff, *Consolation*, 3–4, 12–14.

85. Lerner, 47; McDonnell, 524.

86. The beguine movement never took root in England; the solitary life was far more popular. In light of the connection I am trying to establish between Norwich and the Low Countries, it is interesting that Norwich is the only town in late medieval times where there is evidence of communities resembling beguinages. Yet, in contrast to a plethora of hermits and anchorites living in Norwich between 1370 and 1532, Tanner found only three such communities. They were established at a time when European beguinages were becoming institutionalized, between 1427 and 1472 (Tanner, 64–66; 198–203). Jantzen's speculation that Julian may have been a beguine before her enclosure is highly unlikely (unless she had lived on the continent), given the fact that there is no evidence for the existence of beguinages in Norwich before 1427 (Jantzen, 7, 20).

87. In fact, any unregulated form of religious life, such as Gerhart Groote's Brothers and Sisters of the Common Life, could be suspected of the Free Spirit heresy (Lerner, 195–99; McDonnell, 566–74), as well as some regular forms, such as Dominican or Franciscan tertiaries (McDonnell, 527–38; Kieckhefer, *Repression*, 23–29).

88. On the part played by women in the Lollard movement, see Claire Cross, " 'Great Reasoners in Scripture': The Activities of Women Lollards 1380–1530," *Medieval Women*, Studies in Church History Subsidia I, ed. Derek Baker (Oxford: Basil Blackwell, 1978), 359–80. While much of the material covered here postdates Julian's time, pages 360–61 describe four women suspected of Lollardy between 1389 and 1393. One of them, an anchoress of Leicester named Matilda, was interrogated because of "sophistical answers" to questions put to her. Three others were imprisoned for "consorting with lollards"; of these, one was a laywoman, one a nun, and the third an anchoress. The chronicler Walsingham wrote of "the clergy's alarm at the intrusion by heretical lay people and above all heretical women in the sphere hitherto strictly reserved for the ordained ministry" (Aston, 13).

89. Tanner, 163. The earliest strongholds of popular Lollardy were in the midlands, the western dioceses of Worcester and Hereford, and on the Welsh border, not in the east (Leff, 574).

90. Lerner, 99, 141, 145–49; Kieckhefer, *Repression*, 25–26.

91. The eight errors of "an abominable sect of malignant men known as beghards and faithless women known as beguines in the Kingdom of Germany" were as follows: 1) that humans can achieve such a state of perfection in this life as to be incapable of sin; 2) that such persons need not fast or pray and can allow the body all that is pleasing to it; 3) they are not subject to human obedience or to any laws of the Church because "where the spirit of the Lord is, there is liberty" (2 Cor 3:17); 4) they can find final blessedness in this life; 5) they do not need the light of glory to enjoy the vision of God; 6) virtuous acts are necessary only for imperfect souls, not for those who have achieved the state of perfection; 7) the

sexual act is not sinful when demanded by nature; 8) it is not necessary to show reverence to the eucharist or to Christ's passion since to do so would be a sign of imperfection and a descent from the heights of contemplation (Lerner, 82).

92. This is obviously related to points 1, 2, 3, 6, and 8 of *Ad nostrum*. See note 91 above.

93. An accusation made against Free Spirits in the Swabian Ries' *Determinatio* reads: "that sins committed ought not to be dwelt upon with bitterness and sadness, because by such grief grace within is impeded" (quoted in McLaughlin, "Free Spirit," 43). This is very similar to Julian's teaching.

94. This point is not found in *Ad nostrum*, but in a letter regarding the Free Spirit heresy written by the Bishop of Strassburg before the Council's decrees were implemented in 1317. According to this document, Free Spirit heretics claimed that the human soul is judged at the time of death, at which time it returns from whence it came, and nothing is left except God alone, in effect, denying the existence of hell and purgatory. In such a scheme, not even Jews or Saracens are damned, because their spirits also return to God (Lerner, 85–87). Julian mentions that her revelations suggested the Jews were not damned (33:234). For a description of attitudes towards Jews in Norwich, see Vivian D. Lipman, *The Jews of Medieval Norwich* (London: The Jewish Historical Society of England, 1967) and Alan Webster, *Suffering—The Jews of Norwich and Julian of Norwich* (London: Diocesan Council for Christian-Jewish Understanding, 1981).

95. C&W, 25.

96. Molinari (4, n. 3) and Chambers (57) both make this point. See also Jeffrey, 43–44, and Aston, 131–33. It was in this period that Margery Kempe was accused of heresy and brought to trial (Butler-Bowdon, *The Book of Margery Kempe*, 27–29, 111–37; Clarissa Atkinson, *Mystic and Pilgrim: The "Book" and the World of Margery Kempe* [Ithaca: Cornell University Press, 1983], 103–28).

97. On the other hand, Atkinson notes that one of the church's counter-attacks to Lollardy was to encourage the publication and dissemination of books of orthodox piety, including the writings of female visionaries (105–6). Margery Kempe's own book points to the popularity and influence during her time of writings by or about continental women mystics such as Jacques de Vitry's *Life* of Marie d'Oignies and the *Revelations* of Birgitta of Sweden (ibid., pp. 31–36). The scarcity of extant copies of Julian's work could have been the result of the dissolution of the monasteries in the sixteenth century ("Editing Julian," 407).

Chapter 2: Julian's Theology

1. Aquinas' *Summa Theologiae* is an example of this type of theology from the Middle Ages. Other examples are, in a rudimentary sense, Origin's *De Principiis*, and in a more highly developed sense, Calvin's *Institutes*, or Schleiermacher's *The Christian Faith*.

2. Augustine could be considered a systematic theologian in this sense of the word. Others in this category include Anselm, Luther, and Rahner.

3. Such an understanding can probably be traced to Schleiermacher's precise distinction between the language of dogmatics and that of poetics or rhetoric. See *The Christian Faith*, propositions 15–19 (ed. and trans. H. R. Mackintosh and J. S. Stewart [Philadelphia: Fortress Press, 1976]). In a similar way, Bernard Lonergan discusses systematics as the seventh functional specialty of theology which moves to a level beyond doctrinal

expressions which remain figurative, symbolic, or merely descriptive (*Method in Theology* [New York: Seabury Press, 1979], 132, 335–53).

4. Lonergan defines the function of systematics as follows: "It is concerned to work out appropriate systems of conceptualization, to remove apparent inconsistencies, to move towards some grasp of spiritual matters both from their own inner coherence and from the analogies offered by more familiar human experience" (*Method in Theology*, 132). Julian does all of these things at various places in the Long Text, at least on a rudimentary level.

5. Leclercq, *The Love of Learning*, 233–86.

6. The Short Text is not divided into sixteen revelations; this was first done in the expanded Long Text. The manuscript of the Short Text is divided into twenty-five sections, separations possibly marked by Julian herself, which Colledge and Walsh have numbered as chapters (C&W, 20).

7. For a detailed comparison of Short and Long Texts, see C&W, 18–25, 59–67.

8. Ibid., 24, 66.

9. Julian's parable may owe some of its inspiration to Anselm's *Cur Deus Homo?* which recounts a similar story: "Suppose one should assign his slave a certain piece of work, and should command him not to throw himself into a ditch, which he points out to him and from which he could not extricate himself; and suppose that the slave, despising his master's command and warning, throws himself into the ditch before pointed out, so as to be utterly unable to accomplish the work assigned; think you that his inability will at all excuse him for not doing his appointed work?" (*Cur Deus Homo?* 2.24; trans. S. N. Deane, *St. Anselm: Basic Writings*, 2nd ed. [La Salle, IL: Open Court, 1979], 233). The similarity of detail between the two is somewhat remarkable, and if Julian did know Anselm's story, this might explain some of her amazement when she realized that God did not hold the servant accountable for the fall (51:268).

10. While the Latin word *exemplum* meant "example" in a general sense, by the end of the thirteenth century it had gained the more precise meaning of "an illustrative story" of the type described here. Its use in this sense was very common in Julian's day. See Thomas F. Crane's Introduction to *The Exempla or Illustrative Stories from the Sermones Vulgares of Jacques de Vitry* (The Folk-Lore Society, Publication XXVI, 1878; reprint, Nendeln/ Liechtenstein: Kraus Reprint, 1967), xviii.

11. Ibid., xvii; see also G. R. Owst, *Literature and Pulpit in Medieval England: A Neglected Chapter in the History of English Letters and of the English People*, 2nd ed. (Oxford: Basil Blackwell, 1961), 56–58, 67–68, 89–92, 152.

12. Owst, 149.

13. Ibid., 61–68. Owst is here pointing out how this method could at times reduce the meaning of scripture to triviality and absurdity, a danger which Julian avoids very well.

14. Ibid., 177–78; C&W, 313.35n. See the example in the *Ancrene Riwle* (Pt. 7; Salu, 172–74).

15. The most common sources for the stories in the example books were Jerome's *Vitae Patrum*, Gregory's *Dialogues*, the *Dialogus Miraculorum* of Caesar of Heisterbach, Voragine's *Legenda aurea*, the historical anecdotes of Valerius Maximus, and various historical chronicles of the Middle Ages (Crane, lxx-lxxi).

16. For a glimpse into the style of the *exempla*, see Crane, 1–131; English translations and notes are found on 135–269.

17. Ibid., lxxx.

18. Example books which circulated in Julian's day include the following: The *Gesta*

Romanorum, Summa Praedicantium, and *Le Manuel des Pechiez*, which was rather freely translated into English under the title *Handlyng Synne* (Crane, lxxxv, c-cii, cxiv-cxv).

19. Colledge and Walsh make note, in particular, of two Norwich monks, Adam Easton and Thomas Brinton, whose preaching campaigns were promoted by the Norwich cathedral priory when Julian was a girl (C&W, 39).

20. This epigrammatic couplet was used for teaching the four senses of scripture in Julian's day (C&W, 133–34): "The letter teaches history, allegory what to believe, the moral sense what to do, the anagogical where we are going."

21. Beryl Smalley, *The Study of the Bible in the Middle Ages*, 2nd ed. (Oxford: Basil Blackwell & Mott, 1952; reprint, Notre Dame: Notre Dame University Press, 1978), 1–25.

22. Monastic exegesis has been little studied, in spite of the fact that it is abundant. Leclercq argues that monastic authors set the tone for scholastic bible study (*The Love of Learning*, 87–88 and nn. 2–3). I am indebted to Leclercq's description of *lectio divina* for what follows here.

23. For a full discussion see ibid., 19–22, 88–90.

24. Ibid., 90–91. The phenomenon of reminiscence helps to explain the problem modern scholars face in tracking down the scriptural "sources" quoted by medieval authors. Rather than using older versions of scripture or modifying them, these authors were probably simply quoting scripture from memory in combination with the process of association of texts. Quotations with no actual textual link grouped themselves together in their minds, often resulting in the conflation of several scriptural texts into one. The problem of the unknown quotation "from Holy Writ" which Margery Kempe attributed to Julian can most likely be explained as such a conflation of texts (see Chapter 1 above, p. 8). Colledge and Walsh note many such conflations in Julian's work.

25. Leclercq, *The Love of Learning*, 93–94.

26. Neglecting this point can be very misleading. For example, in his appendix entitled "The Influence of Scripture on the *Revelations*," Brant Pelphrey confines himself to a discussion of whether or not Julian had access to an actual bible in order to use it as a source for her own work (331–49). Many of his points are well taken, but the conclusion one reaches from this way of considering the influence of scripture is that scripture played a minimal role in Julian's thought and in the composition of *Showings*.

27. David C. Fowler, *The Bible in Middle English Literature* (Seattle: University of Washington Press, 1984), xi. Fowler's entire book has the purpose of pointing out the pervasiveness of biblical influences on Middle English literature.

28. C&W, 46.

29. Colledge and Walsh find 152 scriptural allusions in the parable. For their line-by-line analysis, see the notes to pages 513–45 and the list of scriptural citations for those pages on 779–88.

30. For what follows here, see ibid., 130–33.

31. Paul Ricoeur, *The Symbolism of Evil* (Boston: Beacon Press, 1967), 355.

32. The study of scripture in the schools also began with the *lectio*. In the beginning it differed little from monastic study, but gradually emphasis began to be placed upon the page itself—hence the term, *sacra pagina*. Instead of being oriented towards *meditatio* and *oratio*, the *lectio* became a public reading of a passage of scripture together with its glosses (the lecture) which moved in the direction of the *quaestio* and *disputatio*. Eventually the *quaestiones* became more numerous, outweighing the amount of time given to the exposition of scripture, and the subject matter became more objective and speculative. Finally,

the theological *quaestio* and *disputatio* became separated entirely from bible study. By Julian's day this process had been complete for nearly a century. See Smalley, 66–82; Leclercq, *The Love of Learning*, 89.

33. Ricoeur, *Interpretation Theory*, 45–69.

34. Indeed, until the eighteenth century, there was no conception of individual creative theological authorship as we think of it today. On this topic, see John Thiel, "Theological Responsibility: Beyond the Classical Paradigm," *Theological Studies* 47:4 (1986): 573–98.

Chapter 3: The Love of Jesus Christ

1. Letter 101 to Cledonius (*PG* 37, 181C-184A).

2. Pelikan, 106–57; Southern, *The Making of the Middle Ages*, 219–57.

3. I owe this insight to Frans Jozef van Beeck, S.J., who stressed it in the course in Systematic Theology given at Boston College in 1981–82. I do not mean to suggest that reflection upon the person and natures of Jesus Christ came to a halt as a result of this development; see Walter H. Principe, *The Theology of the Hypostatic Union in the Early Thirteenth Century*, 4 vols. (Toronto: Pontifical Institute of Mediaeval Studies, 1963–75) for some very technical discussions of this subject. For the special significance of Christ's humanity for medieval women, see Bynum, *Holy Feast*, 246–49.

4. Southern notes well the connection between popular piety and "academic" theological development: "It was indeed one of the characteristics of our period that the connexion between thought and feeling, between emotional intensity and the formal structure of thought, was close" (*The Making of the Middle Ages*, 234; cf. 240).

5. For a brief outline of the soteriological themes found in the patristic authors, see Walter H. Principe, *Introduction to Patristic and Medieval Theology*, 2nd ed. (Toronto: Pontifical Institute of Mediaeval Studies, 1982), 33–38.

6. Possible sources for Julian's descriptions are far too numerous to mention, but I have found one in particular where the correspondences to Julian's meditations on the passion are striking. It is *A Talkyng of the Loue of God*, a fourteenth century text which is itself a compilation and free rendering of three earlier works: the Introduction to Anselm's *Prayers and Meditations*, and the Middle English treatises *On Ureisun of God Almihti* and *The Wohunge of Ure Lauerd* (see the version edited and translated by Salvina Westra, O.P. [The Hague: Martinus Nijhoff, 1950], Introduction, xiii–xxxi). The details Julian chooses to emphasize are the same as those described in the following citations from this work: "There You were for my love with hard knotty scourges flogged and beaten so painfully and so cruelly that Your fair complexion, which was so bright and so fresh, was utterly defiled and soiled, Your skin torn and rent to pieces. There flowed on each side a stream of water and of red blood. . . . Then there was put on Your head a crown of sharp thorns so that wherever there was a thorn the red blood streamed out" (49). "They . . . led forth Longinus . . . and gave him a sharp spear to pierce Your heart so that it split in two. And from that same spring of life, through that horrible wound, ran two floods: Your rich, precious blood, which bought the whole world, and that precious holy water, which washed this whole world of the guilt and of the sin in which they had fallen" (53). "I see You so piteously hanging on the cross, Your body all covered with blood, Your limbs wrenched asunder, Your joints twisted, Your wounds and Your sweet face, which was so bright and fair, now made so horrible" (61).

7. Imaging Christ's human nature as clothing was a rather common medieval device;

for some examples see C&W, 527.168n, 528.171n, and 536.249n. It was also used frequently by Augustine; for example, the body of Christ is described as the *habitus* of the Word who descended from heaven "naked" but ascended "clothed with our flesh" (*Sermones* 263.3); Jesus' humanity took its shape from the Word and he "wore" humanity like a garment, "that it might be changed for the better" (*De diversis quaestionibus* 83, q. 73.2). See Brian E. Daley, S.J., " 'A Humble Mediator': The Distinctive Elements in Saint Augustine's Christology," *Word and Spirit* 9 (1987): 100–17, esp. 105 and 115, n. 38.

8. Carr, 158–79.

9. Ibid., 174–75.

10. Ibid., 158–64.

11. See Frans Jozef van Beeck, *Christ Proclaimed: Christology as Rhetoric* (New York: Paulist Press, 1979), 395, n. 86 and 423.

12. Julian calls Christ "the spouse" in only two places: 51:278 and 58:293, and in both cases the passages are more accurately read as referring to Christ as the spouse of the church. She refers to the Holy Spirit as spouse of the soul in 52:279. Neither image is predominant in her theology.

13. This description of the servant's suffering recalls the deutero-Isaian suffering servant, especially the fourth servant song, Is 52:13–53:10, and Is 63:3–5.

14. For some examples, see Gertrude the Great's spiritual exercises in honor of the five wounds (Petroff, *Visionary Literature*, 225) and Angela of Foligno's meditations on Christ's wounds (ibid., 256–57). Colledge and Walsh note frequent correspondences between Julian's descriptions of the passion and the *Fifteen Oes*, a popular meditation on the details of Christ's passion extant in both English and Latin in Julian's day (C&W, 52, 58, 86, 201.6n, 217.6n, 394.6n, 418.14n).

15. Bynum, *Holy Feast*, 4.

16. C&W, 85–86.

17. The servant's eagerness to "hasten and run" recalls Ps 19:4–5: "the sun, which comes forth like a bridegroom leaving his chamber, and like a strong man runs its course with joy." The *Glossa ordinaria* traditionally related this verse to the incarnation (C&W, 536.249n). The desire of the servant to do the lord's will also recalls Lk 22:15: "I have earnestly desired to eat this passover with you" and Heb 10:7: "Lo, I have come to do thy will, O God."

18. For other medieval renderings of the spiritual thirst of Christ, see C&W, 418.14n.

19. On the complexity and ambivalence of the symbol of blood, see Bynum, *Holy Feast*, 64–65. There is a strong temptation to link Julian's meditations on Christ's blood with those of Catherine of Siena, whose devotion to the blood of Christ is well known (ibid., 177–79). However, it is difficult to establish an actual textual link between Julian and Catherine, whose works do not seem to have been known in England until the fifteenth century. Doubtless both were drawing upon a widespread devotion as their common source (cf. C&W, 86).

20. The notion of Christ's wounds as a shelter for humankind is found in the *Anima Christi*: "within thy wounds hide me." On the popularity of this prayer in Julian's day, see C&W, 296.24n. The *Ancrene Riwle* has an extended meditation on Christ's wounds as a hiding place from the storms of temptation (Pt. 4; Salu, 129–30). Julian's description of the Sacred Heart of Jesus differs from others of her time because of her emphasis upon the joy with which Jesus views his open side (C&W, 99–100). For other medieval reflections on the Sacred Heart, see C&W, 241.1n, 394.3n and 394.6n.

21. Although the interpretation of the Philippians hymn as descriptive of the incarna-

tion was common in Julian's day, modern scripture scholarship disputes it. See, for example, James D. G. Dunn, *Christology in the Making: An Inquiry into the Origins of the Doctrine of the Incarnation* (London: SCM Press, 1980), 114–21.

22. Julian had referred to this passage even more clearly in the Short Text: "But each soul should do as St. Paul says, and feel in himself what is in Christ Jesus" (x:142).

23. In spite of the incarnational meaning she sees in this passage, Julian also seems to understand the "Adam christology" implicit within it, which is the interpretation given to this passage by Dunn (114–21).

24. Rom 5:12–20; 1 Cor 15:20–23, 45–49.

25. The representation of Christ as a gardener in medieval iconography is relatively rare (C&W, 530.193n).

26. It could also contain an oblique reference to the "useless servant" who buried his talent in the field (Mt 25:24–25). Other scriptural parables which connect gardening images with the kingdom of God are the sower and the seed (Mk 4:1–20 and par.), the seed growing secretly (Mk 4:26–29), the mustard seed (Mk 4:30–32 and par.), the weeds of the field (Mt 13:36–43), the laborers in the vineyard (Mt 20:1–16), and the fig tree (Mk 13:28–29 and par.).

27. Note how this recalls God's commendation: "Behold my servant, whom I uphold, my chosen, in whom my soul delights" of Isaiah 42:1 and its New Testament echo: "You are my beloved Son; with you I am well pleased" (Mk 1:11 and par.).

28. C&W, 203.36n.

29. This fear was realized in the attack of the devil which Julian describes later (67:311–12, 69:315–16, 70:316–17).

30. The theme of the "harrowing of hell" was familiar to everyone in Julian's milieu, literarily through such works as *Piers Plowman* and the pseudo-Bonaventure's meditations on the passion, as well as through the mystery plays (cf. C&W, 534.224n).

31. This is a very rich scriptural image, recalling the righteous remnant of the house of Judah which shall "take root downward and bear fruit upward" (Is 37:31; 2 Kings 19:30) and which Paul calls "the holy root" of Israel (Rom 11:16). Christ himself was identified with the "branch" which would grow from the root or stump of Jesse (Is 11:1) and the "root and offspring of David" (Rev 22:16). The elect of Ephesians are "rooted and grounded in love" (Eph 3:17). See C&W, 47 and 542.300n.

32. The *Ancrene Riwle* counsels that, whatever the devil does, "scorn him. Laugh the old ape loudly to scorn, by virtue of your true faith, and he will be shamed and will soon take to flight" (Pt. 4; Salu, 109). Accordingly, when Julian saw God scorn the devil, she tells us, "I laughed greatly" (13:201).

33. For the notion of the happy fault, see the rite for the blessing of the Paschal candle on Easter Eve: "O certe necessarium Ade peccatum et nostrum quod Christi morte deletum est. O felix culpa que talem ac tentum meruit habere redemptorem," and the second stanza of the medieval lyric, *Adam lay ibowndyn*: "Ne hadde the appil take ben, teken ben,/ Ne hadde neuer our lady a ben heuene qwen;/ Blyssid be the tyme that appil take was, therfore we mown syngyn 'deo gracias!'" (see C&W, 412.12n for references).

34. See Clark, "Predestination in Christ," 88–89, for a comparison between Julian and Duns Scotus on this idea.

35. Julian's treatment of salvation as recreation follows the western tradition described by Gerhard Ladner in *The Idea of Reform: Its Impact on Christian Thought and Action in the Age of the Fathers* (Cambridge: Harvard University Press, 1959). This idea is discussed at greater length in Chapter 5 below, pp. 112–13.

36. The change in Christ's clothing alludes to the transfiguration passages of the synoptic gospels (Mk 9:2–8 and par.).

37. Julian's use of "suddenly" here recalls 1 Cor 15:51–52: "We shall all be changed, in a moment, in the twinkling of an eye."

38. The opening and consistent theme of Paul's first letter to the Corinthians is that what seems to be the weakness and folly of the cross is true power and wisdom from God's perspective and for those who believe (see especially 1:17–2:16). Note Paul's closing words here, in light of Julian's desire through the passion to have the mind of Christ: " 'For who has known the mind of the Lord so as to instruct him?' But we have the mind of Christ" (1 Cor 2:16).

39. This echoes the perspective of Ephesians 1:3–10: "Blessed be the God and Father of our Lord Jesus Christ, who . . . chose us in him before the foundation of the world, that we should be holy and blameless before him. He destined us in love to be his sons through Jesus Christ, according to the purpose of his will, to the praise of his glorious grace which he freely bestowed on us in the Beloved. . . . For he has made known to us in all wisdom and insight the mystery of his will, according to his purpose which he set forth in Christ as a plan for the fulness of time, to unite all things in him, things in heaven and things on earth."

40. The substance and sensuality of the soul are discussed in detail in Chapter 5 below, pp. 109–13.

41. This "double knitting" to Christ through creation and redemption repeats the sentiment of Ephesians and Colossians. We were "chosen in him before the foundation of the world" (Eph 1:4), but in him we also "have redemption through his blood" (Eph 1:7). Christ is "the image of the invisible God, the first-born of all creation" in whom "all things were created" (Col 1:15–16), but he is also "the first-born from the dead" (Col 1:18).

42. 1 Cor 12:12–31, Rom 12:4–8, and Eph 4:11–16, 5:21–32.

43. However, Julian does entertain the possibility of salvation outside the church. This is discussed in Chapter 7 below, pp. 164–66.

44. Pierre Teilhard de Chardin, *The Phenomenon of Man* (New York: Harper, 1959), esp. 291–98; Karl Rahner, "Christology within an Evolutionary View of the World," *TI* V, 157–92.

45. This idea appears to be influenced by the thought of Eph 4:11–13: "And his gifts were that some should be apostles, some prophets, some evangelists, some pastors and teachers, to equip the saints for the work of ministry, for building up the body of Christ, until we all attain to the unity of the faith and of the knowledge of the Son of God, to mature manhood, to the measure of the stature of the fulness of Christ."

46. 39:244, 52:281, and 73:323. Julian has learned well the conditions for a good confession (contrition, confession, and performance of penance levied by the confessor), as prescribed by the Fourth Lateran Council, which were given as instruction to the faithful throughout the thirteenth and fourteenth centuries. For a more complete discussion of this, see Chapter 6 below, p. 117.

47. Recall also the allusion to the eucharist, and probably also to baptism, in Julian's treatment of the water and blood from the side of Christ (12:200). However, in contrast to many women visionaries, Julian exhibits little personal devotion to the eucharist (Bynum, *Holy Feast*, 48–69, 113–49).

48. Carolyn Walker Bynum provides an interesting comparison between men's and women's treatment of this theme in " ' . . . And Woman His Humanity': Female Imagery

in the Religious Writing of the Later Middle Ages" in *Gender and Religion*, 257–88; see Bynum's more general study *Jesus as Mother*, especially 110–69. See also Valerie M. Lagorio, "Variations on the Theme of God's Motherhood in Medieval English Mystical and Devotional Writings," *Studia Mystica* 8 (1985): 15–37; Robert Boenig, "The God-as-Mother Theme in Richard Rolle's Biblical Commentaries," *Mystics Quarterly* 10 (1984): 171–74; Robert J. O'Connell, "Isaiah's Mothering God in St. Augustine's *Confessions*," *Thought* 63 (1983): 188–206; Eleanor McLaughlin, "'Christ My Mother': Feminine Naming and Metaphor in Medieval Spirituality," *Nashotah Review* 15:3 (1975): 228–48; André Cabussut, "Une dévotion médiévale peu connue: la dévotion à Jésus, nôtre mère," *Revue d'ascétique et de mystique* 25 (1949): 231–45.

49. Bynum, "'. . . And Woman His Humanity'," 263.

50. For Julian's treatment of the motherhood image, see Ritamary Bradley, "Mysticism in the Motherhood Similitude of Julian of Norwich," *Studia Mystica* 8 (1985): 4–14; "Patristic Background of the Motherhood Similitude in Julian of Norwich," *Christian Scholar's Review* 8 (1978): 101–13; and "The Motherhood Theme in Julian of Norwich," *Fourteenth Century English Mystics Newsletter* 2:4 (1976): 25–30; also, Kari Elisabeth Børresen, "Christ Nôtre Mère, La Théologie de Julienne de Norwich," *Mitteilungen und Forschungsbeiträge de Cusanus-Gesellschaft* 13 (1978): 320–29; Christine Allen, "Christ Our Mother in Julian of Norwich, *Studies in Religion/Sciences Religieux* 10:4 (1981): 421–28; Paula S. Datsko Barker, "The Motherhood of God in Julian of Norwich's Theology," *Downside Review* 100 (1982): 290–304.

51. Julian thus sees motherhood as an essential attribute of God. See the further discussion of this in Chapter 4 below, pp. 93–94.

52. For a further discussion, see Elizabeth A. Johnson, C.S.J., "Jesus, the Wisdom of God: A Biblical Basis for Non-Androcentric Christology," *Ephemerides Theologicae Louvanienses* 61 (1985): 261–94.

53. Colledge and Walsh find in Julian a strong dependence upon the wisdom literature of the Hebrew scriptures (C&W, 43 and the citations listed on 780–81).

54. This translation is from the Latin Vulgate, which is the bible Julian would have known. Since the passage is not found in the Hebrew originals or earliest Greek translations, it was most likely a Christian gloss later incorporated into the Latin text. It reveals an early Christian reflection on the Wisdom figure, probably as influenced by the gospel of John (cf. Jn 14:6).

55. The *Ancrene Riwle* cites this passage and meditates on it thus: "He [Christ] says Himself, through Isaias, that He loves us more than any mother her child. . . . Can a mother, He says, forget her child? And even if she should, I can never forget you—and then He gives the reason, . . . 'I have painted you,' He says, 'in my hands.' This He did with red blood, upon the cross. . . . Our Lord, because He wished never to forget us, put marks of piercing in both His hands, to remind Him of us" (Pt. 7; Salu, 175).

56. It was not mentioned in the Short Text, nor was it included in the first edition of the Long Text, because it is not in the summary of the revelations in the Long Text's first chapter.

57. The same dual imagery is found in Christ's last discourse in John's gospel, where references to Christ's travelling from heaven to earth and back again (Jn 13:1, 3, 33, 36; 14:2–5, 28; 16:16–19) are combined with the image of a woman in labor: "When a woman is in travail she has sorrow, because her hour has come; but when she is delivered of the child, she no longer remembers the anguish, for joy that a child is born into the world"

(Jn 16:21; cf. C&W, 529.181n). In a similar vein, Paul describes his own missionary labor: "My little children, with whom I am again in travail until Christ be formed in you" (Gal 4:19).

58. This appears to be original to Julian. Clark remarks, "no full antecedent has yet been found for Julian's bold appropriation to Christ of Motherhood in the order of creation as well as of redemption" ("Nature, Grace and the Trinity," 211). See also Bynum, " '. . . And Woman His Humanity'," 266.

59. See, for example, *A Talkyng of the Love of God*: "Ah dear Lord, great is your clemency, who thus spread your arms bodily on the cross. . . . [Christ] calls [the soul] to life and to love-kisses, as a mother does her dear son, who hears him cry and takes him in her arms. . . . She gives him her breast and stops his tears. That breast be my pleasure, my care, my longing, sweet Jesus . . . to suck to satiety, which through the opening by the spear . . . with the moistening by your precious blood relieves all sorrows" (Westra, 7). Bynum points out that in medieval physiology milk was understood as processed blood (*Holy Feast*, 65, 178–79); see her discussion of blood as nourishment, and its particular symbolism for women, 270–75. An unusual variation on this is found in the *Ancrene Riwle* where the mother's blood is not nourishment but a bath: "If a child had some disease such that a bath of blood was necessary to its recovery, the mother who would provide such a bath would indeed love it greatly. This is what Our Lord did for us, when we were so diseased with sin and so marked with it that nothing could heal us or cleanse us except his blood" (Pt. 7; Salu, 175).

60. Julian sees the activities of instruction, discipline, and chastisement as belonging to Christ's office of motherhood along with the exercise of tender love, compassion, and nurturing. Male writers had a tendency to isolate tenderness, nurturing, and mercy as qualities of motherhood, while authority and discipline more adequately described the fatherhood of God. Women, including Julian, were generally much less gender-conscious in this respect (Bynum, " '. . . And Woman His Humanity'," 262–68).

61. Bradley also emphasizes this point ("Mysticism in the Motherhood Similitude," 4, 8).

62. The details here are reminiscent of the *Veni Sancte Spiritu* and the prayer for the gifts of the Spirit (cf. Is 11:2–3) recommended in the *Ancrene Riwle* (Pt. 1; Salu, 11).

63. These sayings in John's gospel indicate Christ's divinity. See especially Jn 8:24, 28, 58, and 13:19, all of which imply that Jesus has been given the name of God revealed in Ex 3:14. See also Jn 6:35, 9:5, 10:7, 11:25, 14:6, and 15:1. For a discussion of divine titles applied to Jesus in John's gospel, see Jerome H. Neyrey, S.J., *An Ideology of Revolt: John's Christology in Social-Science Perspective* (Philadelphia: Fortress Press, 1988), 213–20.

Chapter 4: From the Love of God to the Trinity

1. This image recalls the parable of the marriage feast (Mt 22:1–14, Lk 14:16–24), the celebration over the return of the prodigal son (Lk 15:22–32), and the eschatological banquet (Rev 19:1–9).

2. For a short description of this association, see Sr. Anna Maria Reynolds, " 'Courtesy' and 'Homeliness' in the *Revelations* of Julian of Norwich," *Fourteenth Century English Mystics Newsletter* 5:2 (1979): 12–20.

3. For what follows here I am indebted to W. O. Evans, " 'Cortaysye' in Middle English," *Mediaeval Studies* 29 (1967): 143–57.

4. The word is not used here in a positive light. The anchoress is being warned against

excessive "courtesy" and liberality (*The English Text of the Ancrene Riwle*, EETS 225, ed. Mabel Day [London: Oxford University Press, 1952], Pt. 8, 190; Salu, 184).

5. W. O. Evans, 143.

6. Ibid., 151–54.

7. For a short description of this relationship, see Robert Lewis Schmitt, "The Image of Christ as Feudal Lord in the *Spiritual Exercises* of St. Ignatius Loyola," Ph.D. diss., Fordham University, 1974, especially 47–100. For a more extended discussion, see Francis L. Ganshof, *Feudalism* (London: Longmans, Green, 1964).

8. Reynolds, 15–17.

9. Julian is referring here specifically to the elimination of bodily wastes.

10. Note the allusion to Mt 6:28–30 and Ps 102:25–28. The Pauline corpus often refers to the new life of grace in terms of "putting on" clothing: cf. Rom 13:14; 1 Thess 5:8; Eph 4:24; Col 3:10–14.

11. Judg 9:51; 2 Sam 22:3; Ps 59:17.

12. God as humanity's dwelling place is seen in the fact that God's own Son came into the world that we might have eternal life (Jn 3:16). We enter into this life through Christ, the door of the sheepfold, where we will find pasture (Jn 10:7–10). By remaining attached to the vine who is Christ, we abide in his love (Jn 15:1–11). Eventually we will enter into his Father's house, where Christ has prepared a place for us, and where there are many dwelling places. There we will be with God forever (Jn 14:2–3). But humanity is also God's dwelling place. Julian's description of the homely love of God captures well the Johannine "God so loved the world that he gave his only Son" (Jn 3:16). In his sojourn here in our flesh, Christ did not disdain to serve us in the most menial tasks (Jn 13:1–15). As the seed falling into the ground and dying, he brought forth the possibility of new life to all (Jn 12:24). This means that for those who love him, he and the Father will come and make their home with them (Jn 14:23). For a full description of the relationship between Julian's notion of homeliness and the Johannine theme of indwelling, see James Walsh, "God's Homely Loving: St. John and Julian of Norwich on the Divine Indwelling," *The Month* n.s. 19 (1958): 164–72.

13. For example, "what gave me most strength was that our good Lord, who is so to be revered and feared, is so [homely] and so courteous" (7:188), and "[God] wants to be trusted, for he is very [homely] and courteous" (10:196). Although the words "courteous" and "homely" as descriptive of God's love were used by other medieval writers, Julian's coupling of them seems to be unique (Reynolds, 16; Clark, "*Fiducia*," 100 and 108, n. 16).

14. *ST* 1.Q21.A2.

15. God's work of mercy is described more extensively in Chapter 6 below, pp. 129–47.

16. *ST* 1.Q3.A3–4. See also Augustine's *De trinitate* 5.2.3, citing Exodus 3:14.

17. *ST* 1.Q5.A1,3.

18. Clark, "Nature, Grace and the Trinity," 204, 212, and 216, n. 17; Pelphrey, 88–89.

19. Ex 3:13–14; *ST* 1.Q2.A3.

20. In medieval iconography, the color blue represented constancy or unchangeability (C&W, 526.153n).

21. The theme of God as rest and peace is central to Augustine (cf. *Confessions* 1.1, 13.35–37; *De civitate Dei* 19.10–13, 27).

22. This theme is so constant in Julian's theology, it is impossible to cite all the occurrences of it.

23. Ricoeur, *Interpretation Theory*, 45–69.

24. Mt 19:26; Lk 18:26–27; Lk 1:37.

25. This is discussed again in Chapter 7 below, p. 151, in the context of eschatology.

26. Note the close parallel in Augustine's *De trinitate* 1.9.18–19.

27. Julian could be indebted here to the liturgical tradition which venerated the cross as cause of Christian joy. Recall, for example, the Good Friday hymn: "Crucem tuam adoramus domine, et sanctam resurrectionem tuam laudamus et glorificamus; ecce enim propter lignum venit gaudium in universo mundo," cited in C&W, 294.9n. She could also be remembering the tradition of Christian worship which prayed through the Son to the Father in the Holy Spirit, a sentiment captured still in the doxology of the Eucharist: "Through him, with him, and in him, in the unity of the Holy Spirit, all glory and honor is yours, almighty Father."

28. Julian's understanding of the trinity in the Long Text has undergone considerable development beyond that found in the Short Text. In the twenty-year interim between the two, she must have done some study of the doctrine. We can only speculate as to her sources. Whatever they were, they were firmly rooted in the Augustinian tradition. If it is true, as Colledge and Walsh suggest (C&W, 45), that Julian was familiar with the trinitarian doctrine of William of St. Thierry, expounded in *The Enigma of Faith*, that text contains long passages copied verbatim or nearly so from Augustine's *De trinitate*. See the edition of *The Enigma of Faith* translated and edited by John D. Anderson (Washington, DC: Cistercian Publications, Consortium Press, 1974), especially 16–24.

29. *De trinitate* 8.10.14.

30. Ibid., 8.1.1–8.2.3; 15.17.27–28, 31; 15.19.37.

31. Julian knows her parable is only an analogy for the Godhead, and she is careful not to interpret it too literally. The images of lord and servant could be seen to imply an inequality within the trinity, but Julian clearly stresses the equality of all three persons (22:216, 73:323). At one point Julian explains that because we are blinded in this life we cannot see God as God is; therefore "God shows himself homely, like a man, even though . . . we ought to know and believe that the Father is not a man" (51:272). Again, when at the end of the parable she describes the Son sitting at the right hand of the Father, she explains: "this does not mean that the Son sits on the right hand side as one man sits beside another in this life, for there is no such sitting, as I see it, in the trinity" (51:278). The trinity was sometimes represented in iconography by three men sitting side by side. Augustine counselled that any corporeal representations of the trinity are merely analogies (*De trinitate* 8.2.3). Julian reiterates Augustine's thought here (cf. C&W, 544.324n).

32. In the passages describing the lord's clothing Julian may be trying to symbolize the divine attribute of immensity. The Middle English word Julian uses, "flammyng," has the connotation of "billowing like flame or vapour," intimating that the garment of the lord was so rich in texture that it reflected light. This recalls Ps 104:1–2: "Thou art clothed with honor and majesty, who coverest thyself with light as with a garment." The notion of immensity also recalls Wis 18:24: "For upon his long robe the whole world was depicted" (C&W, 526.155n-527.157n and 543.310n).

33. Augustine, too, makes it clear that the Spirit is the love with which God loves us. The Spirit is God the gift, God as given love. See, for example, *De trinitate* 15.17.31 and 15.18.32.

34. Ibid., 1.4.7.

35. For example, being is a primary attribute of God, the holy trinity (58:293), but the

Father is also specifically called Being (59:296). As Being, God is essential Goodness (5:183), but goodness is often appropriated to the Holy Spirit as a synonym for love (53:283).

36. The discussion here is confined to the expressions as they are reformulated in the Long Text.

37. In Augustine's *De trinitate* the triad "greatness, wisdom, goodness" appears in 6.6.8 along with "truth" and especially in 8.1: "The essence or being of God is the same as his being great, good, wise." It also appears in 7.1.1, but there power and wisdom are both principally appropriated to Christ, following 1 Cor 1:24. In all cases, Augustine is attempting to show that such attributes apply to God's essence, not to any one person. Augustine's most famous triads for the trinity are "mind, knowledge, love" (*De trinitate* 9) and especially "memory, understanding, will" (ibid., 10).

The triad "might, wisdom, love" as used by Julian is obviously a derivation of the Augustinian idea that the human spirit is the image of the trinity. It is found in Hugh of St. Victor's *De sacramentis* 1:2, and in William of St. Thierry's *Disputation against Abelard* 2, where he criticizes Abelard's way of attributing these names to the persons of the trinity (*PL* 180:250AB). William himself uses the triad with caution: "Although the Divine Names of this kind suit the three persons in the Trinity equally because of their unity of nature, . . . certain of them seem to be ascribed more commonly and more frequently to certain persons in the Trinity. . . . namely, power is ascribed to the Father, wisdom to the Son, and goodness to the Holy Spirit. This is done for distinction of persons that they may be distinguished, not that they may be separated" (see Anderson's translation of the *Enigma of Faith*, 81–82 and nn. 207 & 208). Aquinas also considers this triad, among others, in *ST* 1.Q39.A8.

The triad is found in several medieval devotional works, most notably for our study in the *Ancrene Riwle*, where a prayer to the trinity reads: "Almighty God, Father, Son and Holy Ghost, as you three are one God, also you are one might, one wisdom, and one love. And though in holy writ might is ascribed particularly to you, beloved Father, wisdom to you, blessed Son, and love to you, Holy Ghost, give to me, almighty God, you three persons, these same three things: might to serve you, wisdom to please you, love and will to do it; might that I may do, wisdom that I can do, love that I shall do, all that is dearest to you" (Pt. 1; for the Middle English text from the Vernon manuscript, see C&W, 533.217n; cf. Salu, 10). See also quotations from the *Mirror of St. Edmund* (C&W, 483.10n) and the *Horologium* (C&W, 668.29n).

38. In the Long Text, Julian occasionally substitutes the term "truth" for "might" in her trinitarian description of God: "For God is endless supreme truth, endless supreme wisdom, endless supreme love uncreated" (44:256). While love makes God long for us, "his wisdom and his truth with his justice make him to suffer us [to remain] here [in this world]" (81:337). See *De trinitate* 8.1.2 where God's greatness is equated with truth and being.

39. Note the similar use of these three verbs in the quotation from the *Ancrene Riwle*: "*might* that I *may* do, *wisdom* that I *can* do, *love* that I *shall* do, all that is dearest to you" (Pt. 1; Salu, 10). In the first place these verbs appear in Julian's text, they appear as they do in the *Ancrene Riwle*: "may," "can," "shall." But later Julian will substitute "will" for "shall" to indicate the action of the Holy Spirit, which is to desire to do the various works of the trinity. She will then use the word "shall" to indicate the action of the whole trinity (see 31:229).

40. Colledge and Walsh translate "keper" as "protector" or "preserver." It indicates the operation of God's mercy, attributable to the second person, which "keeps" us united to God in spite of sin.

41. Note the allusion to Augustine's "mind, knowledge (or reason), love" (*De trinitate* 9).

42. Lordship is an unusual image for the Spirit. It is not particularly biblical, except for 2 Cor 3:17: "Now the Lord is the Spirit." It could reflect the Nicene-Costantinopolitan Creed: "We believe in the Holy Spirit, the Lord, the giver of life." Julian's connecting the Spirit with the work of eschatological fulfillment could have its source in the Pauline notion of the Spirit as our "guarantee" of salvation (2 Cor 1:22).

43. Note the explicit allusion to Eph 3:18.

44. Eleanor McLaughlin makes this point in " 'Christ My Mother'," 237–39; Colledge and Walsh note that Julian is the first to consider motherhood an essential attribute of God (C&W, 583.20n); Bynum says that Julian exhibits a very sophisticated use of the motherhood theme by allowing it to describe the action of the whole trinity towards us (*Jesus as Mother*, 140, 151); and Sallie McFague notes that Julian considers God as "substantially" not just "accidentally" female (*Models of God: Theology for an Ecological, Nuclear Age* [Philadelphia: Fortress Press: 1987], 115).

45. Rosemary Radford Ruether, *Sexism and God-Talk: Toward a Feminist Theology* (Boston: Beacon Press, 1983), 68–71. See also McFague's discussion of the absence of any nature/history dualism in Julian, 115–16.

46. McFague, 97–180.

47. *De trinitate* 5.15.16.

48. For example, see Aquinas' elaborate doctrine of the immanent trinity (*ST* 1.QQ27–42).

49. Karl Rahner, *The Trinity* (New York: Herder & Herder, 1970).

50. The intimacy between the Spirit and the soul is well expressed through the image of spouse, which Julian uses for the Spirit: "God rejoices that he is our Father, and God rejoices that he is our Mother, and God rejoices that he is our true spouse, and that our soul is his beloved wife" (52:279).

Chapter 5: The Work of Nature

1. For a summary of this basic fact of Christian philosophy, see Etienne Gilson, *The Spirit of Mediaeval Philosophy*, trans. A. H. C. Downes (New York: Charles Scribner's Sons, 1936), 64–83.

2. I have inserted the fourth sentence which is missing from the Paulist Modern English translation (cf. C&W, 300.12–13). Note the similarity of this passage to Wisdom 11:22–26: "The whole world before thee is like a speck that tips the scales, and like a drop of morning dew that falls upon the ground. But thou art merciful to all, for thou canst do all things, and thou dost overlook men's sins, that they may repent. For thou lovest all things that exist, and hast loathing for none of the things which thou hast made, for thou wouldst not have made anything if thou hadst hated it. How would anything have endured if thou hadst not willed it? Or how would anything not called forth by thee have been preserved? Thou sparest all things, for they are thine, O Lord who lovest the living" (cf. C&W, 212.11n).

3. Julian has penetrated here to the root of what Gilson sees as the difference between the God of Greek philosophy and the Christian God: "The God of St. Thomas and Dante is

a God who loves," citing Dante's expression of divine causality from the last line of the *Divine Comedy*: "L'amor che muove il Sole e l'altre stelle" (*The Spirit of Philosophy*, 75).

4. This translation is awkward, but the Middle English construction does not lend itself easily to transcription into Modern English. The Middle English reads: "Of this nedeth vs to haue knowledge, that vs lyketh nought all thing that is made, for to loue and haue god that is vnmade" (C&W, 301.24–26).

5. Note the similarity here to the famous story about Benedict in Gregory's *Dialogues* II (*PL* 66, 198–200) where Benedict "saw a wonderful light shining in the darkness; and the whole world was brought before his gaze, gathered as it were under this one ray of light. . . . It was not that the heavens and earth were contracted but that the soul of the beholder was dilated, because, being rapt in God, he could see without difficulty all that was beneath God" (English translation from C&W, 317.10n).

6. The Christian notion of God as eternal being transcends the notions of dynamism and staticism: "Even in the thought of those who are most attracted to the aspect of realization and perfection which characterizes the Pure Being, we may easily discern the presence of the element of 'energy' which, as we know, is inseparable from the concept of act" (Gilson, *The Spirit of Philosophy*, 57). Julian's emphasis upon the eternity of God's love makes this same point.

7. Julian is consistent here with medieval philosophy as described by Gilson: "Just as it is by His goodness that God gives being to beings, so also it is by His goodness that He makes causes to be causes, thus delegating to them a certain participation in His power, along with a participation in His actuality" (*The Spirit of Philosophy*, 100). There is an echo here of Aquinas' notion that God "is in all things by his power, inasmuch as all things are subject to his power; He is by his presence in all things, as all things are bare and open to his eyes; He is in all things by his essence, inasmuch as He is present to all things as the cause of their being" (*ST* 1.Q8.A3).

8. Julian could owe these ideas to Boethius, probably through Chaucer's translation. On the idea of chance see *The Consolation of Philosophy* V, Prose 1; for the goodness of all that is done, see IV, Prose 6. Sin increases our inability to see things from God's perspective.

9. Note the echo of Genesis 1:31: "And God saw everything that God had made, and behold, it was very good."

10. Cf. 1 Cor 2:7: "But we impart a secret and hidden wisdom of God, which God decreed before the ages"; and Aquinas: "Because the divine wisdom is the cause of the distinction of things, therefore Moses said that things are made distinct by the Word of God, which is the conception of His wisdom; and this is what we read in Genesis [1:3–4]: God said: 'Be light made.'. . . . And He divided the light from the darkness" (*ST* 1.Q47.A1).

11. For a summary of the origins and development of this world view, see Bernard McGinn, *The Golden Chain: A Study in the Theological Anthropology of Isaac of Stella* (Washington, DC: Cistercian Publications, 1972), 51–102; cf. also Augustine, *Confessions* 7.12.18 and *De civitate Dei* 11.22; Aquinas, *ST* 1.Q47.A2.

12. Cf. Mk 1:11 and parallels: "Thou are my beloved Son; with thee I am well pleased."

13. See Ruether, 72–82.

14. This is a development of the synoptic theme that the forces of nature were affected by Christ's death, the most vivid description of which is in Mt 27:45–54. Possible sources for Julian's knowledge of this theme are noted in C&W, 367.15n, 368.27n, and 369.35n.

15. For the notion of microcosm, see McGinn, *The Golden Chain*, 122–33 and Lars Thunberg, "The Human Person as Image of God: Eastern Christianity," in *Christian*

Spirituality: Origins to the Twelfth Century, ed. Bernard McGinn and John Meyendorff (New York: Crossroad, 1986), 295–97. For its development by the twelfth century Cistercians, see the Introduction to *Three Treatises on Man: A Cistercian Anthropology*, ed. Bernard McGinn (Kalamazoo: Cistercian Publications, 1977), 88–89 (representative texts in the Cistercians are listed under note 339).

16. *De genesi ad litteram* 16.60. For a discussion of the proximity of the human soul to God in Augustine, see John Edward Sullivan, O.P., *The Image of God: The Doctrine of St. Augustine and Its Influence* (Dubuque: Priory Press, 1963), 16–22, and McGinn, *Three Treatises*, 58.

17. For example, even the work which may well have been the guide for Julian's life as an anchoress, *The Ancrene Riwle*, strongly emphasizes custody of the senses and protection against temptation to the seven deadly sins that can come from exposure to the world (Pt. 2; Salu, 21–52).

18. Sullivan, 84–93; for the difference between "vestige" and "image" see ibid., 19–20.

19. The classical expression of this is found in Augustine's *Confessions* 10.6.9 through 10.7.11. It was used extensively in medieval texts of spiritual guidance and is most explicitly developed in Bonaventure's *Itinerarium Mentis in Deum*.

20. Compare this to Augustine: "Out of an immoderate liking for . . . the least goods, we desert the best and highest goods, which are you, O Lord our God, and your truth and your law. These lower goods have their delights, but none such as my God, who has made all things, for in him the just man finds delight, and God is the joy of the upright of heart" (*Confessions* 2.5.10).

21. The echo of Augustine is so obvious here that it scarcely needs mentioning: "You have made us for yourself, and our hearts are restless until they rest in you" (*Confessions* 1.1).

22. Cf. "But seek first his kingdom and his righteousness, and all these things shall be yours as well" (Mt 6:33).

23. For the Greeks, see Ladner, 83–107 and Sullivan, 163–95. For Augustine, see Sullivan, 3–162 and Ladner, 185–203. The differences between Augustine and those who preceded him are summarized in Sullivan, 194–95.

24. For some examples, see Sullivan, 204–16 and 288–94. Julian is mentioned on 293. In addition, Sullivan's extensive treatment of the theme in Aquinas is found on 216–72.

25. For example, if Julian knew Augustine's *De trinitate*, as I think highly likely, she surely would have been aware of the fact that Augustine considered women to be deficient images of God: "The woman, together with her own husband, is the image of God, so that the whole substance may be one image, but when she is referred to separately in her quality as a helpmeet, which regards the woman alone, then she is not the image of God, but as regards the male alone, he is the image of God as fully and completely as when the woman too is joined with him in one" (7.7.10; trans. in Ruether, 95). See Ruether's further discussion of this misogynist strain in the *imago Dei* tradition, 93–99.

26. Bynum," . . . 'And Woman His Humanity'," 260–62.

27. Although Julian usually refers to this as human might, at times she calls it truth, mind, or memory, using the terms interchangeably. Augustine's concept of mind or memory designates the foundation or inner essence of human intellectual creation which expresses itself through the operations of understanding and will (Sullivan, 44–49). It was common from the twelfth century on to substitute "power" for "truth, mind or memory." It would be interesting to explore exactly how this change occurred, and how it altered the

meaning of the concept expressed. Julian clearly uses "might," the Middle English equivalent of "potentia," to mean the ability to accomplish what one desires.

28. "Not every thing which is in some way like God in creatures is also to be called his image, but only that to which he alone is superior; namely, that which has been expressed from him, and between which thing and himself no other nature has been interposed" (*De trinitate* 11.5.8, translated and discussed in Sullivan, 16).

29. The beginning of this passage could be subject to a pantheistic interpretation, something Julian seems to be aware of, since she immediately adds a qualification. A striking parallel is found in *The Spirit and the Soul* 24: "The soul is a spiritual substance. . . . We should not believe it to be a part of God nor of the same substance as God, nor yet made out of some elemental matter. Rather, it is a creature of God, created out of nothing" (McGinn, *Three Treatises*, 217).

30. For Augustine's theology of creation, see Ladner, 167–85, in which the most relevant texts are cited. For a shorter discussion, see Sullivan, 17–21.

31. "For I saw that God never began to love humankind; for just as humankind will be in endless bliss, fulfilling God's joy with regard to his works, just so has that same humankind been known and loved in God's prescience *from without beginning* in his righteous intent" (53:283); we find in Christ, the mediator "our full heaven in everlasting joy by the prescient purpose of all the blessed trinity *from without beginning*" (53:283); "In our creation we had beginning, but the love in which he created us was in him *from without beginning*" (86:342–43; emphasis mine).

32. Note how well this idea captures the thought of Augustine: "the concept of image used by Augustine demands the presence of God, not simply as a principle of origin . . . but requires the enduring presence of the exemplar as the term of the dynamic activity found in an image" (Sullivan, 21).

33. Note the conflation of several scriptural texts here: the author of Colossians wishes his readers the knowledge of Christ, "in whom are hid all the treasures of wisdom and knowledge" (Col 2:2–3) and later says: "your life is hid with Christ in God" (Col 3:3). Julian combines these with the idea that God "chose us in him [Christ] before the foundation of the world" (Eph 1:4).

34. For the roots of this idea in the Pauline corpus, see Ladner, 54–59; for the idea in Augustine, see Sullivan, 13–14, 21–22; in Bernard, see Etienne Gilson, *The Mystical Theology of St. Bernard*, translated by A. H. C. Downes (New York: Sheed & Ward, 1940), 52.

35. This is the theme of Col 1:15–20.

36. "I am the Alpha and the Omega" (Rev 1:8) and "I am the first and the last, and the living one" (Rev 1:17–18). Cf. Sullivan, 21.

37. The human body as such is not the image of God. Again, this is a basic Augustinian insight, followed by virtually all medieval thinkers (Sullivan, 44–52).

38. Gilson, *The Spirit of Philosophy*, 168–75.

39. Margaret R. Miles, *Augustine on the Body* (Missoula: Scholars Press, 1979); Sullivan, 48–49; McGinn, *Three Treatises*, 5–10.

40. Miles, 1–8, 127–31.

41. McGinn, *Three Treatises*, 87.

42. For a discussion of the effects of Aristotelian philosophy upon the problem of the unity of soul and body, and for Aquinas' solution, see Anton C. Pegis, *At the Origins of the Thomistic Notion of Man* (New York: Macmillan, 1963) and, more briefly, Gilson, *The Spirit of Philosophy*, 175–88; Bynum, *Holy Feast*, 254.

43. See Bynum's discussion of medieval women's attitudes toward the body (*Holy Feast*, 212–28) and of the medieval view of physicality (245–59).

44. Miles, 22–28.

45. See, for example, *The Spirit and the Soul* 9: "The life of the soul is twofold, for it lives in the flesh and in God. There are consequently two kinds of sense knowledge in man, an interior and an exterior one, each one having its own proper object which is its means of being renewed. The interior faculty is renewed in the contemplation of divine things and the exterior in the contemplation of things human. God became man, then, in order that the total man might find happiness in him" (McGinn, *Three Treatises*, 191).

46. McGinn, *Three Treatises*, 182–83. This treatise, composed almost completely of verbatim quotations from various sources, was very popular (there are 60 manuscripts of it in the British Museum alone) and was cited by many thirteenth century theologians, probably because it was thought to be of Augustinian origin. I think it highly likely that Julian knew its contents, for there are several instances, besides this one, where her thought is remarkably similar. For information on its origins and influence, see ibid., 63–74.

47. Ibid., 242. Cf. also "the sensuality, or animality of the soul is its lower energy which draws with it the sensuality of the flesh as an obedient servant" (244). Both quotations are taken from sections 37 and 38 which are transcriptions of Hugh of St. Victor's *Didascalion*.

48. My source here is Ladner, 177–83, who includes the relevant Augustinian texts in his notes. Augustine's chief source for the idea of the simultaneity of creation, which he cites repeatedly, is the Vulgate's rendering of Ecclesiasticus 18:1: "Qui vivit in aeternum, creavit omnia simul."

49. This explanation allowed Augustine to reconcile the account of Genesis 2 with that of Genesis 1 (Ladner, 183). *The Spirit and the Soul* 41 has an interesting interpretation of this part of Augustine's doctrine: "After the first act of creation, no new bodily materials were created, but all created at one time, bodies are propagated by formation in time. Souls were not essentially all made together in this way, but they were made in a like nature, in the image and likeness of God. Thus they are thought to have been made together but judged not to have been sent out together; not sent out together for the sake of the essence, but made together for the sake of the form that is like to the image and likeness of God. Flesh is passed on to flesh in the act of procreation, but the spirit is in no way begotten by the spirit" (McGinn, *Three Treatises*, 247).

50. For a similar idea in Augustine, see Miles, 95–96. See also *The Spirit and the Soul* 9: "God became man, then, in order that the total man might find happiness in him" (McGinn, *Three Treatises*, 191).

51. Note the similarity of this passage to the thought of Eph 4:4–13: "There is one body and one Spirit, just as you were called to the one hope that belongs to your call. . . . Grace was given to each of us according to the measure of Christ's gift. . . . And his gifts were . . . for building up the body of Christ, until we all attain to the unity of the faith and of the knowledge of the Son of God, to mature manhood, to the measure of the stature of the fulness of Christ" (C&W, 567.31n).

52. Ladner, 184.

53. This difference is marked in a comparison between Augustine and Gregory of Nyssa (ibid., 71–75, 175–77, 184–85).

54. To cite only one example, Hugh of St. Victor developed the theme elaborately; see

Ford Lewis Battles, "Hugo of Saint-Victor as a Moral Allegorist," *Church History* 18 (1949): 220–40, esp. 231–39.

55. See, for example, "Concerning the Relationship between Nature and Grace," *TI* I, 297–317, esp. 311–15.

56. Again Julian follows the mature Augustine, who saw that the divine image remains in its roots in humanity in spite of sin, since it belongs to the very nature of the intellectual soul to be the image of God (Sullivan, 42–44).

57. I have deleted the words "restored by grace" here, following the suggestion that this phrase is a scribal addition (C&W, 475.3n). If one understands Julian's idea of the image of God, this is a superfluous addition.

58. See Bernard McGinn's introduction to *On Grace and Free Choice* in *Treatises III: The Works of Bernard of Clairvaux*, ed. and trans. by Daniel O'Donovan, O.C.S.O. and Conrad Greenia, O.C.S.O. (Kalamazoo: Cistercian Publications, 1972), 28–29 and Gilson, *Mystical Theology*, 46–59. For another parallel to Julian's idea see *The Spirit and the Soul* 48, where the author writes: "Free will was committed to man. After Eve was seduced by the serpent and fell, man lost the goodness of his nature and the vigor of his judgment but not the power of choice, lest he not have the means to emend his sin. It remained to him to seek salvation by free will, that is by rational choice; but first he had to be helped and inspired by God to seek salvation. That we accept the inspiration to salvation is within our power; that we attain what we desire to attain is a divine gift" (McGinn, *Three Treatises*, 256).

59. These words are an exact repetition of 37:241.

60. See Karl Rahner's discussion on this in "On the Theology of the Incarnation," *TI* V, 177; cf. Carr, 150.

Chapter 6: The Work of Mercy

1. Thomas Tentler, *Sin and Confession on the Eve of the Reformation* (Princeton: Princeton University Press, 1977); Mary Flowers Braswell, *The Medieval Sinner: Characterization and Confession in the Literature of the English Middle Ages* (East Brunswick/London/Toronto: Associated University Presses [Teaneck, NJ: Fairleigh Dickinson University Press], 1983).

2. See Georgianna, 70–110 for a good discussion of the awareness of the role of the individual conscience which developed in the twelfth and thirteenth centuries.

3. These differed from the old manuals, originating from the Celtic monks, which had included merely external lists of sins and penances appropriate to each (see John T. McNeill and Helena M. Gamer, *Medieval Handbooks of Penance* [NY: Columbia University Press, 1938]). One of the most influential of the new type of manual was the *Liber Poenitentiales* of Robert of Flamborough (see the critical edition of J. J. Francis Firth, C.S.B [Toronto: Pontifical Institute of Mediaeval Studies, 1971]), which Braswell describes in detail (38–45).

4. For the development of the tradition of the seven cardinal or deadly sins in Western thought, see Morton W. Bloomfield, *The Seven Deadly Sins: An Introduction to the History of a Religious Concept, with Special Reference to Medieval English Literature* (Lansing: Michigan State College Press, 1952). The *Ancrene Riwle* is the first important work in English to treat the seven deadly sins in any kind of detail (ibid., 148–51). The *Riwle* was strongly influenced by the penance manuals, a correspondence that is discussed by Braswell (45–51) and by Gerard Sitwell in his introduction to Salu's translation of the *Riwle* (xviii–xxi). Georgianna

calls Part 5 of the *Ancrene Riwle* the first vernacular penance manual directed towards penitents rather than priests (102). A good example of the categorization of sins and their remedies can also be found in *The Book of Vices and Virtues* (EETS 217, ed. W. Nelson Francis [London: Oxford University Press, 1942]), a fourteenth century Middle English translation of Lorens D'Orleans' *Somme le Roi*, originally written in 1279.

5. A good example of this instruction can be found in *The Lay Folks' Catechism*, EETS OS 118, ed. Thomas Frederick Simmons and Henry Edward Nolloth (London: Kegan Paul, Trench, Trübner, 1901).

6. Robert Mannyng of Brunne's *Handlyng Sin* is an example book for preachers devoted entirely to sermons about sin and its remedies. See the version edited by Idelle Sullens (Binghamton, NY: Medieval and Renaissance Texts and Studies, 1983). Cf. Braswell, 52–57.

7. Braswell, 61–129.

8. Ibid., 25–30, 52.

9. By the time Julian wrote the Short Text, England had suffered through three episodes of the plague: 1348–49, 1361–62, 1369; there was a final outbreak in 1379 (McKisack, 331–33). See Philip Ziegler, *The Black Death* (New York: Harper & Row, 1969) and Robert S. Gottfried, *The Black Death: Natural and Human Disaster in Medieval Europe* (New York: The Free Press, 1983).

10. See Dunne's description of this (*A Search For God*, 76–83).

11. This is the exact line of reasoning followed in *The Consolation of Philosophy*: "No one can doubt . . . but that God is almighty. . . . There is nothing that the almighty cannot do. . . . Can God do evil? . . . Wherefore . . . evil is nothing, since God cannot do it who can do anything" (III, Prose 12, lines 74–82). It is also the position of Augustine; see *Confessions* 7.3–5, 7.11–16, and Gillian Evans, *Augustine on Evil* (Cambridge: Cambridge University Press, 1982), esp. 1–6.

12. By contrast, Augustine very definitely sets the origin of sin in Adam's will (*De Nuptiis et Concupiscentia* 2:48, 50).

13. The similarity here to Romans 5:20–21 has been noted in Chapter 3 above, p. 57. Augustine also substantially developed the view that God subsumes evil into good. See, for example, *De Ordine* 2.4, 2.7; *De Nuptiis* 2.48; G. Evans, 93–97.

14. The origin of evil has been an incomprehensible problem for the whole history of thought. See, for example, Paul Ricoeur's discussion of the ambiguity of the Adamic myth in *The Symbolism of Evil*, 243–52. Augustine came to the unsatisfying conclusion that evil came mysteriously out of good, in the case of both angels and humanity (*De Nuptiis* 2.48, 50).

15. By contrast see Aquinas' extensive treatment of human nature in the state of original justice (*ST* 1–2.QQ 94–101).

16. See Wis 10:1–2: "Wisdom protected the first-formed father of the world, when he alone had been created; she delivered him from his transgression, and gave him strength to rule all things." Augustine, citing this text, links it to Christ's descent into hell where he liberated Adam (*Epistolae* 164.6).

17. See Claus Westermann, *Creation*, trans. John J. Scullion, S. J. (Philadelphia: Fortress Press, 1974), 89. This is certainly also true of Augustine, whose theological construction allowed for the simultaneous influence of both sin and grace on the human soul. In the *Confessions*, for example, he reflects upon how God's grace was ever at work in his life, even before his baptism, leading and drawing him to conversion (*Confessions* 13.1). God's blessing (grace) continues to attend the creation of human nature, even though that

creation is conceived under the influence of original sin: "God's gift is bestowed on the seminal elements of His creature with the same bounty wherewith 'He maketh His sun to rise on the evil and on the good, and sendeth rain on the just and unjust.' It is with so large a bounty that God has blessed the very seeds, and by blessing has constituted them. Nor has this blessing been eliminated out of our excellent nature by a fault which puts us under condemnation. . . . God's work continues still good, however evil be the deeds of the impious" (*De Gratia Christi et de Peccato Originali* 2.46).

18. While Augustine generally emphasizes the "willfulness" of sin more strongly than Julian does, he too considers sin "a wound" or a "bad state of health" afflicting an essentially good nature (*De Nuptiis* 2.57).

19. This is how Jesus can be said to have been "made sin" for us, following 2 Cor 5:21. Augustine, too, was interested only in moral evil (G. Evans, 97–98).

20. *De diversis*, Sermo 42.2; *PL* 183, 662. The Latin phrase Bernard employs, "regio dissimilitudinis," is taken from Augustine (*Confessions* 7.10.16), although Bernard uses it slightly differently. See the discussion of this in Gilson, *Mystical Theology*, 45–46.

21. Julian does not use this terminology, though she does distinguish between Adam's sin and personal sin.

22. Julian follows Augustine's anti-Pelagianism here, especially as developed in *De Peccatorum Meritus et Remissione* and *Contra Duas Epistolas Pelagianorum* (G. Evans, 128–32, 137–38).

23. For example, some things appear to be "chance" in human sight because of human "blindness" (11:197), and Julian questions the existence of evil because of her "folly" (27:224).

24. The phrase "the old root of our first sin" recalls the action of the servant of the parable, raising up "the great root out of the deep depth" (51:277), that is, rescuing sinful human nature from the powers of hell. See the discussion of this in Chapter 3 above, p. 56 and n. 31.

25. The barrenness of the earth recalls many scriptural references to the effect of sin upon the earth: for example, Gen 3:17–18, Ex 16:3, Lev 16:22, Mt 24:15, Lk 15:14. It also recalls Bernard's *regio dissimilitudinis* (n. 20 above, this chapter).

26. Julian could be indebted here to the *Salve Regina*: "To thee do we send up our sighs, mourning and weeping in this valley of tears."

27. By the "exterior part" Julian says she means "our mortal flesh," but by extension includes the soul's sensuality in which she feels "regret." The "interior part" is the soul's substance.

28. Note how the body "without shape and form" recalls Gen 1:2: "The earth was without form and void"; Julian frequently draws a parallel between the nothingness before creation and the nothingness of sin. This passage is one of the few times that Julian even approaches the language frequently used in her day to describe the miseries of the flesh. Usually she shows more restraint. The picture of the oppressive, fearsome, stinking body of pain from which we need to be rescued could owe its graphic detail to the actual dead bodies of plague victims which Julian may have viewed first-hand. Colledge and Walsh note an interesting parallel to Julian's imagery: in a manuscript of Hildegard of Bingen's *Scivias*, there is an illustration of "a young woman from whose mouth a naked child emerges to fly up to welcoming angels, escaping the devils who lurk in wait for it" (C&W, 622.32n and 623.33n).

29. Rom 8:2–17; Gal 5:16–24.

30. For example, see Augustine, *De Nuptiis* 1.25, 30, 34; Aquinas, *ST* 1–2.Q77.A5,

Q82.A3. While Augustine most frequently associates concupiscence with temptation to covetousness and lust, he describes it generally as "a languor after illness" (*De Nuptiis* 1.28), similar to Julian's "heaviness of body."

31. "For I delight in the law of God, in my inmost self, but I see in my members another law at war with the law of my mind and making me captive to the law of sin which dwells in my members" (Rom 7:22–23).

32. It was a commonplace in the Middle Ages to regard the hour of death as a time when one was particularly susceptible to the torments of evil spirits, who were always lying in wait for the soul. Medieval crucifixion iconography often depicted devils surrounding the bad thief, or even the cross of Christ (C&W, 209.37n).

33. For a study of medieval belief in the devil, see Jeffrey B. Russell, *Lucifer: The Devil in the Middle Ages* (Berkeley: University of California Press, 1984). See also C&W, 635.2n, 7n; 636.9n, 10n, 12n.

34. This is similar to the conflict of wills described by Paul in Rom 7:15–25 and by Augustine in Book 8 of the *Confessions*, esp. 8.5.10–12 and 8.9.21.

35. Julian may have been familiar with what Walter Hilton had to say on this subject: that sensuality draws the soul's reason down to its level (*The Scale of Perfection* 2.14).

36. This could be an allusion to the Free Spirit heresy, which supposedly claimed it was possible to attain perfection in this life. Julian relates several times in her revelations that she herself shall continue to sin (37:241, 79:333).

37. One's "empty affections" for the "pomps and pride and the vainglory of this wretched life" need to be broken down, along with one's "vicious pride" (28:226). Furthermore, "if we are moved to be careless about our way of life or about the custody of our heart," presuming on the strength of God's love for us, we "need to beware of this impulse," for "it is false . . . and has no resemblance to God's will" (79:334). Compare the *Ancrene Riwle* where the first "rule" of life is the "right directing" or custody of the heart; this interior rule is much more important than rules governing external conduct (Intr.; Salu, 1).

38. "Let us . . . neither on the one side fall too low, inclining to despair, nor on the other side be too reckless, as though we did not care; but let us meekly recognize our weakness, knowing that we cannot stand for the twinkling of an eye except with the protection of grace" (52:281). The tension between presumption and despair is an important theme in the *Ancrene Riwle* (Georgianna, 125–26).

39. The connection Julian makes between sloth and despair is interesting. By her day, sloth was considered one of the seven deadly sins, and it had acquired the meaning it has today, signifying laziness. But in the cardinal sin tradition, which came to the West through Cassian and Gregory, this sin was referred to variously as *accidia*, implying an apathy or listlessness about spiritual matters, and/or as *tristitia*, undue sadness or melancholy (Bloomfield, 70, 72, 96, 112–13). In linking despair to sloth, Julian betrays some awareness of this earlier stage of the tradition. In the *Ancrene Riwle*, despair is the eighth cub of sloth (Pt. 4, Salu, 90).

40. The tradition of pride as root of the seven cardinal sins seems to have originated with Gregory, whose teaching on the sins became dominant in the Middle Ages (Bloomfield, 73–75). This influence is seen in Walter Hilton, Julian's contemporary, to cite one example. He warns against the danger of "the movements of melancholy" (*Scale* 1.90), but not to the extent that he emphasizes the dangers of pride, which he considers "the beginning of every kind of sin" (1.85; cf. also 1.56–63). See also Braswell, 39–41, 69–70, 79.

41. See, for example, Valerie Saiving [Goldstein], "The Human Situation: A Feminine View," *The Journal of Religion* 40:2 (1960): 100–12; Carr, 57–58, 186.

42. Compare this to the opening pages of the *Ancrene Riwle*, where the author's purpose in writing a rule for the "right directing of the heart" is to keep it "untroubled and free . . . from overscrupulous self-accusations which say: 'In this matter you are committing sin,' or 'that is not yet amended as well as it ought to be.'" (Intr.; Salu, 1).

43. Part 4 of *The Ancrene Riwle* graphically describes the seven deadly sins as beasts, each of which has numerous offspring representing the many sins that follow from these seven. Those who fall victim to the deadly sins are described as members of the devil's court, married to each of the "seven hags" and responsible for the offspring (Salu, 85–93; cf. Georgianna, 126–31). Walter Hilton has an extensive treatment of temptations to the seven deadly sins in *The Scale of Perfection*; see especially Book 1, chapters 52–73. However, Bloomfield has found that, while most mention the seven deadly sins, the fourteenth century English mystics, notably Rolle and the *Cloud* author (and, we might add, Julian), "show a dissatisfaction with the overclassification of sin which is the forerunner of an attitude to become fairly common in the next century," revealing "an independent attitude and a carelessness about detailed enumeration and analysis which are refreshing, if unusual" (Bloomfield, 176; cf. 177–82).

44. "Let anyone who thinks that he stands take heed lest he fall" (1 Cor 10:12).

45. The hiddenness of sin is treated extensively in the *Ancrene Riwle* (Georgianna, 131–38).

46. On the importance of shame for the remission of sins, see Georgianna, 96–97, 110–111.

47. Note the reference in this passage to the "three wounds" that Julian had prayed to attain for herself: contrition, compassion, and longing for God ("holy desires to God for him").

48. Compare the Song of Songs 8:6–7: "Love is strong as death, . . . Many waters cannot quench love, neither can floods drown it."

49. Romans 6:1–4. Colledge and Walsh acknowledge that this is one place where Julian betrays an awareness of contemporary heresy, notably that of the Free Spirit (C&W, 456.28n, 29n).

50. *De Peccato Originali* 34. English translation by Peter Holmes and Robert Wallis (*Nicene and Post-Nicene Fathers*, Vol. V: *Saint Augustin: Anti-Pelagian Writings* (New York: Charles Scribner's Sons, 1908), 249.

51. The possibility of salvation for those not in the church is discussed in Chapter 7 below, pp. 164–66.

52. Note the economic trinitarian construction of this passage, wherein the works of nature, mercy, and grace are visible.

53. This recalls Augustine's famous line "Noverim me, noverim te" (*Soliloquies* 2.1.1) and it is essential to his thought. Gilson calls it "Christian Socratism" (*The Spirit of Philosophy*, 209–28). See also McGinn, *The Golden Chain*, 109–12 (a list of twelfth century authors who developed this popular theme are found at note 27).

54. Paul prays that the Ephesians may be "rooted and grounded in love" (Eph 3:17).

55. These prayers correspond to the devotions listed in the *Ancrene Riwle*, Pt. 1; Salu, pp. 7–8 (C&W, 77–78).

56. "But rejoice in so far as you share Christ's sufferings, that you may also rejoice and be glad when his glory is revealed" (1 Peter 4:13).

57. The penitential manuals invariably listed the ten commandments and the sins

connected with each. See, for example, *The Lay Folks' Catechism* (Simmons and Nolloth, 31–60).

58. Jn 14:5–6; Ps 23:1–3.

59. These three virtues are singled out and mentioned together at the beginning of the *Ancrene Riwle* (Intr.; Salu, 3).

60. One of the most famous treatises on humility was written by Bernard of Clairvaux: "The Steps of Humility and Pride" in *Treatises II: The Works of Bernard of Clairvaux*, ed. M. Basil Pennington, O.C.S.O, trans. M. Ambrose Conway, O.C.S.O. (Washington, DC: Cistercian Publications, 1974).

61. This passage may owe its inspiration to the *Ancrene Riwle*: "Our Lord, when He allows us to be tempted, is playing with us as a mother with her darling child. She runs away from him and hides, and leaves him on his own, and he looks around for her, calling 'Mama! Mama!' and crying a little, and then she runs out to him quickly, her arms outspread, and she puts them round him, and kisses him, and wipes his eyes" (Pt. 4; Salu, 102). Note, however, that Julian has not kept the image of God as a playful deceiver (Georgianna, 134–35), although elsewhere she does say that God allows us to experience distress for our profit (cf. 28:226; 61:300).

62. In Mt 18:1–4, Jesus singles out the humblest, the little child, as the greatest in the kingdom of heaven.

63. Ralph Hanna III, "Some Commonplaces of Late Medieval Patience Discussions: An Introduction," in Gerald J. Schiffhorst, ed., *The Triumph of Patience* (Orlando: University Presses of Florida, 1978), 65–87. See also Elizabeth D. Kirk, " 'Who Suffreth More Than God?': Narrative Redefinition of Patience in *Patience* and *Piers Plowman*," in the same volume, 88–104.

64. See note 39 above in this chapter.

65. This is an aspect of medieval piety extremely difficult for moderns to understand. Bynum provides an insightful discussion of the motivations behind ascetical practices in *Holy Feast*, 208–18. While asceticism has been practiced in Christianity since its origins, Kieckhefer notes that there was an intensification of ascetical practices in the fourteenth century, probably due to the effects of the Black Death: *Unquiet Souls: Fourteenth Century Saints and their Religious Milieu* (Chicago: University of Chicago Press, 1984), 1–3.

66. Note the difference between Julian in her maturity and the way she had been in her youth, desiring extraordinary suffering in order to share Christ's passion (2:177–78).

67. "And we all, with unveiled face, beholding the glory of the Lord, are being changed into his likeness from one degree of glory to another" (2 Cor 3:18).

68. "For my yoke is easy and my burden is light" (Mt 11:30).

69. Jn 17:21–26; 1 Jn 4:12–16.

70. "I am the least of the apostles" (1 Cor 15:9).

Chapter 7: The Work of Grace

1. Leclercq, *The Love of Learning*, 65–86.

2. Note how this image recalls scriptural passages about the eschatological banquet, such as Mt 22:1–10 and Rev 19:9.

3. This passage is full of scriptural echoes. For example, the joy and honor of the first heaven recall the reward promised in the beatitudes to those who suffer for righteousness (Mt 5:6, 11–12), the parable of the talents (Mt 25:14–30; Lk 19:11–27) and the parable of the last judgment (Mt 25:31–34), and John 12:26: "if anyone serve me the Father will

honor him." The second heaven recalls Ps 90:16 and the joy of all heaven over repentant sinners of Lk 15:7, 10.

4. Note how this picks up the theme of the parable of the workers in the vineyard (Mt 20:1–16).

5. This recalls Christ's transfiguration: "and his garments became glistening, intensely white" (Mk 9:3).

6. The image of the crown symbolizes that Christ, the faithful servant, receives the reward of the just, as in Isaiah 61:10: "he has clothed me with the garments of salvation, he has covered me with the robe of righteousness, as a bridegroom decks himself with a garland," and James 1:12: "Blessed is the man who endures trial, for when he has stood the test he will receive the crown of life which God has promised to those who love him." See also Heb 2:9: "But we see Jesus, who for a little while was made lower than the angels, crowned with glory and honor."

7. The use of "city" in this context, recalls Rev 21:2–3: "And I saw the holy city, new Jerusalem, coming down out of heaven from God, prepared as a bride adorned for her husband; and I heard a loud voice from the throne saying, 'Behold the dwelling of God is with men. He will dwell with them, and they shall be his people, and God himself will be with them.'" See Leclercq's comments on the symbol of the heavenly Jerusalem (*The Love of Learning*, 66–70, 76–83).

8. This is the union desired by Jesus in John 17:21: "That they may all be one; even as thou, Father, art in me, and I in thee, that they also may be in us."

9. This passage provides a clear example of the kind of sensual language frequently used in the Middle Ages for describing the experience of God (cf. Bynum, *Holy Feast*, pp. 150–52). It lists the "spiritual senses," which were often elaborately described in mystical literature (See, for example, Karl Rahner, "The Doctrine of the 'Spiritual Senses' in the Middle Ages," *TI* XVI, 104–34). The end of the passage has scriptural ties; see 1 Cor 13:12: "For now we see in a mirror dimly, but then face to face" and 1 Jn 3:2: "Beloved, we are God's children now; it does not yet appear what we shall be, but we know that when he appears we shall be like him, for we shall see him as he is."

10. This is an elaboration on the promise of Rev 21:4: "He will wipe away every tear from their eyes, and death shall be no more, neither shall there be mourning nor crying nor pain any more, for the former things have passed away."

11. The trembling of the pillars of heaven is a scriptural image: "the pillars of heaven tremble, and are astounded" (Job 26:11); also, in Isaiah's vision of God, "the foundations of the thresholds shook at the voice of him who called" (Is 6:4).

12. Colledge and Walsh point out that Julian may have in mind here the resurrection appearances of Christ in which peace is offered and fear is dispelled (Mt 28:10; Lk 24:36–38; Jn 20:19–21, 26; C&W, 506.13n).

13. Note how this parallels Mt 11:28–30, especially "For my yoke is easy and my burden is light."

14. The "friendly welcoming" recalls the welcome given to the prodigal son in Lk 15:20.

15. Compare with Col 3:2: "Set your minds on things that are above, not on things that are on earth."

16. See the discussion of this in Chapter 3 above, pp. 56–57.

17. This passage could owe its inspiration to Phil 4:4–6: "Rejoice in the Lord always; again I will say, Rejoice. . . . Have no anxiety about anything, but in everything by prayer and supplication with thanksgiving let your requests be made to God," and Heb 12:28:

"let us be grateful . . . and let us offer to God acceptable worship, with reverence and awe."

18. This echoes the phrase "una voce dicentes" of the Preface, the preamble to the prayer of the heavenly host taken from Isaiah 6:3: "Holy, holy, holy is the Lord of hosts." It is also reminiscent of the picture of heaven given at the end of Augustine's *De civitate Dei* (22.30).

19. Aquinas also distinguishes between Uncreated Charity, which is the Holy Spirit dwelling in us and created charity, whereby we participate in the mutual love between Father and Son (*ST* 2–2.Q23.A2). He also understands charity as a virtue infused into the soul (*ST* 2–2.Q24.A3). See C&W, 727.10n for other references.

20. Julian is obviously applying the message of 1 John 4:17–18: "In this is love perfected with us, that we may have confidence for the day of judgment. . . . There is no fear in love, but perfect love casts out fear. For fear has to do with punishment, and he who fears is not perfected in love." This thought underlies the teaching of Cassian, Augustine, and Bernard on the "filial fear" of God (cf. Clark, "*Fiducia,*" 101).

21. See Chapter 4 above, pp. 74–79.

22. Note here how grace builds on nature. Colledge and Walsh consider this to be one of Julian's finest rhetorical and theological passages. See their comment at 673.20n.

23. Note the parallel to the thought of Is 11:3: "His delight shall be in the fear of the Lord."

24. See the discussion of this in Pelikan, 174–84.

25. Such extremes were brilliantly satirized by Erasmus (cf. *Ten Colloquies,* trans. Craig R. Thompson [Indianapolis: Bobbs-Merrill, 1957]). For a discussion of medieval popular devotions, see Ronald C. Finucane, *Miracles and Pilgrims: Popular Beliefs in Medieval England* (Totowa, NJ: Rowman & Littlefield, 1977).

26. Julian obviously expects John of Beverly to be known to her readers, but his fame has not extended to the present day. See C&W, 51 and 447.22n for information about him.

27. The last line of this passage is an obvious paraphrase of Lk 1:38.

28. Note how this passage expresses the sentiment of the Magnificat (Lk 1:46–55). It also contains an allusion to the angel's greeting of Lk 1:28.

29. The notion of *Apocatastasis panton* is found in Clement of Alexandria, Origen, and Gregory of Nyssa. It was strongly attacked by Augustine. Julian, so thoroughly Augustinian in other respects, parts from him here, as she does with her teaching on sin. *Apocatastasis* was formally condemned by the Council of Constantinople in 543. Julian was correct in understanding this to be against church teaching (see the discussion of this in Chapter 1 above, pp. 18–22, with respect to the danger of heresy). For a bibliography on *apocatastasis*, see Gotthold Müller, *Apocatastasis Panton: A Bibliography* (Basel: Basler Missionsbuchhandlung, 1969).

30. Cf. Mt 25:41; Is 14:12–14.

31. Lk 18:27: "What is impossible with men is possible with God" and par. in Mt 19:26, and Lk 1:37: "For with God nothing will be impossible" (cf. also Gen 18:14; Job 42:2; Jer 32:17).

32. Note the congruence here with Ps 69:28: "Let them be blotted out of the book of the living; let them not be enrolled among the righteous."

33. Clark makes this interpretation ("*Fiducia,*" 105).

34. Lk 15:3–10.

35. Julian never even considers the solution advanced by Calvin a century and a half later, that God predestines some to damnation. This would be irreconcilable with her understanding of God's love.

36. Note 1 Cor 2:7: "But we impart a secret and hidden wisdom of God, which God decreed before the ages for our glorification"; Rom 11:33: "O the depth of the riches and wisdom and knowledge of God! How unsearchable are his judgments and how inscrutable his ways!" and Sir 11:4: "For the works of the Lord are wonderful, and his works are concealed from men."

37. This deed is not to be confused with another deed Julian speaks of which pertains to the future salvation of the individual Christian, referring especially to how God will make human sinfulness the cause of heavenly bliss, something which remains a mystery to us in this present life, but which we will understand immediately upon entering heaven. Julian makes a special effort to distinguish this deed from the one mentioned earlier (36:238–40).

38. See the discussion of this in Chapter 6 above, p. 127.

39. Julian is trying to counteract the great fear of death and final judgment which permeated the popular religion of her day, made explicit, for instance, in the *Dies Irae* and the *Libera Me* of the Mass for the Dead. This fear is, as Colledge and Walsh note, contrary to her spirit of trust (C&W, 729.11n).

40. This is similar to Karl Rahner's conclusion about universal salvation. See "The Hermeneutics of Eschatological Assertions," *TI* IV, 338–40. See also John R. Sachs, S.J., "Current Eschatology: Universal Salvation and the Problem of Hell," *Theological Studies* 52:2 (1991):227–54.

Bibliography

Editions of *Showings:*

A Book of Showings to the Anchoress Julian of Norwich. Edited by Edmund Colledge, O.S.A. and James Walsh, S.J. Toronto: Pontifical Institute of Mediaeval Studies, 1978.

Showings. Edited and translated into Modern English from the Critical Text by Edmund Colledge, O.S.A. and James Walsh, S.J. New York: Paulist Press, 1978.

A Revelation of Love. Edited by Marion Glasscoe. Exeter: Exeter University Press, 1976.

Revelations of Divine Love. Edited and translated by Clifton Wolters. Harmondsworth: Penguin Books, 1966.

Revelations of Divine Love Shewed to Devout Ankress by Name Julian of Norwich. Edited by Dom Roger Hudleston, O.S.B. London: Burns & Oates, 1927.

XVI Revelations of Divine Love Shewed to Mother Juliana of Norwich. Edited by George Tyrell. London: Kegan Paul, Trench, Trübner, 1902.

Revelations of Divine Love. Edited by Grace Warrack. London: Methuen, 1901.

Other Sources:

Allen, Christine. "Christ Our Mother in Julian of Norwich." *Studies in Religion/Sciences Religieux* 10:4 (1981): 421–28.

Ancrene Riwle. *The English Text of the Ancrene Riwle*. EETS 225. Edited by Mabel Day. London: Oxford University Press, 1952.

———. Edited and translated by Mary B. Salu. London: Burns & Oates, 1955.

Anselm of Canterbury. *St. Anselm: Basic Writings*. 2nd ed. Translated by S. N. Deane. La Salle, IL: Open Court, 1979.

Aquinas, Thomas. *Summa Theologica*. 3 vols. Translated by the Fathers of the English Dominican Province. New York: Benziger Brothers, 1947.

Archer, John and Barbara Lloyd. *Sex and Gender*. Cambridge: Cambridge University Press, 1985.

Aston, Margaret. *Lollards and Reformers: Images and Literacy in Late Medieval Religion*. London: Hambledon, 1984.

Atkinson, Clarissa. *Mystic and Pilgrim: The "Book" and the World of Margery Kempe*. Ithaca: Cornell University Press, 1983.

Augustine of Hippo. *Concerning the City of God against the Pagans*. Translated by Henry Bettenson with an Introduction by David Knowles. Harmondsworth: Penguin Books, 1972.

———. *The Confessions of St. Augustine*. Edited and translated by John K. Ryan. Garden City: Doubleday, 1960.

———. *Saint Augustin: Anti-Pelagian Writings*. Nicene and Post-Nicene Fathers. Vol. V. Translated by Peter Holmes and Robert Wallis. New York: Charles Scribner's Sons, 1908.

———. *The Trinity*. Translated by Stephen McKenna, C.SS.R. Washington, DC: Catholic University of America Press, 1963.

Barker, Paula S. Datsko. "The Motherhood of God in Julian of Norwich's Theology." *Downside Review* 100 (1982): 290–304.

Battles, Ford Lewis. "Hugo of Saint-Victor as a Moral Allegorist." *Church History* 18 (1949): 220–40.

Bernard of Clairvaux. *Treatises II: The Works of Bernard of Clairvaux.* Edited by M. Basil Pennington, O.C.S.O. and translated by M. Ambrose Conway, O.C.S.O. Washington, DC: Cistercian Publications, 1974.

———. *Treatises III: The Works of Bernard of Clairvaux.* Edited and translated by Daniel O'Donovan, O.C.S.O. and Conrad Greenia, O.C.S.O. Kalamazoo: Cistercian Publications, 1977.

Bloomfield, Morton W. *The Seven Deadly Sins: An Introduction to the History of a Religious Concept with Special Reference to Medieval English Literature.* Lansing: Michigan State College Press, 1952.

Boenig, Robert. "The God-as-Mother Theme in Richard Rolle's Biblical Commentaries." *Mystics Quarterly* 10 (1984): 171–74.

Bolton, Brenda M. "Mulieres Sanctae." In *Sanctity and Secularity: The Church and the World.* Studies in Church History X. Edited by Derek Baker. Oxford: Basil Blackwell, 1973: 77–95.

The Book of Vices and Virtues. EETS 217. Edited by W. Nelson Francis. London: Oxford University Press, 1942.

Børresen, Kari Elisabeth. "Christ Nôtre Mère, La Théologie de Julianne de Norwich." *Mitteilungen und Forschungsbeiträge de Cusanus-Gesellschaft* 13 (1978): 320–29.

Bradley, Ritamary. "The Motherhood Theme in Julian of Norwich." *Fourteenth Century English Mystics Newsletter* 2:4 (1976): 25–30.

———. "Mysticism in the Motherhood Similitude of Julian of Norwich." *Studia Mystica* 8 (1985): 4–14.

———. "Patristic Background of the Motherhood Similitude in Julian of Norwich." *Christian Scholar's Review* 8:2 (1978): 101–13.

Braswell, Mary Flowers. *The Medieval Sinner: Characterization and Confession in the Literature of the English Middle Ages.* East Brunswick/London/Toronto: Associated University Presses [Teaneck, NJ: Fairleigh Dickinson University Press], 1983.

Brigid of Sweden. *The Revelations of St. Birgitta.* EETS 178. Edited by W. P. Cumming. London: Oxford University Press, 1929.

Butler, Cuthbert. *Western Mysticism: The Teaching of Ss. Augustine, Gregory and Bernard on Contemplation and the Contemplative Life.* 2nd ed. London: Constable, 1926.

Bynum, Caroline Walker, Stevan Harrell, and Paula Richman, eds. *Gender and Religion: On the Complexity of Symbols.* Boston: Beacon Press, 1986.

Bynum, Caroline Walker. *Holy Feast and Holy Fast: The Religious Significance of Food to Medieval Women.* Berkeley: University of California Press, 1987.

———. *Jesus as Mother: Studies in the Spirituality of the High Middle Ages.* Berkeley: University of California Press, 1982.

Cabussut, André. "Une dévotion médiévale peu connue: la dévotion à Jésus, nôtre mère." *Revue d'ascétique et de mystique* 25 (1949): 231–45.

Carr, Anne E. *Transforming Grace: Christian Tradition and Women's Experience.* San Francisco: Harper & Row, 1988.

Chambers, P. Franklin. *Juliana of Norwich: An Introductory Appreciation and An Interpretive Anthology.* New York: Harper & Bros., 1953.

The Chastising of God's Children and the Treatise of Perfection of the Sons of God. Edited by Joyce Bazire and Eric Colledge. Oxford: Basil Blackwell, 1957.

Chaucer, Geoffrey. *Chaucer's Translation of Boethius's 'De Consolatione Philosophiae.'* EETS ES 5. Edited by Richard Morris. London: N. Trübner, 1868; reprint 1969.

Clark, John P. H. *"Fiducia* in Julian of Norwich." *Downside Review* 99 (1981): 97–108, 214–29.

———. "Nature, Grace and the Trinity in Julian of Norwich." *Downside Review* 100 (1982): 203–20.

———. "Predestination in Christ According to Julian of Norwich." *Downside Review* 100 (1982): 79–91.

Clay, Rotha Mary. *The Hermits and Anchorites of England.* London: Methuen, 1914; reprint, Detroit: Singing Tree Press, 1968.

Coleman, Janet. *English Literature in History, 1350–1400: Medieval Readers and Writers.* London: Hutchinson, 1981.

Coleman, Thomas. *English Mystics of the Fourteenth Century.* London: Epworth Press, 1938.

Colledge, Edmund and James Walsh. "Editing Julian of Norwich's *Revelations:* A Progress Report." *Mediaeval Studies* 38 (1976): 404–27.

Constable, Giles. "The Popularity of Twelfth-Century Spiritual Writers in the Late Middle Ages." *Renaissance Studies in Honor of Hans Baron.* Edited by Anthony Molho and John A. Tedeschi. DeKalb, IL: Northern Illinois University Press, 1971: 5–28.

———. "Twelfth-Century Spirituality and the Late Middle Ages." *Medieval and Renaissance Studies* 5. Edited by O. B. Hardison, Jr. Chapel Hill: University of North Carolina Press, 1972: 27–60.

Cross, Claire. " 'Great Reasoners in Scripture': The Activities of Women Lollards 1380–1530." In *Medieval Women.* Studies in Church History Subsidia I. Edited by Derek Baker. Oxford: Basil Blackwell, 1978: 359–80.

Daley, Brian E., S.J. " 'A Humble Mediator': The Distinctive Elements in Saint Augustine's Christology." *Word and Spirit* 9 (1987): 100–17.

Darwin, Francis D. S. *The English Medieval Recluse.* London: SPCK, 1944.

Deanesly, Margaret. *The Lollard Bible and Other Medieval Biblical Versions.* Cambridge: Cambridge University Press, 1920.

Dunne, John. *A Search for God in Time and Memory.* Notre Dame: Notre Dame University Press, 1977.

Egan, Harvey D., S.J. *Christian Mysticism: The Future of a Tradition.* New York: Pueblo Publishing Company, 1984.

Evans, Gillian. *Augustine on Evil.* Cambridge: Cambridge University Press, 1982.

Evans, W. O. " 'Cortaysye' in Middle English." *Mediaeval Studies* 29 (1967): 143–57.

Finucane, Ronald C. *Miracles and Pilgrims: Popular Beliefs in Medieval England.* Totowa, NJ: Rowman & Littlefield, 1977.

Fowler, David C. *The Bible in Middle English Literature.* Seattle: University of Washington Press, 1984.

Ganshof, Francis L. *Feudalism.* London: Longmans, Green, 1964.

Georgianna, Linda. *The Solitary Self: Individuality in the "Ancrene Wisse."* Cambridge: Harvard University Press, 1981.

Gilson, Etienne. *The Mystical Theology of St. Bernard.* Translated by A. H. C. Downes. New York: Sheed & Ward, 1940.

———. *The Spirit of Mediaeval Philosophy.* Translated by A. H. C. Downes. New York: Charles Scribner's Sons, 1936.

Gottfried, Robert S. *The Black Death: Natural and Human Disaster in Medieval Europe.* New York: The Free Press, 1983.

Grundmann, H. *Religiöse Bewegungen im Mittelalter*. 2nd ed. Hildesheim, 1961.

Guarnieri, Romana. "Il Movimento del Libero Spirito." *Archivio Italiano per la storia della pieta* 4 (1965): 351–708.

Hilton, Walter. *The Stairway of Perfection*. Edited and translated by M. L. Del Mastro. Garden City: Doubleday, 1979.

Jacques de Vitry. *The Exempla or Illustrative Stories from the Sermones Vulgares of Jacques de Vitry*. Edited by Thomas F. Crane. The Folk-Lore Society, Publication XXVI, 1878; reprint, Nendeln/Liechtenstein: Kraus Reprint, 1967.

Jantzen, Grace M. *Julian of Norwich: Mystic and Theologian*. New York: Paulist Press, 1988.

Jeffrey, David Lyle, ed. *The Law of Love: English Spirituality in the Age of Wyclif*. Grand Rapids: William B. Eerdmans, 1988.

Johnson, Elizabeth A., C.S.J. "Jesus, the Wisdom of God: A Biblical Basis for Non-Androcentric Christology." *Ephemerides Theologicae Lovanienses* 61 (1985): 261–94.

Kempe, Margery. *The Book of Margery Kempe*. Edited and translated by W. Butler-Bowdon. New York: The Devin-Adair Company, 1944.

————. *The Book of Margery Kempe*. EETS 212. Edited by Sanford Brown Meech and Hope Emily Allen. London: Oxford University Press, 1940.

Kieckhefer, Richard. *Repression of Heresy in Medieval Germany*. Philadelphia: University of Pennsylvania Press, 1979.

————. *Unquiet Souls: Fourteenth Century Saints and Their Religious Milieu*. Chicago: University of Chicago Press, 1984.

Knowles, David. *The English Mystical Tradition*. London: Burns & Oates, 1961.

Knowlton, Sr. Mary Arthur. *The Influence of Richard Rolle and Julian of Norwich on the Middle English Lyrics*. The Hague: Mouton, 1973.

Ladner, Gerhard. *The Idea of Reform: Its Impact on Christian Thought and Action in the Age of the Fathers*. Cambridge: Harvard University Press, 1959.

Lagorio, Valerie M. "Variations on the Theme of God's Motherhood in Medieval English Mystical and Devotional Writings." *Studia Mystica* 8 (1985): 15–37.

Lambert, M. D. *Medieval Heresy: Popular Movements from Bogomil to Hus*. London: Edward Arnold Publishers, 1977.

The Lay Folks' Catechism. EETS OS 118. Edited by Thomas Frederick Simmons and Henry Edward Nolloth. London: Kegan Paul, Trench, Trübner, 1901.

Leclercq, Jean. *The Love of Learning and the Desire for God*. 2nd ed. Translated by Catharine Misrahi. New York: Fordham University Press, 1974.

Leff, Gordon. *Heresy in the Later Middle Ages: The Relation of Heterodoxy to Dissent c. 1250–c. 1450*. Manchester: Manchester University Press/New York: Barnes & Noble, 1967.

Lerner, Gerda. *The Majority Finds Its Past: Placing Women in History*. Oxford: Oxford University Press, 1979.

Lerner, Robert E. *The Heresy of the Free Spirit in the Later Middle Ages*. Berkeley: University of California Press, 1972.

Lipman, Vivian D. *The Jews of Medieval Norwich*. London: The Jewish Historical Society of England, 1967.

Lonergan, Bernard. *Method in Theology*. New York: Seabury Press, 1979.

Mannyng, Robert, of Brunne. *Handlyng Sin*. Edited by Idelle Sullens. Binghamton, NY: Medieval and Renaissance Texts and Studies, 1983.

McDonnell, Ernest W. *The Beguines and Beghards in Medieval Culture*. New Brunswick: Rutgers University Press, 1954.

McFague, Sallie. *Models of God: Theology for an Ecological, Nuclear Age*. Philadelphia: Fortress, 1987.

McFarlane, K. B. *John Wycliffe and the Beginnings of English Nonconformity*. London: English Universities Press, 1952.

McGinn, Bernard. *The Golden Chain: A Study in the Theological Anthropology of Isaac of Stella*. Washington, DC: Cistercian Publications, 1972.

————. *Three Treatises on Man: A Cistercian Anthropology*. Kalamazoo: Cistercian Publications, 1977.

McGinn, Bernard and John Meyendorf, eds. *Christian Spirituality: Origins to the Twelfth Century*. New York: Crossroad, 1986.

McIlwain, James T. "The 'Bodelye syeknes' of Julian of Norwich." *Journal of Medieval History* 10 (1984): 167–80.

McKisack, May. *The Fourteenth Century: 1307–1399*. Oxford: Clarendon Press, 1959.

McLaughlin, Eleanor. " 'Christ My Mother': Feminine Naming and Metaphor in Medieval Spirituality." *Nashotah Review* 15:3 (1975): 228–48.

————. "The Heresy of the Free Spirit and Late Medieval Mysticism." *Medievialia et Humanistica*, n.s. 4 (1973): 37–51.

McNeill, John T. and Helena M. Gamer, eds. *Medieval Handbooks of Penance*. New York: Columbia University Press, 1938.

Merton, Thomas. *Conjectures of a Guilty Bystander*. Garden City: Doubleday, 1966.

————. *Mystics and Zen Masters*. New York: Farrar, Strauss & Giroux, 1961.

Miles, Margaret. *Augustine on the Body*. Missoula: Scholars Press, 1979.

Molinari, Paul. *Julian of Norwich: The Teaching of a 14th Century English Mystic*. London: Longmans, Green, 1958; reprint 1979.

Müller, Gotthold. *Apocatastasis Panton: A Bibliography*. Basel: Basler Missionsbuchhandlung, 1969.

Murphy, James J. *Rhetoric in the Middle Ages: A History of Rhetorical Theory from Saint Augustine to the Renaissance*. Berkeley: University of California Press, 1974.

Oakley, Ann. *Sex, Gender and Society*. New York: Harper & Row, 1972.

O'Connell, Robert J. "Isaiah's Mothering God in St. Augustine's *Confessions*," *Thought* 63 (1983): 188–206.

Orme, Nicholas. *English Schools in the Middle Ages*. London: Methuen, 1973.

Owst, G. R. *Literature and Pulpit in Medieval England: A Neglected Chapter in the History of English Letters and of the English People*. 2nd ed. Oxford: Basil Blackwell, 1961.

Pantin, W. A. *The English Church in the Fourteenth Century*. Cambridge: Cambridge University Press, 1955.

Pegis, Anton C. *At the Origins of the Thomistic Notion of Man*. New York: Macmillan, 1963.

Pelikan, Jaroslav. *The Christian Tradition: A History of the Development of Doctrine*. Vol. 3: *The Growth of Medieval Theology (600–1300)*. Chicago: University of Chicago Press, 1978.

Pelphrey, Brant. *Love Was His Meaning: The Theology and Mysticism of Julian of Norwich*. Salzburg: Institut für Anglistik und Amerikanistik, 1982.

Pepler, Conrad. *The English Religious Heritage*. St. Louis: B. Herder Book Co., 1958.

Petroff, Elizabeth. *Consolation of the Blessed*. New York: Alta Gaia Society, 1979.

————, ed. *Medieval Women's Visionary Literature*. New York/Oxford: Oxford University Press, 1986.

Power, Eileen. *Medieval English Nunneries c. 1272 to 1535*. Cambridge: Cambridge University Press, 1922.

————. *Medieval Women*. Edited by M. M. Postan. Cambridge: Cambridge University Press, 1975.

Principe, Walter H. *Introduction to Patristic and Medieval Theology*. 2nd ed. Toronto: Pontifical Institute of Mediaeval Studies, 1982.

————. *The Theology of the Hypostatic Union in the Early Thirteenth Century*. 4 vols. Toronto: Pontifical Institute of Mediaeval Studies, 1963–75.

Rahner, Karl. *Theological Investigations*. 20 vol. New York: Crossroad, 1982/83.

————. *The Trinity*. New York: Herder & Herder, 1970.

Reynolds, Sr. Anna Maria. "'Courtesy' and 'Homeliness' in the *Revelations* of Julian of Norwich." *Fourteenth Century English Mystics Newsletter* 5:2 (1979): 12–20.

Richardson, H. G. "Heresy and the Lay Power under Richard II." *English Historical Review* 201 (1936): 1–25.

Ricoeur, Paul. *Interpretation Theory: Discourse and the Surplus of Meaning*. Fort Worth: Texas Christian University Press, 1976.

————. *The Symbolism of Evil*. Boston: Beacon Press, 1967.

Riehle, Wolfgang. *The Middle English Mystics*. London: Routledge & Kegan Paul, 1981.

Robert of Flamborough. *Liber Poenitentiales*. Edited by J. J. Francis Firth, C.S.B. Toronto: Pontifical Institute of Mediaeval Studies, 1971.

Ruether, Rosemary Radford. *Sexism and God-Talk: Toward a Feminist Theology*. Boston: Beacon Press, 1983.

Russell, Jeffrey B. *Lucifer: The Devil in the Middle Ages*. Berkeley: University of California Press, 1984.

Saiving, Valerie. "Androcentrism in Religious Studies." *The Journal of Religion* 56:2 (1976): 177–97.

————. "The Human Situation: A Feminine View." *The Journal of Religion* 40:2 (1960): 100–12.

Schiffhorst, Gerald J., ed. *The Triumph of Patience*. Orlando: University Presses of Florida, 1978.

Schmitt, Robert Lewis. "The Image of Christ as Feudal Lord in the *Spiritual Exercises* of St. Ignatius Loyola." Ph.D dissertation, Fordham University, 1974.

Smalley, Beryl. *The Study of the Bible in the Middle Ages*. 2nd ed. Oxford: Basil Blackwell & Mott, 1952; reprint, Notre Dame: Notre Dame University Press, 1964.

Southern, Richard W. *The Making of the Middle Ages*. New Haven: Yale University Press, 1959.

————. *Western Society and the Church in the Middle Ages*. Harmondsworth: Penguin Books, 1970.

Stacey, John. *John Wyclif and Reform*. London: Lutterworth Press, 1964.

Stone, Robert Karl. *Middle English Prose Style: Margery Kempe and Julian of Norwich*. The Hague: Mouton, 1970.

Sullivan, John Edward, O.P. *The Image of God: The Doctrine of St. Augustine and Its Influence*. Dubuque: Priory Press, 1963.

A Talkyng of the Loue of God. Edited by Salvina Westra, O.P. The Hague: Martinus Nijhoff, 1950.

Tanner, Norman. *The Church in Late Medieval Norwich, 1370–1532*. Toronto: Pontifical Institute of Mediaeval Studies, 1984.

Tentler, Thomas. *Sin and Confession on the Eve of the Reformation*. Princeton: Princeton University Press, 1977.

Thiel, John. "Theological Responsibility: Beyond the Classical Paradigm." *Theological Studies* 47:4 (1986): 573–98.

Thompson, William M. *Fire and Light: The Saints and Theology.* New York: Paulist Press, 1987.

Thouless, Robert H. *The Lady Julian: A Psychological Study.* London: SPCK, 1924.

Tuchman, Barbara W. *A Distant Mirror: The Calamitous 14th Century.* New York: Ballantine Books, 1978.

Underhill, Evelyn. *The Mystics of the Church.* New York: Schocken Books, 1964; reprint 1971.

Van Beeck, Frans Jozef. *Christ Proclaimed: Christology as Rhetoric.* New York: Paulist Press, 1979.

Walsh, James. "God's Homely Loving: St. John and Julian of Norwich on the Divine Indwelling." *The Month,* n.s. 19 (1958): 164–72.

Warren, Ann K. "The Nun as Anchoress: England 1100–1500." In *Distant Echoes: Medieval Religious Women.* Vol. 1. Edited by John A. Nichols and Lillian Thomas Shank. Kalamazoo: Cistercian Publications, 1984.

Webster, Alan. "Suffering—The Jews of Norwich and Julian of Norwich." London: Diocesan Council for Christian-Jewish Understanding, 1981.

William of St. Thierry. *The Enigma of Faith.* Edited and translated by John D. Anderson. Washington, DC: Cistercian Publications, Consortium Press, 1974.

Wilson, Katharina M., ed. *Medieval Women Writers.* Athens: University of Georgia Press, 1984.

Woolf, Virginia. *A Room of One's Own.* New York: Harcourt Brace Jovanovich, 1957.

Ziegler, Philip. *The Black Death.* New York: Harper & Row, 1969.

Index

Index of Scriptural References

Genesis, 33, 35, 52–53, 67, 105, 110, 196 n. 49, 199 nn. 25 & 28, 204 n. 31
Exodus, 81, 188 n. 63, 189 n. 19, 199 n. 25
Leviticus, 199 n. 25
Judges, 189 n. 11
2 Samuel, 189 n. 11
2 Kings, 185 n. 31
Job, 203 n. 11, 204 n. 31
Psalms, 184 n. 17, 189 nn. 10–11, 190 n. 32, 202 n. 58, 203 n. 3, 204 n. 32
Proverbs, 61, 66
Song of Songs, 14, 201 n. 48
Wisdom, 66, 190 n. 32, 192 n. 2, 198 n. 16
Sirach, 205 n. 36
Ecclesiasticus (Vulgate), 66, 196 n. 48
Isaiah, 47, 53, 66, 184 n. 13, 185 nn. 27 & 31, 188 n. 62, 203 nn. 6 & 11, 204 nn. 18 & 23 & 30
Jeremiah, 204 n. 31
Matthew, 53, 185 n. 26, 188 n. 1, 189 n. 10, 190 n. 24, 194 n. 22, 199 n. 25, 202 nn. 2–3 & 62 & 68, 203 nn. 4 & 12–13, 204 nn. 30–31
Mark, 47, 185 nn. 26–27 & 36, 193 n. 12, 203 n. 5
Luke, 83, 184 n. 17, 188 n. 1, 190 n. 24, 199 n. 25, 202 n. 3, 203 nn. 3 & 12 & 14, 204 nn. 27–28 & 31 & 34

John, 35, 48, 78–79, 187 nn. 54 & 57, 188 n. 63, 189 n. 12, 202 nn. 3 & 58 & 69, 203 nn. 8 & 12
Romans, 8, 36, 57, 60, 92, 185 nn. 24 & 31, 186 n. 42, 189 n. 10, 199 n. 29, 200 nn. 31 & 34, 201 n. 49, 205 n. 36
1 Corinthians, 20, 36, 65, 185 n. 24, 186 nn. 37–38 & 42, 191 n. 37, 193 n. 10, 201 n. 44, 202 n. 70, 203 n. 9, 205 n. 36
2 Corinthians, 47, 189 n. 17, 192 n. 42, 199 n. 19, 202 n. 67
Galatians, 60, 188 n. 57, 199 n. 29
Ephesians, 36, 185 n. 31, 186 nn. 39 & 41–42 & 45, 189 n. 10, 192 n. 43, 195 n. 33, 196 n. 51, 201 n. 54
Philippians, 35, 50–52, 60, 68, 141, 203 n. 17
Colossians, 36, 61, 186 n. 41, 189 n. 10, 195 nn. 33 & 35, 203 n. 15
1 Thessalonians, 189 n. 10
Hebrews, 46, 184 n. 17, 202 n. 6, 203 n. 17
James, 203 n. 6
1 Peter, 201 n. 56
1 John, 39, 202 n. 69, 203 n. 9, 204 n. 20
Revelation, 36, 53, 185 n. 31, 188 n. 1, 197 nn. 2 & 36, 203 nn. 7 & 10